PRAISE FOR THE FIRST EDITION . . .

☆ ***A REAL-LIFE SAGA OF WORLD WAR II TEXAS***. "This book provides a worthwhile survey of the role of military aviation . . . anecdotal details keep the text lively . . . vintage and contemporary photographs make the book valuable for anyone interested in the military buildup that affected Texas communities."—JUDYTH RIGLER, *San Antonio Express-News*

☆ ***NEW HISTORY FOR AN OLDER TEXAN***. "I am a native Texan and history buff, but I was never aware of the important role many small Texas towns played in the aerial war efforts of the United States. What a revelation this book provided.

"Very well written, interesting, informative, humorous and sometimes tragic, *The Stars Were Big and Bright* is one book that will remain in my personal library for years to come. It is sure to be reread whenever the urge to revisit the history of Texas' contribution to the U.S. Army Air Force's efforts during WWI and WWII.

"I was impressed also with the numerous vintage photographs, maps, descriptions of the relevant airfields, aircraft photos and specifications, as well as the high level of documentation from primary source documents.

"This book absolutely has to be the best book on this topic yet written. Perhaps the author, Thomas E. Alexander, will treat us to another great book in the future."—JAMES W. BAILEY, Fredericksburg, Texas.

☆ ***WOW—WHAT A FASCINATING BOOK***. "I thoroughly enjoyed the portrayal of the life and times of Sweetwater as well as what it was like to be a WASP in a small Texas town!"—NANCY MARSHALL DURR of The Woman's Collection at TWU, Denton, Texas.

☆ ***I DIDN'T WANT TO PUT IT DOWN***. "I really enjoyed reading *The Stars Were Big and Bright.* There was so much informative and humorous information in a well-written format. It was very interesting learning about the diversity in the locations of the air bases and I loved the old pictures. It was a book I didn't want to put down."—J. CARLILE, Whitehouse, Texas

☆ ***A COMPELLING READ***. "*The Stars Were Big and Bright* is a compelling read about a time when people of the United States banded together in a common cause and about the Texas homefront during wartime. What makes this book an interesting read is that it contains not just the facts but the reactions of soldiers and Texans alike."—DD TURNER, *The Brownsville Herald*

☆ ***THOSE TEXAS BASES***. "Alexander's subject is treated with both factual authority and writing skill . . . the prose style is graceful . . . makes good use of material, including quotations from veterans present at reunions in recent years. The book is comprehensive, fair, and a pleasure to read."—MARY KATE TRIPP, *Amarillo Globe-News*

☆ ***HISTORIAN DESCRIBES ROLE AIR STATIONS HAVE PLAYED IN TEXAS***. "Aviation buffs and fans of 20th-century Texas history will find plenty to please them in this well-written and often entertaining work."—*Dallas Morning News*

☆ ***A FASCINATING STORY***. "It's a facinating story. I've already purchased copies to send to some friends who grew up in the aviation business during the wartime period."—STANLEY MARCUS, Chairman Emeritus of Neiman Marcus and author, Dallas, Texas.

Silver Wings

The U.S. Army Air Force in Texas, 1940-1946

By Thomas E. Alexander

State House Press
Abilene, Texas

SECOND EDITION
First edition printed as *The Stars Were Big And Bright: The United States Army Air Forces and Texas During World War II, Volume II*

State House Press
1 McMurry University #637
Abilene, Texas 79697-0001
325-793-4686

Printed in the United States of America
Distributed by Texas A&M University Press Consortium
800-826-8911
www.tamupress.com

ISBN-13: 978-1-933337-73-9
ISBN-10: 1-933337-73-7

Cover Design by Rosenbohm Graphic Design

Publishing Offices at McMurry University

Library of Congress Cataloging-in-Publication Data

Alexander, Thomas E., 1931–
The Stars Were Big and Bright : The United States Army Air Forces and Texas During World War II, Volume II / Thomas E. Alexander.
p. cm.
Includes bibliographical references and index.
ISBN 1-57168-554-5
1. World War, 1939–1945--Aerial operations, American. 2. United States. Army Air Forces--History. 3. World War, 1939–1945--Texas. 4. Texas--History, Military. I. Title
D790.A783 2001
940.54'4973--dc21

99-29958
CIP

For Capy, again and always

"The stars at night
Are big and bright
(clap clap clap clap)
Deep in the heart of Texas

The prairie sky
is wide and high
(clap clap clap clap)
Deep in the heart of Texas"

Contents

LIST OF MAPS AND PHOTOGRAPHS

Maps:

Photographs:

Acknowledgments

If everyone who helped make this volume possible were to be properly thanked, this acknowledgment section might well be not only the lengthiest chapter in the book but quite likely also the most interesting. Historians, librarians, archivists, students, and a host of other good folk with vivid memories, supercharged computers, warm hearts, and willing hands have all contributed significantly to the weaving of this tiny tapestry that represents but a small sampling of the World War II experience in Texas.

Just as their comrades-in-arms helped shape my first volume on this subject, the veterans who came to the Lone Star State nearly six decades ago to learn the skills of war were foremost among the contributors. They are eager to share their memories, and if the tales of their adventures grow ever so slightly broader with each telling, what of it? These men and women clearly believe each and every word of the stories they so earnestly relate about the war years, and because they believe them, they must be true. If ever there were a reason to accept the old adage that perception is reality, the recollections of the veterans of that great and terrible war most surely provide it.

The wives and widows of those veterans have stories of their own to tell. The women are an exceptional lot, the likes of which will never be seen again. Reminiscences of hardships shared, small victories won, and heavy losses overcome are voiced in an anthology of proud tales now leavened by rays of laughter or sometimes dampened by tiny drops of tears.

There is little if any self-pity evident in the recollections of these remarkable people, although the magnitude of the sacrifices they made and the hardships they endured so many years ago are beyond the comprehension of most living Americans. In short, this greatest of generations simply overcame it all. United by bonds of patriotism and a powerful sense of duty, the men learned to fly and to fight, while the women, no less united, learned to cope with anxiety, separation, and all too often, grief.

Many of them are still here to tell about their experiences through stories that put into sharp perspective the wondrous power of the human spirit against a bleak backdrop of a world torn asunder by the ravages of war. In the broadest possible sense, this book is respectfully dedicated to each and every one of them.

In addition to the veterans and their spouses, many others have enthusiastically assisted in the preparation of this second volume. Mike Porter in Pampa, for example, was of great help due to his unique position as both an ex-cadet at that city's World War II airfield and now as a volunteer official at Pampa's Freedom Museum USA. He shared not only his memories and the museum's collection of vintage photographs, but his time as well. Together, we visited the once-mighty air base that is now an equally mighty, if odiferous, cattle feed lot. Mike pointed out where he had stood on that proud day in 1944 when he received his pilot's silver wings, even though the moment of reverie quickly lost some of its poignancy when a mini-herd of Holsteins decided to re-enact for our benefit the famous stampede scene from John Wayne's immortal movie *Red River*. We swiftly withdrew, leaving the thousands of bovines to trample the still-existent old air-force runways as they wished.

Others in Pampa were of invaluable assistance and were spared the dubious adventure of visiting a feedlot. John Mead, at the Lovett Memorial Library, used his day off from work to photocopy more than three hundred pages of the *Pampa News* from the war years. Ann Davidson, director of the White Deer Land Company Museum, dug out old photographs of the base and obligingly made copies for inclusion in this book.

In Hondo, the late John R. Wentz provided access to all military artifacts and photos in the Medina County Museum and trusted us to freely borrow whatever photos we wanted for copying with the good-faith understanding that they would be returned. (They were.) John conducted a tour of what remains of Hondo's old airfield, pointing out the few World War II buildings that remain. He shared memories, too, of his many visits to the airfield as a boy growing up during the war years, and of life in Hondo in the early 1940s. John is gone now, but his memories live on.

Close to the runway on the airfield is Betsy Hermann's Flight Line Cafe, where general-aviation pilots and townfolk alike frequently dine. In a corner of her eatery, Betsy maintains a small treasure trove of memorabilia from Hondo's military air-glory days. Those not interested in finding historical nuggets in this collection might well focus on devouring one of Betsy's traditional Texas-skillet breakfasts. The staff at Hondo's newspaper, *The Anvil Herald*, and at the city's municipal library, were most generous with their time and material.

At Del Rio, on the Rio Grande, interest runs high in the history of Laughlin Field. The only active Air Force base written about in this book, Laughlin is both well-managed and a pleasure to visit. Carolyn Hay, a historian with the 47th Fighter Training Wing, supplied books and photographs of the World War II airfield that preceded today's sleekly modern facility. She also referred us to Jim Long, who as chairman of the Laughlin Heritage Foundation does a first-rate job of keeping the field's historical legacy alive. His mother, who lived in Del Rio during the World War II years, contributed colorful tales of life along the border sixty years ago. Ms. Lee Lincoln oversees the fascinating Whitehead Memorial Museum in Del Rio and opens the doors to the museum's research center to anyone interested in the history of the city and the region.

In Midland, Dot Erwin, archivist at the American Airpower Heritage Museum, provided access to an impressive array of photographs and records. In downtown Midland, the inestimable Nancy Rankin McKinley holds sway over the Midland County Historical Museum. She opened the building for us on a day that it was supposed to be closed and then trustingly permitted scores of photographs to be borrowed for reproduction purposes. Her willingness to cooperate and to share her priceless recollections of Midland Army Airfield is greatly appreciated.

In nearby Odessa, Ms. Bobbie Klepper arranged access to a valuable collection of vintage photographs of the base that was almost as close to Odessa as it was to Midland. As archivist emeritus of Special Collections at the University of Texas of the Permian Basin's J. Conrad Dunagan Library, Ms. Klepper can always find at least one more old picture to be considered. Fredericksburg's Mimi Walmsley devoted an afternoon to telling of her life in Midland during the war as the wife of Major Bill Walmsley, a pilot and bombing-range officer. Her picture of the major's plane being flown over a Midland target is included in this book.

To find the full story behind Marfa's World War II airfield, a researcher must visit Alpine as well as Marfa itself. Melleta R. Bell, archivist at Sul Ross University's Bryan Wildenthal Memorial Library in Alpine, tracked down old airfield publications filled with photographs and data. Her assistants, Troy M. Solis and Bennie Joe Gallegos, provided both technical help and directions to buildings that had been moved to Alpine from the Marfa airfield many years ago.

In Marfa, C. M. "Fritz" Kahl, the mayor himself, was generous with his time in recounting his experiences as a flight instructor at the airfield during the war. The mayor's memories are rich with recollections about the history of the city he now governs. There are not enough hours in a year to hear them all, and each is a gem in its own right. The staff at Marfa's fine library was very helpful, and when their research resources had been tapped out, they wisely suggested that we visit the mayor for the rest of the story.

In El Paso, about as far west as Texas goes, legends and truths about Biggs Field can be found in the Border Heritage Branch of that city's public-library system. Other military documents may be seen in the Southwest Collections Department on the University of Texas El Paso campus. The main source for regional military history, however, is Floyd "Twister" Geery at the Fort Bliss Museum. Twister knows inside-out the story of Fort Bliss and its attached Biggs Field, and his willingness to share that knowledge is appreciated.

Fort Worth has enjoyed a long relationship with military airpower, and there are many historians in the city eager to share their views and their research on the subject. Dr. J'nell Pate of Tarrant County Community College was quick to answer a request for a copy of her paper on Carswell Air Force Base and its predecessor, Fort Worth Army Airfield. Jane Dees, at the Fort Worth Museum of Science and History, provided access to reams of papers and documents relating to the World War II airfield that became Carswell AFB. Donita Maligi at the Special Collection Division of the University of Texas at Arlington Library System exhibited both great patience and professional perseverance in checking the *Fort*

Worth Star-Telegram archives for airfield material. At the Tarrant County Historical Commission Archives, Susie Murrin Pritchett enthusiastically aided our search for research material. The staff at the main library in downtown Fort Worth led the way to valuable clipping files even though a major tornado had only recently turned the library's carpets into mini-swamps.

Lubbock Army Airfield, which eventually became Reese Air Force Base, has many champions. Among these is Sally Still Abbe, a planner for the city of Lubbock and an authority on the story of the field. She provided names, films, and documents, while Victoria Jones, an archivist of the Southwest Collection in Texas Tech University's Special Collections Library, found interesting photographs of the old base and persevered until the United States Postal Service managed to get them properly delivered. Mike DeLano, director of operations at Slaton's Texas Air Museum, loaned us an extremely rare copy of the *U.S. Army Air Force Directory of Airports* for reproduction purposes with no questions asked. Such trust is rare.

In Austin, artist-to-the-Air Force Bill Lacy let us browse through the Bergstrom Austin Heritage Association's collection of photographs to choose what we wanted for reproduction in the book. His generosity is appreciated. At the city's magnificent new air facility, where the legacy of the old army field is perpetuated as Austin Bergstrom International Airport, public relations whiz Jackie Mayo took great delight in pointing out what remains of the old military field while singing the praises of the new air center.

Susan Lewis at Big Spring's Hangar 25 Museum could not have been friendlier or more helpful in providing information about the military air base that once flourished where the refurbished hangar now stands. Jim Little, who served at the base during its postwar years, offered helpful insights into base history. In downtown Big Spring, the enthusiastic and cordial ladies of the Howard County Heritage Museum searched through the archives to find interesting photographs of the World War II era. Director Angie Way and her associates Tammy Schrecengost and Nancy Raney devoted much time to this project. Bobby and Gloria McDonald, friends of Hangar 25, were also generous with time and with before-and-after photographs of the hangar during its dramatic restoration.

Finally, the excellent staff in the Texas Room of the Houston Public Library collected much background material for the Ellington chapter, while historian Glenn Swanson at the Lyndon B. Johnson Space Center offered key suggestions about the location of even more reference information. Dr. Erik Carlson, now at the University of Texas in Dallas, provided a copy of his short history of Ellington Field through the years. Special thanks goes to Mitchell T. "Tom" Hail, historian of Austin's Texas Military Forces Museum, for his persistence in seeking information about Ellington Field. Once he found what he was looking for, he made certain it arrived in time to beat the deadline for this book.

Keeping the author well-supplied with overall Air Force historical material has become something of a cottage industry for Bruce Ashcroft, historian at the Air Education and Training Command Headquarters at Randolph Air Force Base. Using his computer as a fencing master might use a saber, Bruce is always quick to enthusiastically respond with just the right stuff. I appreciate that.

I am grateful to all those who have gone the extra mile to be of assistance. Without the help of each of them, this work could not have been completed. Despite their best efforts, however, I know there are errors lurking within these pages, and every one of them is mine.

One person, again, stands out as the real moving force behind this work. Her contributions to the very successful first volume in this series are surpassed only by her tireless efforts on my behalf in this second book. For that, and for all of the marvelous things she does, I dedicate this volume of *The Stars Were Big and Bright* to Capy, my typist, editor, critic, wife, and best friend ever.

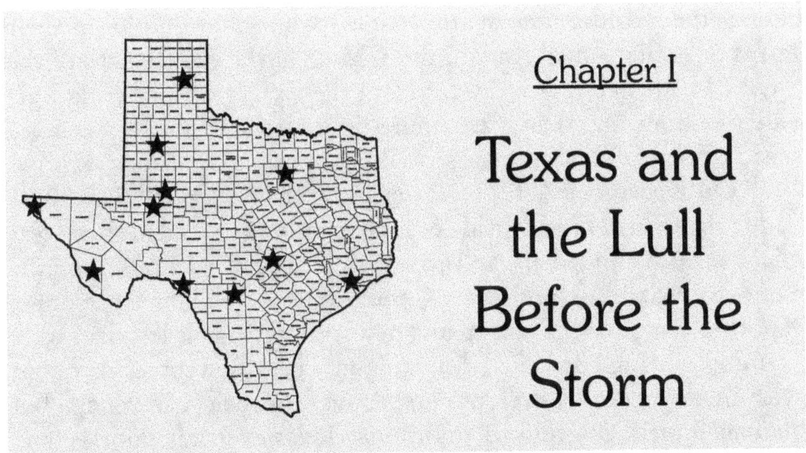

Chapter I

Texas and the Lull Before the Storm

Texas isn't geography. It's history. It's a world in itself.

Edna Ferber
Giant, 1952

Every ten years or so, a prominent American writer seems to come to the startling conclusion that somehow Texas moves in an orbit altogether different than her sister states. Zane Grey apparently was the first to use the "world in itself" description of the Lone Star State in 1934 in his novel *West of the Pecos.* Native Texan George Sessions Perry waited eight years before borrowing the line as the title for his book, and then came Ms. Ferber's use of it in *Giant,* her less-than-affectionate novel dedicated to the gigantic foibles of Texas as she perceived them in 1952. A full decade passed before John Steinbeck came around to the "world in itself" revelation as he traveled the state with his dog, Charley.

A quick study of the attitudes and conditions that prevailed throughout Texas in the years prior to World War II tends to support the different-world status attributed to it by such a diverse battery of noted authors. Particularly in the rural areas of the state, which was far more rural than it was urban until the mid-1940s, residents preferred to keep their way of life exactly as it had been for generations. They were essentially isolationists, content to let the rest of the world go about its business while they stayed on their farms or in their small communities. Most of the rural Texans of the day had little cause to stray far from their place of birth, and outsiders seldom found any sustaining reason to attempt to penetrate what quickly proved to be essentially a tightly closed society.

On December 7, 1941, however, when the United States was suddenly thrust into World War II, profound elements of great change, both immediate and irreversible, began to surge into the Lone Star State. Hundreds of thousands of military personnel reported for duty at the many new training facilities that were seemingly being constructed overnight. These newcomers brought with them not only different perspectives on society in general but also alien attitudes toward traditional Texas customs, morals, and values. Many of these differences, through difficulty, were gradually integrated into, or at least superimposed upon, the nineteenth-century frontier traditions that had long endured in the state.

As a very positive countering effect to the often negative disruption created by this horde of uniformed invaders was the warmly welcomed and sorely needed prosperity almost instantly generated by a massive and free-flowing infusion of war-produced federal capital. Many Texans, long-ravaged by the Great Depression, suddenly found steady employment readily available at military construction projects. Further, the newly arrived soldiers who carried with them the seeds of social change also brought quantities of cash that quickly found its way into the nearly dry economic mainstream of the state.

Of the agents of change that the war introduced to Texas, arguably the most significant was the Air Force. It is important to note here that in June 1941, the official name of the Army's air branch was changed from the Army Air Corps to the United States Army Air Forces. The new designation was used until September 18, 1947, when the U.S. Air Force was established as a separate service. During World War II, however, the air branch was commonly if erroneously referred to as the U.S. Army Air Force, and for purposes of simplicity and grammatical expediency, this technically incorrect colloquialism will be used throughout this book.

Attracted by wide-open spaces and good flying weather, the Army operated nearly seventy airfields in virtually every corner of the state during the war, with many of those fields located in relatively less populated West Texas. The bases seemed to be everywhere, and the personnel assigned to both teach and learn the deadly skills of war hailed from all parts of America. That was where the problem often lay.

This book is about eleven of those airfields, their neighboring communities, and the men and women who lived and worked on them. Each of the eleven has been selected for inclusion because there was something unique about how it came into being, about its World War II mission, or simply because it has interesting stories to tell. Fort Worth Army Airfield is in the book because of the unusual military and industrial partnership it represented. Biggs Field is included because of its colorful history and its curious pattern of intra-service allegiance. First an Army field, then an Air Force base, and now an Army field once again, Biggs may perhaps be as one well-spoken daughter of a former Air Force officer recently described it as being. "Poor Biggs," she lamented, at least half-facetiously, "it's like a bald-headed stepchild, and I don't think anybody wants it." [1]

Old Marfa Field affords an excellent opportunity to study an air base that rapidly grew in the West Texas desert, only to bloom brightly before falling into neglect and eventual total obliteration. It is a true ghost base today, with even its former location known but to a few. Pampa was selected because it presents a dramatic, if powerfully fragrant, example of swords becoming plowshares in the finest traditions of the vast Texas Panhandle. So the old fields each have a unique story to pass along, sometimes heartening and sometimes haunting, yet of all eleven World War II airfields included in this book, only Laughlin Field at Del Rio continues to function as a fully operational modern air base. The others have either disappeared or been transformed—into sites including a prison, a twenty-first century international airport, a museum, or, in Pampa, a massive cattle feedlot.

There were, of course, certain formulaic factors involved in the government's initial decision to place wartime bases at certain locations throughout Texas. The partnerships that evolved between the bases and their neighboring towns were distinctly unique, however, and at least in the short term, mutually beneficial. This book traces the evolution of those partnerships and provides a brief capsule history of each community to illustrate what caused its relationship with its airfield to be different from any other. In telling the story of each base, the book often relies on the reminiscences of some of those who shared the experiences of Texas at war. They were eyewitnesses to a turbulent half-decade of nearly revolutionary change.

NEW FACES AND NEW BUILDINGS

> *I was about twenty-six years old when they started building that big base out west. I'd never lived anyplace else but Hondo, and I knew every face in town. All of a sudden, there were new faces everywhere, and I was kind of scared.*
>
> Mary Kate Oliphant
> San Antonio, Texas

There can be no question that the coming of war in December 1941 and the immediate opening of the airfields brought an instant and indelible change to what had long been the cloistered world of Texas. The challenges to the state's sheltered traditions first began when construction workers thronged into even the smallest rural community, almost always successfully seeking employment on the bases. As the construction work neared completion, the first of more than a million uniformed temporary residents began to occupy the just barely completed facilities. In all likelihood, these newcomers would not have given much if any consideration to traveling to the Lone Star State at all had not a stern War Department firmly ordered them to promptly do so. Yet come to Texas they did, in what began as a stream and quickly became a veritable rushing torrent of khaki-clad humanity. The floodgates had been forced open by war, and some startling new ways of looking at life were flowing in at a dizzying rate.

A great many Texans suddenly found themselves face to face with strangers as construction on the airfields accelerated and military personnel began to arrive soon after Pearl Harbor. It is interesting to note, however, that what appeared to be a burst of airfield-building activity prompted by the war was in fact the final phase of a long-range federal master plan that had been developing for nearly a decade.

As early as 1932, newly elected President Franklin D. Roosevelt had begun using relief funds appropriated by Congress to ease the economic burden of the Great Depression by employing long-idle workers for various government construction projects. Foremost among these projects was the building, improving, and expanding of key Air Corps facilities nationwide. According to one source, political interests initially were the main determining factor in the location of the federal projects rather than any future strategic importance the new airfield might have.[2]

Although the Roosevelt administration was in fact merely carrying out the mandate of a federal five-year plan that had been approved for air-facility improvement in 1926, the use of relief appropriations to fund the improvement projects can only be viewed as a stroke of political genius. By putting America's growing army of unemployed men back to work, the administration was able to reverse the tide of the Great Depression. Further, in putting those men to work building airfields, Roosevelt moved the nation toward a higher degree of readiness for the worldwide clash of arms so clearly in the making by the late 1930s.

When the portents of the impending world crisis grew even more ominous, Roosevelt called for vast sums to be directly used for the building of new aircraft for the Army. He had, after all, been laying a firm foundation for this new air armada through his airfield-facilities-building program funded by relief-work dollars.

Within a short three-month period after the president had outlined his plans for a vastly accelerated national defense program to Congress, the legislature voted to approve virtually everything Roosevelt had requested. Known as Public Law 18, the plan called for an initial 6,000 aircraft, 3,203 pilots, and 45,000 enlisted men, and a $300 million appropriation package to pay for it all.[3]

For the president, it was a win-win-win situation. He had used relief funds to build new air facilities, in one masterstroke breaking the backbone of the Depression and propelling the country into a far better state of preparedness for the war that was by now sure to come. Also, the beginning of the end of the Great Depression had increased the president's popularity among the electorate. As another plus, the improved economic situation had muted outcries that it had come about despite the perceived risks involved in moving the nation forward on an irreversible track toward the brink of full-scale involvement in yet another foreign war.

A significant portion of Roosevelt's accelerated airpower expansion program was of direct importance to Texas. In 1940, following his earlier congressional victory, the president next asked for a massive production schedule designed to deliver to the War Department an astonishing armada of 50,000 aircraft. More airplanes clearly meant more pilots, and that in turn called for even more training fields. Texas, the longtime home of such highly successful air bases as Randolph and Kelly fields at San Antonio, was easily the leading contender for many of the new airfields that the president's program would require. Blessed with good flying weather, at least usually, and seemingly endless uncrowded skies, the Lone Star State had already proved to be an excellent host for the U.S. Army Air Force. If further enticements were needed, Texas could also readily provide vast quantities of relatively inexpensive land that was for the most part free from any natural vertical impediments to the forward progress of airborne fledgling pilots.

When the air branch itself had been a fledgling and largely experimental military service at the beginning of the twentieth century, it had been the vast and clear skies that attracted the attention of military authorities to Texas. To avoid the frequent clouds and foul weather on the East Coast, Lt. Benjamin Foulois had brought the Army's sole aeroplane to San Antonio's Fort Sam Houston in 1914 to establish the nation's very first military aviation training center. The area had been selected by the Army because of its climate, its relatively flat terrain, and, as one historian notes, "because Texas skies seemed to have been created just for flying."[4] This short-lived but fortuitous early introduction of military aviation to San Antonio would prove to be a major factor in shaping the dominant role Texas would assume in World War II.

The construction of the new air bases that would be needed for the war was for a time thinly disguised as a peacetime endeavor. Shortly after Roosevelt's easily won Public Law 18 had gone into the records, representatives of the Civil Aeronautics Authority (CAA) were dispatched to all parts of the United States to survey likely prospects as sites for either new airfield construction or existing airports that could be readily expanded and modernized.

As the historical leader in the nation's military flight-training program and home to a surprisingly large number of airports that could easily be expanded, Texas received what seems to have constituted a lion's share of the CAA's interest. When the airport survey was completed, it also appeared that the state had likely received even more than a lion's share of the government spending recommended by the study. Of the 191 sites visited by CAA officials, 149 were initially chosen to receive federal funding for either construction or expansion of airport facilities. Of those 149 sites, nearly half were located in Texas.[5]

The soon-to-be-allocated funds were to flow through Mr. Roosevelt's Works Projects Administration (WPA) and therefore ostensibly were to be used for immediate relief purposes and longer-range civilian aeronautical activities. Few if any observers, however, failed to recognize that the approved airports were in fact being developed for military purposes. Further, it was widely assumed that in the future, when the Army had exhausted its need for the facilities, they would in all likelihood become the property of the nearest community as an unquestionably valuable commercial asset to any town in the peacetime that would follow victory in the war.

In addition to the long-range value to be realized if one of the airport projects could be obtained, Texas communities also recognized the positive impact a government construction contract would have on their immediate Depression-created economic woes. As a result, cities and towns across the state entered into a vigorous and often heated competition to gain the blessing of the CAA site-selection authorities. Politicians at the local, state, and federal levels lobbied mightily to convince Washington that their favorite community was, without a doubt, far and away the superior choice for one, or maybe more, of the promised new installations.

AN END TO ISOLATION

Saturday nights around here before the war were pretty wild, we'd always thought, until the soldiers came and showed us that we hadn't even known what wild was. Those boys just stood this town on its ear.

Ardell Foster
Odessa, Texas

Although there is evidence that at least some of the citizens in the hotly competing communities voiced their concerns about the social implications that might arise should a newly built airport be suddenly transformed into a military air base, the alluring prospect of a mighty flow of federal dollars was clearly more important to the majority. However, when the construction was completed just as the outbreak of war did indeed cause the facilities to become military training fields, the initial concerns of the few became the shared fears of all. Texas, or so it seems in retrospect, was not fully ready to abandon many of its nineteenth-century ways merely because a decidedly twentieth-century war had been brought to its doorstep on December 7, 1941.

Everyone knew that Texas was the largest state in the Union. Its 263,000 square miles in area made it bigger than the combined land area of Germany and Japan, soon to be America's two principal wartime foes. Yet for all of its tremendous size, Texas had a population of only 6.5 million people in 1940. Nearly a million more human beings lived in New York City at the time than lived in the entire Lone Star State. About six of every ten of those Texans lived in rural areas.[6]

The sheer vastness of the state created something of a natural isolationism. People born on farms or in small towns tended to stay close to their birthplaces. Only a minority of them held college degrees, and a reported 60 percent of those living in smaller communities had not received a high-school diploma.[7] A majority of Texas men labored in agriculture, while women worked almost exclusively in the home. Together they raised their relatively large families in such a way that, absent any such radical upheaval as war, the children were more than likely to lead their lives in much the same way as had their parents and grandparents.

Churches were at the center of all community life. One of every three Texans belonged to an established religious organization of some denomination or another. Not surprisingly, all of the churches placed great importance on such long-held traditional values as morality, honor, fidelity, honesty, charity, and temperance. The largest of the religious denominations statewide was that of the Baptists, which claimed well over a third of all churchgoers in 1940. At the same time, there were more than a half-million confirmed

Roman Catholics, which amounted to slightly less than 10 percent of the state's population.[8]

There were more men than women in Texas just before the war started, but that statistic was soon to change. Only one of every five adults owned an automobile, even though the state boasted in excess of 15,000 miles of hard-surfaced roadways. Of the 693,323 telephones in use in 1940, more than half were to be found in the state's fifteen larger urban population centers. Forty-one radio stations broadcast their daily programs to the mere one million radio receivers located in homes and offices throughout the state. While regular radio broadcasts served to penetrate the isolation of rural Texas to some degree, a core of opposition to American involvement in any foreign military dispute still existed.[9]

Motion pictures offered a welcome diversion from the traditionally dull routine of small-town existence. Virtually every town had at least one movie theater, and people flocked in to see such popular stars as Shirley Temple, Clark Gable, and Carole Lombard. Saturday matinees gave younger Texans a way to escape small-town boredom when they could ride side by side with Hopalong Cassidy and Gene Autry, at least in their popcorn-fueled imagination. The dashing Errol Flynn swashbuckled his way into the hearts of ladies of all ages. The laconic Jimmy Stewart, who would soon be flying bombers over Hitler's Germany, had just won an Academy Award for *The Philadelphia Story,* while Orson Welles, who would never win any significant Academy Award, was completing work on his classic film *Citizen Kane.* The newsreels, heavily edited though they were, gave moviegoers at least a general visual idea of what was happening outside the invisible but very real gates of their small community. To most, it mattered little, for they were isolated by either choice or circumstance, shackled to the ways of the past both by the heavy chains of the economic depression and a lack of desire to break away from all that was familiar to them.

TEXAS RESPONDS TO PEARL HARBOR

Like most old-timers, I guess, I can remember exactly where I was when the news about Pearl Harbor came through. We—my sisters and me—were all sitting on Granny Ruth's porch when our cousin ran up and told us what had happened. I didn't know where Pearl Harbor or even Hawaii was, but I did know that something terrible had taken place.

Lorene Schnelling
San Antonio, Texas

After aircraft of the Imperial Japanese Navy attacked Pearl Harbor, Hawaii, on Sunday, December 7, 1941, life in Texas, indeed life everywhere, was never to be as it had been before. What President Roosevelt had called a day of infamy also proved to be the herald of years of profound and irreversible change.

On the Monday after the Pearl Harbor attack, the effects of the day-old war could already be felt across Texas. Young men lined up to volunteer for military service, and by the time the conflict had ended four years later, some 750,000 Texans had been in uniform. Many of those too old to enlist soon set out for the larger cities to find employment in vital war-related industrial plants. Nearly a half-million Texans were employed at many such plants near Houston and Fort Worth.[10]

Construction workers on partially completed military installations went on round-the-clock schedules to prepare barracks for the thousands of trainees who would be heading for Texas in just a matter of days. Oil field and refinery employment levels rose rapidly, and expanded highway crews worked twenty-four-hour shifts to bring the state's highways up to military requirements.

Workers flocked into Texas from other states, and they were quickly joined by a vanguard of what would soon be virtual armies of soldiers. As a result, the population began to increase rapidly, growing at a faster rate during the first two years of the war than it had in the whole ten-year period between 1930 and 1940.[11]

As might be expected, this explosive growth and sudden prosperity were not realized without serious problems. Housing was woefully inadequate in nearly all small communities near the growing military installations. Servicemen and their families competed with construction workers to occupy almost any kind of dwelling. In Hondo, families outbid other families for the right to live in an only slightly modified chicken house. Barns became dormitories, and front porches were rented as bedrooms to desperate workingmen on an eight-hour-shift basis. Rents for any type of housing, be it house, shed, or barn, rose to ridiculous levels, forcing the government to place rent-ceiling restrictions in most of the affected communities.[12]

Food prices rose as well. The cost of meat nearly doubled in Alpine almost overnight, for example, while commodities everywhere became increasingly scarce and therefore increasingly expensive. One grocery store ran an ad in the *Hondo Anvil Banner* to apologize for the serious disruption to decades-old laws of supply and demand created by a soaring population and diminishing transportation capabilities.[13] Black market activities flourished in nearly every city and town, as the shortages grew more acute and the needs of the military accelerated. The whole problem of imbalance between the need for and the availability of foodstuffs was for the most part exacerbated when the government initiated a rationing program early in the war.

The onrush of newcomers to Texas towns brought other problems as well. Off-duty soldiers and construction workers alike streamed into the nearby communities at every opportunity, seeking relaxation and diversion from their tiring and often dull daily routines. With many of the local males gone away to war, the fun-seekers reveled in the abundance of unattached, or seemingly unattached, girls. Inevitably, this meant trouble. Their male classmates often ostracized high-school girls who dated servicemen from the airfields. The girls who ignored such punishment usually found their new escorts far less restricted than were the local men by what was considered proper dating decorum. There was a war on, after all, and the men training to go into it had neither the patience nor the time to observe what had long been the traditional ground rules for sexual behavior. It was obviously not all just wartime fun and games, however, as local newspapers were soon carrying reports of weddings between hometown girls and the temporary Texans. As visits to such one-time military towns as Hondo, Marfa, and Lubbock will easily prove, many of those marriages have successfully withstood the test of six decades of time.

Quite often, the population of the rapidly expanding airfields quickly outstripped that of their neighboring towns. Military communities with from eight to ten thousand uniformed inhabitants were not unusual throughout rural Texas. As more than a few civic leaders had feared and expected even before the bases were fully operational, the explosive growth caused many problems. The sale of alcohol, still illegal in many parts of Texas when the war started, proved to be one of the most vexing concerns to the city fathers. The newcomers, be they lonely and homesick or just looking for an alcohol-fueled good time, had little patience with what they considered to be laughably oppressive rules governing the sale of ardent spirits. Bootlegging became a prosperous business in many communities, while the operators of illegal stills found a booming market among airfield personnel in town for a Saturday night's fling.

The problem created by the excessive consumption of alcohol by servicemen during the war years was apparently not limited to Texas, however. On May 27, 1942, the beginning of what it perceived to be a nationwide alcoholic binge prompted the National Conference of the Presbyterian Church to beseech President Roosevelt to close all distilleries, breweries, and retail liquor stores for the duration of the war. The president, fond of his traditional evening martini and still gloating over the defeat of the national prohibition law a few years earlier, simply chose to completely ignore the church group's earnest request.[14]

Despite the sudden presence of thousands of high-spirited young strangers in their midst, the leaders of most Texas communities made a sincere effort to make their wartime visitors feel at home while still trying to maintain something of the pre-war order of things. Ladies' groups held social events for the soldiers, and the local United Service Organization (USO) provided entertainment and even Saturday-night dances. Churches, long the mainstay of community life, opened their doors to the servicemen and encouraged parishioners to do the same. Sunday dinners for the soldiers after church were popular events throughout the war.

To their credit, airfield commanders took strong measures to protect both their personnel and the residents of neighboring towns from each other. Suspicious and potentially troublesome business locations were promptly placed off-limits to all personnel, and cafes with unacceptable standards of sanitation were given strict orders to clean up their premises or be closed to military patronage. Stringent measures were taken to prevent the spread of venereal disease, and the military police worked closely with the local law-enforcement officers to control if not eradicate prostitution, which somehow seemed to flourish nonetheless.

It speaks well for military and civilian authorities alike that very few major outbreaks of violence occurred in Texas towns where the potential for serious trouble clearly existed. It is tempting to speculate, however, that if economic conditions in Texas had been stronger at the very outset of the war, things might have been considerably more confrontational.

Many of the old-timers who lived in towns near the newly established airfields recall that, for the most part, residents were so overjoyed at what the coming of the Army had meant to their pocketbooks that they tended to ignore all but the most outrageous misdeeds of the individual soldiers. The prevailing attitude among those Texans with airfields as neighbors seems to have been a heady mix of gratitude and forbearance wrapped in patriotism and a heartfelt pride that their town had an Army installation right next door. According to one old-time resident of a small Texas town, this curiously benign attitude allowed miscreant soldiers "to get away with murder just as long as nobody got hurt."[15] Even Yogi Berra could not have said it better.

Although there were occasions when the relationship between a community and its neighboring airfield with its often-rowdy component of restless young men did erupt, the association in general was compatible and mutually beneficial. The towns grew and prospered and looked forward to the end of the war that would bring them, among many other things, a civilian airport donated by a victorious and grateful United States government. The military, on the other hand, found exactly what it needed in Texas. The flying weather had for the most part been as ideal as predicted, and the civilians had been relatively tolerant, if not downright hospitable. More important, the combination of favorable conditions had permitted the massive wartime flight-training programs to proceed at a commendable and occasionally record-breaking pace. From 1942 through mid-1945, the Army Air Force training schools in Texas had produced thousands upon thousands of pilots, navigators, bombardiers, aerial gunners, and aircraft mechanics.[16]

Each community seemed to embrace its airfield in its own unique way. In Pampa, for example, rumors about the coming of the airfield occupied the local newspaper's front page for months in advance, and when the base was formally announced, headlines nearly five inches high broke the news to excited Pampans. In Fort

Worth, the announcement of the coming of a big bomber base was treated in a far more cosmopolitan and restrained manner, but there can be no misreading of the fact that the big city was every bit as ecstatic as the small town in being chosen as the site for an army airfield. Little could the local residents grasp that the coming of the bases would serve as a watershed in their history, the dividing line between the old and the new Texas.

Visitors to such towns as Hondo, Marfa, and Big Spring can still locate some of those people whose lifetimes were irreversibly altered by the war and the opening of an airfield near their hometown. They can remember when once slow-paced communities were abruptly transformed into crowded and bustling hives of activity, with trainloads of strangers arriving at all hours of the day and night.

While a few of the reminiscences of the old-timers are a bittersweet mix of hope, anxiety, and grief, for the most part the memories revealed in oral-history accounts are pleasant ones. Whatever friction and social upheavals might have occurred nearly sixty years ago appear to have become blurred and muted with the passage of time.

What does remain clear in the minds of those who choose to comment on the war years, however, is how exciting it all was. Time, which had seemingly stood still in the decades before the war, appeared to abruptly accelerate. Everything seemed to be happening faster, and the little towns came alive with a vigor never before experienced. The legendary uncrowded Texas skies were now filled with literally thousands of airplanes of all shapes and sizes, each proudly bearing the big and bright star emblems of the U.S. Army Air Force. Even the once deeply quiet country nights were shattered by the throbbing chorus of massed aircraft engines being revved to full throttle.

It was an exhilirating time. With the coming of war, new life had also come to Texas, and when that war came to a close, the face of the state would be forever changed.

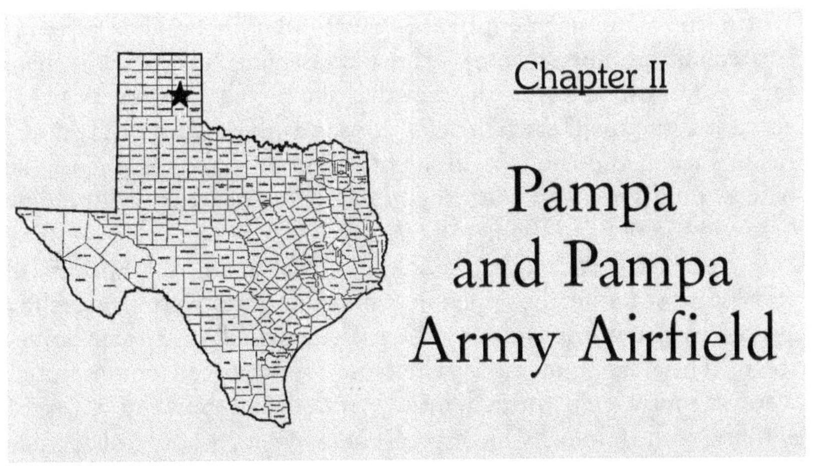

Chapter II

Pampa and Pampa Army Airfield

I asked a guy in town once why they called this place Pampa, and he said it was because it looked something like Argentina around here. I told him if that was so, I didn't think I wanted to go to Argentina.

S/Sgt. Ernest Hewlett

In 1887, when the Southern Kansas Railway selected a spot in the Texas Panhandle to build a station, local rancher George Tyng was asked to suggest a suitable name for the windswept and dusty site. Tyng, manager of the giant White Deer Land Company, on whose property the station was to be built, relied on memories from his early travels to convince himself that the barren landscape of the Panhandle somehow resembled the lush pampas of Argentina. Vague though the comparison might have seemed, the railroad accepted the premise and Pampa, Texas, was born.[1]

Even with a romantic-sounding name and a railroad running through it, tiny Pampa remained little more than a boxcar station house and a few dugout homesteads for the first five years of its existence. A post office finally opened in late 1892 and George Tyng, perhaps feeling the pride of authorship, soon convinced the owners of his company that Pampa should become the firm's headquarters city. The first frame building to be erected at the site, in 1902, was the White Deer Land Company's boarding house.

Worth, the announcement of the coming of a big bomber base was treated in a far more cosmopolitan and restrained manner, but there can be no misreading of the fact that the big city was every bit as ecstatic as the small town in being chosen as the site for an army airfield. Little could the local residents grasp that the coming of the bases would serve as a watershed in their history, the dividing line between the old and the new Texas.

Visitors to such towns as Hondo, Marfa, and Big Spring can still locate some of those people whose lifetimes were irreversibly altered by the war and the opening of an airfield near their hometown. They can remember when once slow-paced communities were abruptly transformed into crowded and bustling hives of activity, with trainloads of strangers arriving at all hours of the day and night.

While a few of the reminiscences of the old-timers are a bittersweet mix of hope, anxiety, and grief, for the most part the memories revealed in oral-history accounts are pleasant ones. Whatever friction and social upheavals might have occurred nearly sixty years ago appear to have become blurred and muted with the passage of time.

What does remain clear in the minds of those who choose to comment on the war years, however, is how exciting it all was. Time, which had seemingly stood still in the decades before the war, appeared to abruptly accelerate. Everything seemed to be happening faster, and the little towns came alive with a vigor never before experienced. The legendary uncrowded Texas skies were now filled with literally thousands of airplanes of all shapes and sizes, each proudly bearing the big and bright star emblems of the U.S. Army Air Force. Even the once deeply quiet country nights were shattered by the throbbing chorus of massed aircraft engines being revved to full throttle.

It was an exhilirating time. With the coming of war, new life had also come to Texas, and when that war came to a close, the face of the state would be forever changed.

Blizzards and financial woes eventually convinced Timothy Hobart, Tyng's successor, that the company's 700,000 acres of land holdings would prove more lucrative than its 70,000 head of cattle. Consequently, the firm's acreage was soon being promoted as a potentially fertile wheat belt in an effort to attract farmers to the area.

The land-promotion venture proved to be successful, and homesteaders began arriving in Pampa by the wagonload and on the railroad. Much of the once-mammoth ranch property was promptly divided and subdivided, fenced and crossfenced, with wheat farmers replacing the cowboys on the White Deer spread. By 1910 the prospering little town had a population of more than four hundred people and boasted a school, a bank, and several churches.[2]

By 1926, the population had risen to 987, a newspaper was being published, and the White Deer Land Company headquarters had been permanently established in the city. Timothy Hobart, manager of the land company, oversaw the firm's continuing success in marketing its land to settlers.

When oil was discovered in the area around Pampa in 1926, the steady flow of settlers became a flood, but Hobart's insistence on carefully screening applicants who sought to buy White Deer acreage spared the city from traditional boomtown vices. Several petroleum-processing plants were built near the town in 1927 and shortly thereafter, Pampa became the county seat of Gray County.

Other railroads, attracted by the spectacular growth in petroleum activity, soon reached the town, and by 1931 the population exceeded 10,000, having grown tenfold in a mere five years. As the oil boom continued well into the late 1930s, the economic conditions in Pampa and Gray County were for the most part better than in many other Texas towns. However, the coming of an Army airfield to the city, shortly after World War II started, gave Pampa an economic boost that would linger long after the war had come to a close in 1945.

PAMPA'S AIRFIELD AN UNEXPECTED BOON

I have always been proud to have been a pioneer at Pampa [Army Airfield] in those memorable years. We never forgot the friendliness and hospitality we encountered from everyone in Pampa.

Vernon Baumgart, Lt. Col. USAF (Ret.)
Cadet Class 43-B, Sheboygan, Wisconsin

Unlike most Texas cities that hosted Army airfields during World War II, Pampa apparently did not aggressively pursue a military installation until after the war had in fact commenced. The first published evidence of any organized effort to obtain a base appeared in the March 14, 1942, edition of the *Pampa News*. The article noted that a committee of local citizens, headed by Mayor Fred Thompson, was on its way to Washington, D.C., to make contact with unspecified governmental authorities to explore ways in which the Pampa area's low-cost natural gas could be employed in the war effort. The mayor and his committee were seeking to convince federal government officials that a major "war production" facility would find the area's cheap fuel and other natural resources a sufficient reason to come to the Panhandle.[3]

It is easy to speculate that the mayor's committee, or some other unidentified but powerful civic-minded group, had in fact long been engaged in extensive behind-the-scenes lobbying efforts on behalf of the city to attract a war-related entity. Any suspicion of a long-standing lobbying campaign might well be confirmed by an announcement that appeared just two months after the appearance of the article about the mayoral visit to Washington in March. Dated May 15, 1942, a news story with three-inch headlines trumpeted that Pampa was to receive a major Army air installation within a very short period of time. The newspaper carried copies of telegrams from Washington, D.C., confirming the good news.[4] On May 17 it was further announced that advance construction officials were soon to arrive in Pampa to survey the site of what was eventually to become a gigantic twin-engine flying school.[5]

Some 2,544 acres of land twelve miles east of Pampa near the tiny community of Heaton had been acquired by the War Department as the site for the base. Reportedly, the principal factors taken into consideration by the government officials in placing the flight school near Pampa were the city's "excellent location," its housing facilities, its water supply, and its schools and churches. Conspicuously absent was any mention of Mayor Thompson's highly touted inexpensive natural gas. Construction costs were estimated to be in excess of $5 million, with the overall project to be supervised by the Army Corps of Engineers. On May 22, 1942, the first group of engineers arrived in the city.[6]

The first contract let for work on the new base was for a test water well that it was hoped would supply the 700,000 gallons per day that the War Department had specified as being required by a base of the magnitude of the one to be constructed. The City of Pampa had pledged to fund the costs of drilling the tester and any subsequent water wells. A $15,000 bond-issue campaign opened on July 5, 1943, and one week later it was announced that the bond issue had carried by an overwhelming margin. The easy passage of the bond issue, according to the *Pampa News*, "reflected Pampans' earnestness to cooperate in every way possible in the development of the new air base."[7]

Once the water wells were successfully drilled, other contracts were let. The firm of Poole Brothers in Shawnee, Oklahoma, was the successful bidder on many of the site-preparation contracts, including excavating, fence building, and pipe laying. It was estimated that 540,000 yards of dirt would be excavated to construct the runways and aprons and that 26,000 feet of pipe and over eight miles of fence would be required. The dollar amount of the initial contracts was not disclosed.[8]

The city's eagerness to be a good host to its new neighbor was reflected in a welcome party it staged in mid-July to greet the Army's senior project officer and his engineering and construction company associates. Held in the high school gymnasium in order to accommodate the large crowd that attended, the party provided Col. Norman B. Olen, project officer for the new base, with a forum to outline the government's plans for a "gigantic Air Force" and Pampa's role in those plans.

The months following the big welcome party saw evidence that the city was indeed destined to share significantly in the Army's plans for its Air Force. All grading work, plumbing, and water systems were completed, and construction of the runways, hangars, barracks, and classrooms proceeded at a rapid rate. The almost frantic pace of the work resulted in the first of what would be many fatal accidents on the base. John Mack Armistead was killed instantly when a ditch caved in on him early in September 1942. The sides of the ditch, which was sixteen feet deep and ten feet wide, collapsed when a heavy crane was driven too close to the edge.[9]

Despite the accident, the construction continued at top speed, and contractors issued urgent pleas for more employees. Desperately needed were general mechanics' helpers who could expect to earn $115 per month, sheet metal workers who would be paid $1,500 to $1,860 a year, and blacksmiths, electricians, and draftsmen whose compensation packages were not divulged.[10]

As buildings were just being finished and before the paint was even dry, military personnel began filtering in to occupy them. Once completed, the base would be home to an average of 4,000 personnel at any given time.

On November 22, 1942, with the completion of the base's principal 6,500-foot concrete runway, a ceremony was planned to feature the first landing at the field. Lt. Col. Daniel S. Campbell, newly appointed commander of the base, circled the runway just long enough for a sizable crowd to gather to witness his landing of the first aircraft. An Army pilot for more than ten years, the thirty-two-year-old colonel most likely anticipated the landing as a moment of glory. Unfortunately, the drama of his touchdown was lost when the pilot of a plane based in Chickasha, Oklahoma, was directed to Pampa because of inclement weather at his original destination. Probably unaware that he was ruining Colonel Campbell's grand entry, the Oklahoma pilot landed his plane on the new runway just three minutes before the base commander's plane touched down, to the cheers of only slightly disappointed onlookers.

On November 29, the very day the first full flight of training planes arrived on the base, soldiers from the field were offered an orientation tour of Pampa. It was declared by Mr. J. R. Martin, organizer of the tour, that the event absolutely had to take place on the same day the scheme was announced, because gasoline rationing was scheduled to start the next day.

Those who wished to act as chauffeurs were instructed to leave the Tex Evans Buick Company lot at 1:30 P.M. and drive to the base in a caravan. Once the soldiers were in the cars, the procession set out on a fifteen-mile circle tour that would give the newcomers a glimpse of such exciting attractions as the ballpark, the high school, the hospital, and an oilfield. Following the trip, the civilian drivers were told to either take their passengers back to the base or let them remain in town if they so chose.

It was estimated that at least three hundred vehicles would be required to make the four-hour tour an unqualified success. The volunteer drivers were assured that they need not worry about losing their way, as Mr. Martin himself would be driving the procession's lead car. The trip, said its organizer, would impress the soldiers with Pampa's resources, its hospitality, and its beauty. Martin ended his urgent call for civilian drivers with a somewhat rhetorical question. "With gasoline rationing starting tomorrow," he stated, "you won't be making any long trips anyway, so why not mark the last of the carefree gasoline days by using the fuel in the tank of your car to give a treat to the soldiers?" [11]

Following their exciting sightseeing tour, the newly arrived cadets began their rigorous training routine. From reveille at 0530 until lights out at 2230, each cadet's day was packed with both ground and in-flight instruction. The mornings, from 0700 to 1130, were devoted to classroom work or time in the Link trainer. After an hour of calisthenics and a quick lunch, the cadets took to the air for nearly seven hours, flying with or without instructor pilots until 2045 and the evening meal. Leisure time lasted less than an hour, until taps was sounded at 2230. This schedule was strictly followed for five days of the week, with Saturday mornings reserved for a formal parade and review. Following that weekly event, the cadets were dismissed until Sunday evening curfew and the beginning of another routine week of training.[12]

The first Christmas at the new airfield was celebrated in grand style and afforded a welcome break in the schedule. To help ensure enough kitchen workers to prepare the gala feast that was planned, squadron officers devised a clever trap. All personnel who did not believe in Santa Claus were asked to sign a sheet of paper posted in the day rooms. Those whose signatures appeared on the sheet were then advised that they had voluntarily assigned themselves to Christmas Day KP duty.

The behind-the-scenes duty in the airfield's kitchens on Christmas 1942 must have been daunting, to say the least. The menu included fresh shrimp cocktail, roast turkey, baked Virginia ham, candied Louisiana yams, whipped Idaho potatoes, and a tossed salad with French dressing. Also offered were fresh broccoli, creamed onions, buttered peas, and carrot strips. To conclude the feast, soldiers were served Wisconsin cheese sticks, assorted nuts, old-fashioned fruitcakes, homemade pumpkin pie, and mixed ice creams. It was all washed down with gallons of coffee, hot chocolate, milk, and tea and topped off with complimentary cigars and cigarettes.[13]

By nearly all accounts, the off-duty time spent by the cadets in Pampa was pleasant. Some forty-five years later, former Cadet W. C. "Dub" Ferguson, Jr., Class 45-B, recalled that "the Pampa Army Airfield was a great place to be stationed, the friendly citizens were dedicated to the men and women in uniform. I appreciated them then, and now, forty-one years later, more so."[14]

Mike Porter, of Class 44-G, who married a Pampa girl while he was assigned to the field, remembers how outgoing all the local citizens were with the base personnel. Porter left Pampa for active duty in the European theater and received a Distinguished Flying Cross for his heroism in combat. Due to a postwar fire at the Army's St. Louis Records Center, however, it took more than fifty years for the medal to be presented to him.[15]

The only significant problem encountered by military personnel in town was a shortage of housing for those airmen with families. Jamie Gough, who later retired from the United States Air Force as a major general, recalls that the only accommodations he could find for his family had formerly been used as a funeral home. There were, the general wrote, "discarded caskets in the basement plus a long, slanting metal counter and sink in the kitchen."[16] Harold H. Noah, an enlisted radio mechanic, lived in the back of Wilson's Drug Store with his wife and two children. His wife's lasting impression of her days in Pampa was her astonishment at the size of the Texas roaches that shared their quarters.[17]

Roger G. Ritchey, a retired Air Force colonel, was not particularly impressed with the Texas Panhandle and Pampa when he was first assigned to the airfield in early 1945, but after he finally found a home for his family, his opinion changed. "We thoroughly enjoyed our stay in Pampa," the colonel recollects, "we met many wonderful people there and I . . . still do have many happy memories of Pampa."[18]

William T. Wagner of Cadet Class 44-T invited his father to come to the base from New Jersey to attend his graduation. After the long trip by bus, the senior Mr. Wagner stayed in a Pampa home. Long after the visit, he continued to be impressed with Texas hospitality and the friendliness of all the people he met in Pampa. "He told everyone about it when he got home," recalls the former cadet, "he talked about nothing but Pampa for years."[19] According to the *Pampa News* of February 23, 1943, one cadet class grew so fond of Pampa and its citizens that it formally expressed a desire to be adopted, en toto, by the city's residents.[20]

The first class of cadets arrived in Pampa some three days later than expected. Heavy traffic on the nation's railways was cited as the cause of the seventy-two-hour delay. When the train carrying them finally arrived at 2:00 A.M. on a Saturday morning, it was met by a somewhat bedraggled but excited group of cadets' wives who had arrived in Pampa well ahead of their husbands. The women had met every arriving train for three days, and when the long-awaited cadet section finally "snorted into" town, as the *Pampa News* reported, the wives "bounced into the arms of their husbands with whoops of delight as they marched from their section of the train." Despite this long-awaited reunion, all cadets were promptly marched to waiting buses and transported directly to the airfield. After consuming coffee, sandwiches, and soup, the men were ordered to bed in anticipation of the first day of training, which began the very next morning.[21]

This first cadet class to arrive at Pampa airfield graduated on February 16, 1943, receiving their commissions and wings from Brig. Gen. Isaiah Davies, commanding general of the 34th Flying Training Wing. Just four days later, Class 43-D arrived and began its training in advanced flying instruction. The second cadet class was made up of young men from forty-two states, the District of Columbia, and Puerto Rico.

On February 28, 1943, plans were announced for an open-house event to be held on March 7 at the less-than-one-year-old air base. According to Col. Daniel S. Campbell, the purpose of the open house was to thank Pampans for their cooperation and hospitality.[22] In a letter that appeared in the newspaper, Campbell wrote, "Pampa people, and those of the entire Panhandle, have time and again demonstrated their willingness and desires to make us feel at home and to cooperate with us in every way." More than forty years later, as a retired Air Force major general, Campbell continued to regard his welcome in Pampa as one of the warmest he received throughout his long military career.[23]

On Sunday, March 7, the day of the open house, the *Pampa News* published a special airfield supplement to commemorate the event and to salute the new base and its personnel. Copies of the supplement were made available to all officers and men through the post exchange at no cost.

It was anticipated that at least 10,000 civilians would visit the base during the three hours that it was open to the public. According to all reports, the number flocking to the airfield greatly exceeded the original estimate, resulting in massive traffic congestion and many overheated automobiles. If the size of the crowd attending the event was as large as the newspaper claimed, nearly half of Gray County's residents visited the base.[24]

Security measures for the open house were quite stringent. All visitors were required to enter the south gate to be directed to parking areas where they left their vehicles to tour the field on foot in groups accompanied by military guides. No cameras were permitted, and a strictly enforced 20 mph speed limit was in effect for the short distance from the gate to the parking lots.

Although most of the field was included on the tour, certain areas were restricted to the visitors. They were allowed to see the chapel, the recreation building, theater, barracks, and day rooms. Also open for inspection were the parachute building, the Link trainer rooms, the instrument building, and certain of the base's five hangars.

For the benefit of the civilians, the Sunday was designated a regular training day, giving them an opportunity to see the cadets march to classrooms and engage in calisthenics. The visitors were also treated to demonstrations of the cadets' flying abilities, as in-flight training continued despite the open-house activities.

When the invitation to the open house was received by the citizens of Pampa, the response was more than enthusiastic. Mayor Fred Thompson, who had played such an important role in bringing the base to the city, wrote an open letter to all military personnel assigned to the installation. In his seemingly heartfelt message, the mayor noted that "we [the city of Pampa] cannot offer you the entertainment facilities or other attractions you might find in other cities, but we do offer you our hospitality and 'what we have' for your entertainment." Mayor Thompson concluded, "In our homes, our business houses, or churches—anywhere in our city, we hope to make you feel that you are a citizen of Pampa."[25]

Local businesses placed ads in the newspaper welcoming the airmen assigned to the field. Some of the advertising copy was all but rhapsodic in extending a warm "Top O' Texas" greeting to the new arrivals. Banks, grocery stores, dry cleaners, and G. S. Shirley's combination liquor store and filling station placed large ads to demonstrate their willingness to be of service to military customers. The Diamond Shop, a leading jewelry store, took a full page to remind the soldiers that "here on the Virgin Plains [*sic*] at the Top O' Texas the cream of American youth is receiving its final training in the art of handling one of Uncle Sam's modern flying warships . . . training that will fit [*sic*] them to carry *The Star Spangled Banner* to ultimate victory over the Axis." The ad also pointed out that before carrying the nation's flag to ultimate victory, the cadets were welcome to make the Diamond Shop their headquarters when in town.[26]

The cadets who served at Pampa came from a variety of prewar backgrounds. Represented in the ranks were former drug clerks, farmers, salesmen, mechanics, and, of course, students. Cadet George R. Montgomery had been a dance instructor, whereas George H. Brown was a glass cutter. John R. Steward built elevators for a living prior to enlisting, and Raymond A. Duran was once a page for a New York City radio company. Robert Dietz was a stress analyst for an aircraft corporation, while Cadet Kenneth E. Proctor of Evanston, Illinois, had been a licensed embalmer.[27]

In addition to the *Pampa News*, which had served the community since 1926 and which reported airfield happenings with great thoroughness, another community newspaper began publishing later in the war. Named *The Pampa Flyer*, it began publication on November 1, 1944, as the voice of Pampa Army Airfield. Like many base newspapers, the small journal carried mainly items about sporting events, inoffensive gossip concerning enlisted personnel, and, without fail, a presentation of inane jokes that would have embarrassed even the most tasteless vaudeville comedian.

Occasionally, however, *The Pampa Flyer* did offer tidbits of statistical information that likely were of little interest to its readers, yet prove fascinating in retrospect. For example, it was reported that airmen and their families had purchased 359,924 tickets to attend movies at the base theater in the twenty-two-month period from January 13, 1943, through October 31, 1944. At 15 cents per ticket, the theater had grossed nearly $54,000 in sales. A poll taken among those attending the movies had shown Gary Cooper to be the most popular star, with Clark Gable, Spencer Tracy, and Betty Grable following close behind. "It was no landslide," the paper noted, as none of the four leaders garnered more than 8 percent of the vote. Other popular stars included Bob Hope, Bing Crosby, and Gene Autry, but the paper found it remarkable that "such masters as Charles Laughton, Thomas Mitchell, and Leslie Howard received not a single vote."[28]

The base newspaper also conducted a poll to determine the favorite authors among its enlisted readers. First on the list was Zane Grey. In second place was Edgar Allan Poe, with Jack London coming in third. Locked in a rather unlikely tie for fourth-favorite authors were Ernest Hemingway and William Shakespeare.

When the first contingent of the Women's Army Corps (WAC) arrived on the base in late 1944, *The Pampa Flyer* dutifully reported that Dorothy Braud, who hailed from Lake Jackson, Texas, was a sheet-metal worker, while Alice M. Doyle, from Edenborn, Pennsylvania, was a welder. Mary S. Sutkins, of Rochester, New York, was employed as a control-tower operator, and Lena E. Vertucci was a surgical technician. While still on the subject of WACs, the base paper saw fit to announce that the army had decided that it was providing too much food to its female soldiers. Rather than continue with the 3,750 calories per day that each WAC was being given, new regulations ordered that only 3,100 calories per day would be served until the end of the war. It is a wonder that existing photographs of Pampa WACs on parade show that the women were, for the most part, far trimmer than their recommended daily intake of calories might suggest.

The Pampa Flyer was also used by base headquarters to carry messages from senior ranking Army Air Force officers. For example, the December 29, 1944, edition reported that Lt. Gen. Barney Giles, deputy commander of the Air Force, had ordered that Army aircraft were under no circumstances to be referred to as "ships," as doing so in the past had led to "serious confusion between Army personnel" and their Navy, Marine Corps, and Coast Guard counterparts.[29]

Other edicts from high command were also printed in the base newspaper. Personnel were sternly reminded in the December 27, 1944, edition not to run on the base's icy boardwalks, as many accidents had been suffered by speeding airmen. All minors on the field were advised in November 1944 that they were required to wear a two-inch red button with the word "minor" imprinted on it in large letters. No follow-up article reported how well this measure was enforced, if at all.[30]

Seemingly fascinated by statistics, *The Pampa Flyer* reported that 91,000,000 cigars per month were being supplied to GIs around the world. Unfortunately, the source of this astonishing quantity of stogies was not named in the article.[31]

Among the subjects seldom covered by the reporters of *The Pampa Flyer* were aircraft accidents. The pages of the civilian-published *Pampa News*, however, presented tragic proof of the dangers of flight training. The first fatal crash occurred on January 27, 1943, when two aircraft collided on a taxiway at an auxiliary field. Killed was Cadet William H. Kidd, age twenty-one, who had been scheduled to graduate in three weeks.[32]

A midair collision claimed the life of instructor William A. Gibbons on May 10, 1943. Three other aviators parachuted to safety while debris from the two destroyed aircraft fell to earth among oil derricks located two miles north of Pampa.[33] Five weeks later, another midair crash was fatal for four more fliers.[34]

On December 15, 1943, two cadets were killed when their plane crashed just after taking off from the field. They were both scheduled to graduate within weeks.[35] Another midair collision took the lives of three fliers on January 5, 1944.[36]

This tragedy was followed by three more fatal crashes within a month's time. In total, ten aviators from the airfield were killed during the four-week period.

Despite what seems to have been a high incidence of fatal accidents, the pace of training did not begin to slacken until much later in the war. Until then, all activities on the base continued at what must have been an almost fevered pace.

In a strikingly non-military occurrence, the Army sought to reap an agricultural windfall from the vast acres it owned surrounding the airfield itself. The entire area had been planted in wheat long before the government had acquired the acreage and built the base, and the crop continued to flourish on the land not covered by the airfield's concrete. In a rare example of federal practicality, it was decided to permit civilian operators to bid on a contract to harvest the wheat.

Not fully versed in commodity pricing, the Army anticipated that it would earn at least $4,000 from its agrarian endeavor. As it soon developed, the estimate was overly optimistic by nearly $1,500 as a result of lower-than-anticipated prices and yields. A total of 3,344 (and a half) bushels were harvested.[37]

When it came to entertaining its personnel, the Army was more in its element. The Pampa Airfield Band and Orchestra, for example, gave concerts, played for formal parades and reviews, and spun off smaller musical groups that entertained at dances both on the base and in town. Members of the band included musicians who had been featured performers with big-name aggregations before the war. Corp. Arthur Rose, for example, had been with Bunny Berrigan's famous orchestra, and Albert Fish had played trumpet for Bobby Hackett. Warrant Officer Ken Carpenter, the band's director, held a musical degree from Drake University. He went on to fame as a popular orchestra leader after the war.[38]

For those soldiers whose leisure-time preferences centered more on outdoor activities than on music, the base provided an ample schedule. In early September 1943 a true Texas event was staged with airfield personnel as participants. Offering Victory Bonds as the prizes for top performers, the base presented a full-scale rodeo, much to the delight of real Panhandle cowboys who came as spectators to watch Eastern greenhorns try their luck at various rodeo events. Calf roping, bull and bronco riding, and bulldogging were featured, as were horse racing and wild-cow milking. As an added attraction, a contest was held seeking the best-dressed cowgirl in attendance, with the winner receiving a $25 Victory Bond.[39]

Among those who had been assigned to the base during the war and perhaps watched these events were William P. Clements Jr., a future governor of Texas; George McGovern, a future Democratic presidential candidate, United States senator, and ambassador; as well as movie star Jack Palance. Both McGovern and Palance saw combat action in the multi-engine aircraft they learned to fly in Texas.

The names of some of the men who had trained at Pampa were enshrined in the airfield's Hall of Fame, which opened on November 2, 1944. If a pilot had been killed, wounded, or was missing in action, his photograph and combat record were given a place of honor in the exhibit. Prisoners of war and those cited or decorated for valor were also included.

Seventy-seven Pampa Hall-of-Famers had received the Distinguished Flying Cross, two had been given Distinguished Service Crosses, and three had been awarded the Silver Star. Forty-one men had received the Purple Heart. In all, 507 Pampa graduates were honored in the Hall of Fame when it opened, including 92 who had been killed in action, 62 who were missing, and 81 who were known to be prisoners of war.[40]

The airfield continued to train pilots for combat on a regular schedule until early May 1945 immediately following the surrender of Nazi Germany. A letter from Lt. Gen. Barton K. Yount notified base personnel that the aviation cadet program was to be "drastically cut back." Those personnel awaiting air-crew training were notified that they were being diverted into other branches of the Army, including the infantry. Probably sensing that this diversion might be unsettling to those who had enlisted to become pilots, the general made reference to their likely "keen disappointment" while assuring them that each man still had a big job to do in "battles yet to be fought." Though probably well-intentioned, General Yount's words most likely did little to assuage the former aviation cadets' disappointment.[41]

By June, all enlisted men over the age of forty were given permission to request separation from the service. Because of this order and the discontinuation of the cadet program, well-founded rumors predicting the imminent closing of the airfield circulated throughout the community, despite denials by base authorities.

There was not the slightest hint of any plans to close the base in a public announcement made by its commander, Col. James A. DeMarco, on July 30, 1945. Speaking on behalf of all his personnel, the colonel invited residents of Pampa and other nearby communities to attend what he promised would be "the greatest Army Air Forces celebrations ever held" at the airfield.[42]

The event, which was being staged to mark the thirty-eighth anniversary of "the world's largest Air Force," had been in the planning stages for months. Nearly thirty of the field's B-25 bombers were scheduled to fly over the crowd at a low altitude, with P-38 fighters to follow close behind. A formal military review and parade was to take place in the early afternoon, with martial music provided by the band from Lubbock Army Airfield. No mention was made about why Pampa Field's own highly vaunted band was not slated to perform. Following a full day of flying, parading, and athletic events, the day ended with a dance in the recreation center.

Despite such festivities, which were highly successful, it became increasingly apparent that the base would soon be found unnecessary. On September 6, 1945, following the surrender of Japan, the announcement Pampans had long feared came from base headquarters, stating that the airfield would indeed become inactive no later than September 30. Although the base commander had stated only a week earlier that he had not been informed of any impending closure, personnel on the base were not surprised at the news.[43]

On September 13 it was announced that the airfield's Hall of Fame was to be moved to Pampa's Kerley-Crossman American Legion Post before the base closed. Two weeks later, it was disclosed that the USO that had performed such yeoman service during the war years would cease operations on October 15.[44]

Finally, on September 23, under a banner headline just slightly smaller than the one that had announced the coming of the base, the *Pampa News* declared that only a skeleton crew would remain on the field by the end of the week. The aircraft were already on their way to a base at Enid, Oklahoma, and the few cadets still in training had been transferred to Houston and Bryan, Texas; Enid, Oklahoma; and Kearns, Utah. It was also announced, in error as it developed, that the buildings on the base were going to be sold.[45]

There was still time for some last-minute public relations, however. In his final message to the people of Pampa, the base commander said, "your neighborliness, hospitality, and helpfulness has not been excelled by any community in which I have been stationed in my Army career." Colonel Ronin concluded his remarks with a rousing tribute to the little Panhandle city that had been such a good neighbor for nearly three years. "I am sincere," said the colonel, "when I say that I consider that no community in the United States could be more patriotic, public spirited, and downright American than this." Colonel Ronin had very likely spoken the truth.[46]

After the base was finally closed, the economic impact on its host city was cushioned to some degree by the tremendous wartime growth that had occurred in the region's numerous petroleum-related industries. The town's population had doubled to nearly 25,000 during the war years and in the following decade. The cyclical nature of the oil business took its toll on the community over the ensuing years, however, and by 1990, the population had decreased to roughly 20,000.[47]

Pampa's airfield fell into disrepair virtually overnight. Despite the earlier announcement to the contrary, the buildings were for the most part razed or moved away to be used elsewhere. The post chapel was moved twelve miles into Pampa, where it continues to be used for Church of Christ Sunday services. The base material upon which the main runway had been constructed was removed when the runway's concrete surface was air-hammered into dust. It was reused to build some eighteen miles of Texas Highway 152.[48]

In 1952 the City of Pampa, which had acquired the entire airfield property from the federal government at no cost, sold it for $2.60 per acre to a feedlot operation. Today, a daily average 15,000 head of cattle occupy the property, making exploration of the old base a somewhat challenging and at best a very brief undertaking.[49] The taxiways make excellent paved livestock alleys, and the few remaining concrete foundations provide a substantial flooring for pens and water troughs. The field's long-idle compass rose still exists, understandably of no interest to the cattle, who apparently do not particularly care to know what direction they face as they contentedly chew their cud.

The heritage of Pampa Army Airfield is not completely lost, however. Annual reunions of former base personnel bring the one-time pilots back to Pampa to reminisce and, if they are hardy enough, to visit all that remains of their once-bustling military home.

Some years ago, "Doc" Savage, of Cadet Class 44-K, came

back to Pampa while on a vacation trip to Kansas from his home in Washington state. His memories of "ten very tense, cold weeks" spent on the base in the winter of 1944 were clearly less than pleasant ones, but curiosity compelled him to take one last quick look at what was left of the old airfield.

Arriving in town, Savage found it difficult to make contact with anyone old enough to know an airbase had ever existed nearby, let alone provide him with directions to the site. He persevered, however, and finally found himself standing where he had not been since February 1945. At first, the ex-cadet who eventually became an Air Force captain was struck with how small the base site looked compared to his memories of it. Then, perhaps with a capricious change in wind direction, Savage was made fully aware that what had once been an airfield was now a cattle feedlot. The transformation of the site was impressive, if not downright overpowering. "It was," Savage wrote, "the best example I've seen of beating swords into plowshares." With that acute observation, the veteran turned his back on Pampa for the last time. "So I've seen it," he wrote, "and that's enough; I'll continue to live in the present."[50]

Most other veterans of the Pampa experience have a different viewpoint. They enjoy returning to the city to attend reunions and tell their tales of war. The former pilots applaud the efforts of ex-cadet Mike Porter and his colleagues at the Freedom Museum USA as they prepare a B-25 for permanent display in Pampa and work to move the old post chapel onto the grounds of the museum.

To these veterans, memories of Pampa are for the most part good ones and the comradeship of old flying buddies important. Life in the present tense is fine, of course, they seem to say, but reliving the unforgettable flying experiences of fifty years ago can be sweet indeed. To many of them, it was the greatest adventure of their lives.

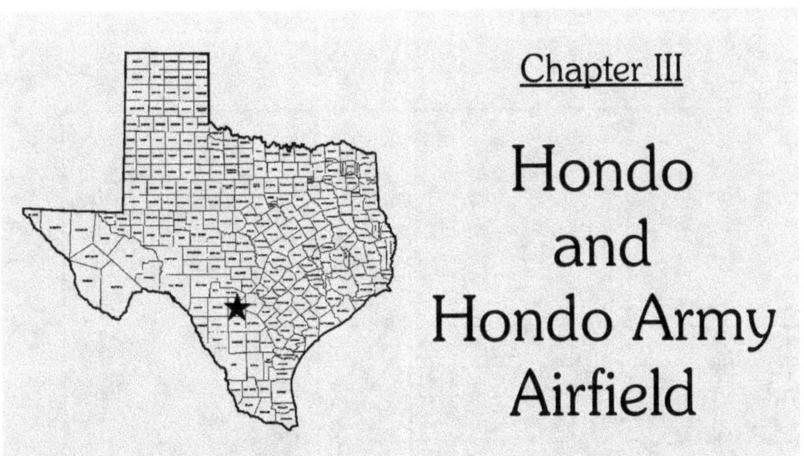

Chapter III

Hondo and Hondo Army Airfield

What I remember most are all those fast-moving trains that just tore right through the middle of that little town constantly, day and night, almost on the half-hour.

Ernest E. Arnschuler
San Antonio, Texas

The noisy smoke-billowing railroad locomotives that had so impressed ex-aviation cadet Arnschuler were symbols of what had initially put Hondo firmly on the map of Texas. In August 1881 Thomas W. Peirce, the president of the Galveston, Houston and San Antonio Railroad Company, had privately acquired 160 acres of land some forty miles due west of San Antonio for a mere $450. The very next year, the shrewd executive sold the parcel of land, conveniently platted, to his own railroad for $15,257, and the laying of company track westward toward Hondo soon began.[1]

By 1884 the newly formed community with trains running through it had twenty-five residents and a two-year-old post office. By 1915 Hondo had become the booming county seat of Medina County and its population had increased a hundredfold.[2]

With the advent of the automobile in the early 1900s, motor cars soon competed with the railroad in comparatively high-speed travel east and west along U.S. 90, the highway that had been built

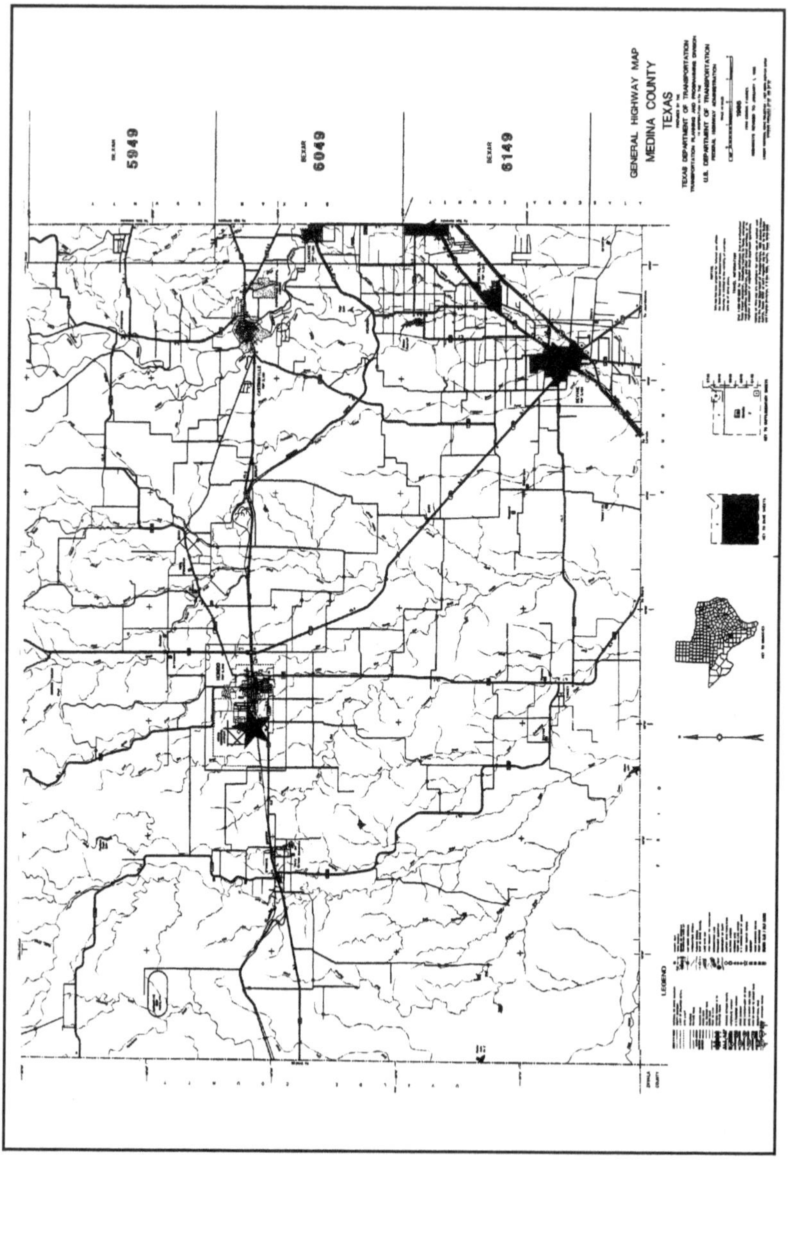

Medina County Map

This map of Medina County shows the location of Hondo Army Airfield during the war years. An inset map of Texas shows the location of the county within the state.

parallel to the train tracks. By the 1930s Hondo's town leaders grew concerned that the increasing flow of speeding vehicular traffic along the highway constituted a mounting peril to Hondoans. Through the auspices of the local Lions Club, what was clearly intended to be a warning sign to speeding motorists was posted on the eastern edge of town. "This is God's country," sternly advised the newly erected billboard, "Don't drive through it like hell." Some longtime residents recall that the sign was in fact meant to be something of a joke, and nearly all old-timers concede that it might just as well have been, as the message had no apparent impact whatever on those who chose to speed like hell through the little city.[3]

Not surprisingly, however, the highly unusual sign did attract considerable attention among visitors to the city, and pictures of it soon appeared in newspapers and magazines all across the country. As might also be expected, there were some in Hondo who were highly offended by the sign's mildly profane wording, and after much often acrimonious debate at citywide meetings, the billboard was taken down, presumably never to be seen again.

However, according to the *Hondo Anvil Herald*, visiting motorists missed seeing the uniquely admonishing signboard, and community leaders soon came to realize that their city had surrendered one of its more famous tourist attractions. Consequently, after even more heated debate, a curious compromise was struck between town boosters and those who had taken offense at the original wording, and the sign was promptly placed back at its old location. It now read "This is God's country—Please don't drive through it like hell." The addition of the polite "please" apparently satisfied those who had been in opposition to "hell." The sign, with its revised wording, remains in its original place on U.S. 90 to this day.[4]

The leaders of the little community had other far more important things to deal with than mildly offensive signboards when the Great Depression struck Medina County in the 1930s. As demand for the area's rich agricultural products diminished along with America's buying power, city fathers desperately sought some enterprise that would infuse new dollars into Hondo's stagnant economy and, they hoped, perhaps even stimulate the town's growth, as Hondo had remained at the 2,500 population level for more than a quarter of a century. As history was to show, the wholly unsolicited enterprise that brought boom times back to Hondo was World War II.

HONDO ARMY AIRFIELD

My memories of Hondo are not particularly favorable, though I could say the same for some of the other places I was stationed.

William H. Rehnquist, Chief Justice
Supreme Court of the United States

Although the nineteen-year-old man who would go from his days as a soldier in World War II to the nation's highest judicial post had other-than-fond memories of his days in Hondo, other soldiers found life in the small Texas town to be more than just tolerable. "I sort of liked it," recalled Amos O. Beasley some fifty years after the fact. "The folks there were friendly and the city welcomed us with open arms."[5]

Town and county leaders had good reason to welcome the Army Air Force to the region when it arrived in 1942. Through their elected representatives in Washington, they had been aggressively lobbying the War Department to construct a military installation near Hondo for some time. That effort, ultimately successful, brought an economic surge to the community that even the most ardent booster could not possibly have imagined.

The government's ultimate decision to build and operate a navigator-training facility at Hondo was based on several factors, the most obvious one being that Army Air Force leaders had suddenly realized that navigators were needed, and needed immediately. In the pre-war build-up of the nation's air arm, the emphasis had been on more and more aircraft with, logically, enough pilots to fly them.

As the prospects for a global war grew ever more ominous in 1940, however, it became increasingly apparent that a huge armada of bombers flown by well-trained pilots would be of little value in combat without equally well-trained navigators and bombardiers on board who could successfully direct and complete the bombers' sole mission, which was to first find an enemy target and then drop bombs on it. Clearly, a large group of such well-trained flying officers would be required very soon. Further, no longer would navigator trainees be only former pilot candidates who had washed out of flight training. The new generation of navigators would emerge from eager young men who enthusiastically wanted to be navigators, not disappointed ex-pilots settling for what they grudgingly perceived as merely the next-best thing.

Navigation schools began to open at Army airfields all across the nation prior to America's entry into the war in December 1941. One such training facility was in operation at San Antonio's giant Kelly Field, located just a short distance east of Hondo. The size of Kelly Field and its proximity to other busy San Antonio air bases were factors in the selection of Hondo as a site for a navigation school. Blessed with usually good flying weather, San Antonio's clear skies were soon crowded with training aircraft from its many local bases as the pre-war build-up accelerated, and the city's rapid urban growth outward toward these once-rural airfields made the resulting congested air traffic over the city increasingly hazardous.[6]

In order to alleviate the problem of crowded air space, while still continuing to enjoy good flying conditions and not materially disrupt the navigational training courses already in session at Kelly, nearby Hondo seemed a likely choice for a new navigator school. Hints of the impending move soon leaked to the public. The *Hondo Anvil Herald* reported on January 23, 1942, some seven weeks after the attack on Pearl Harbor, that "several Army officials were here today, scouting for a location for an air training field."[7]

Rumors continued to swirl that a big Army flying installation for the community was soon to be announced, although indications were that Army officers were seriously concerned that the little town did not have adequate housing to accommodate even the first wave of construction workers and the advance guard of military personnel. To offset these concerns, the town's leaders guaranteed the government that four hundred housing units would be immediately available for base workers.[8]

On March 2, 1942, the speculation about the airfield reached an even higher level when the local newspaper reported that "a force of some nine or more Army engineers arrived here Monday and began a survey for a location of the site for the proposed Aviation Navigation School." The newspaper account then pinpointed the "proposed" location precisely and surmised that the total area involved would be "four thousand acres" in size. The well-informed *Anvil Herald* missed the field's final total acreage by a mere 325 acres.[9]

By April 3, all speculation ended when Robert L. Kollman, president-manager of the Hondo Chamber of Commerce, received the following joyous telegram from U.S. Senator W. Lee "Pappy" O'Daniel:

> WAR DEPARTMENT ANNOUNCES TODAY AUTHORIZATION FOR CONSTRUCTION OF AIR FORCE TRAINING SCHOOL AT HONDO TO COST IN EXCESS OF FIVE MILLION DOLLARS.[10]

Apparently not wishing to be outdone, Texas's other senator at the time, Tom Connally, simultaneously sent a telegram of his own to announce the Army's decision to an already exuberant Hondo. Subsequent communications from Washington revealed that some 6,000 navigator candidates would be training at the new facility, including many of the cadets then being trained at Kelly Field. Realizing that the fruit borne of their labor to acquire the new base was sweet indeed, the city fathers wasted no time in using the War Department's announcement to set about formally incorporating the City of Hondo. It was important that the city receive the coveted designation of "defense area" from the federal government in order to obtain Washington's financial assistance in improving streets and expanding utilities to provide service to the soon-to-be-built facility. As an incorporated entity, such a designation was far more likely to be obtained. On April 17, 1942, fewer than three weeks following the confirmation of the airfield's approval, Hondo voted to become an incorporated city.[11]

If the town moved rapidly to incorporate, its speed was pallid when compared with the alacrity with which contractor H. B. Zachry of San Antonio undertook his airfield-construction duties. Within a week of the senators' twin telegrams, Zachry had his men on site and, having promptly and unceremoniously unhoused the site's few occupants, he personally oversaw the demolition of houses, fences, trees, and literally anything else that stood in the way of his massive undertaking.

The local newspaper reported that those residents who had been suddenly and summarily dispossessed of their homes and even their personal belongings were "taking it gracefully."[12] Other reports, however, clearly indicate that all was not a gracious compliance with the twenty-four-hour eviction notices. Some residents physically resisted orders to vacate their lands, only to have bulldozers rip out their fences, setting livestock free, and then watch helplessly as their homes and even their personal belongings were crushed beneath the onslaught of the giant earth-moving machines.[13]

Mr. Zachry had a seemingly impossible timetable to maintain, and he was clearly determined to succeed no matter the cost in human relations. He had been given only 100 days by the War Department to turn nearly 4,000 acres of Texas farmland into a functioning flying field with an anticipated 8,000 inhabitants. Plans called for more than 600 buildings, a complete utility network, and a system of streets, runways, and taxiways requiring 650,000 square yards of concrete.[14] Zachry imported or locally hired more than 3,000 construction workers, who were clearly given to understand that they would be working around the clock to accomplish the massive task that the company had been given.

Tons of supplies and thousands of men flooded into Hondo, and the Southern Pacific trains carrying construction materials all but choked off north or southbound automobile traffic trying to cross its east/west-running roadbed. Despite Hondo's earnest pledge to find housing for the massive influx of humanity, many workers were forced to find accommodations as far away as San Antonio, D'Hanis, Tarpley, Castroville, and other communities.

Zachry and his crews, while clearly overzealous on several occasions, were unquestionably focused and efficient. Working day and night for forty days, all concrete work was soon completed. Simultaneously, the construction of hangars, barracks, classrooms, and administrative offices went on at a feverish pace.

In a masterpiece of understatement, the *Hondo Anvil-Herald* announced, "this is a big job that the government wants done in a hurry." [15] If any Hondoans wondered what their role would be in the frantic hubbub that surrounded them, the newspaper admonished, "You best do your part by accepting conditions as they are and keep smiling," [16] although those whose lifelong homes had been forcibly and instantly taken from them might have found it difficult to maintain a happy smile. By most accounts, the citizens of Hondo seemed to recognize what the base meant, not only to their town, but also to the entire nation suddenly at war.

When the dust finally settled on the huge site just west of

town, only eighty-nine days after the clearing of the ground had commenced, what had been small farms and homesteads in April had become a gigantic air base in July. H. B. Zachry had somehow accomplished his goal, and the navigation school was ready to train cadets.

Following a trend that was well underway even at the time and would long continue in government-contract fulfillment throughout the war and beyond, costs incurred in the project ran appreciably higher than the $5 million originally quoted by Senator Pappy O'Daniel. The land itself had cost a mere $300,000, or nearly $82 per acre, but the buildings had been constructed for about $5.5 million, and all that rapid concrete-laying for more than a month of days and nights added another cool $1.5 million. Despite the cost and the social upheaval created, it remains that the Zachry Company had wrought a near miracle in building what would soon become the world's largest navigator school for $7 million in just one day short of three months' time.[17]

Reports indicate that on occasion, the contractor had found it necessary to modify War Department building specifications in order to make facilities on the new base more livable. The late John Wentz remembered that the original plans for the soldiers' barracks called for dirt floors, which would have made living conditions all but intolerable in South Texas. Fortunately, the same plans called for barrack roofs that could support the weight of an accumulated snow depth far greater than had ever fallen in the Hondo area. Zachry simply poured the concrete floors for the barracks and paid for the alteration to the specifications by installing less supportive and proportionally less expensive roofs for the buildings.[18]

With Zachry's miracle now one for the 1942 record books, it was the Army's turn to create some miracles of its own. The new facility, under the command of Lt. Col. G. B. Dany, officially opened its gates on July 4, 1942, and began training student navigators five weeks later. Classes that were already in session at Kelly Field made the transition to the new base in such an orderly manner that not one hour of scheduled training was lost in moving the school from San Antonio to Hondo. The first of the hastily transferred classes graduated in late August 1942.[19]

The new cadets were initially welcomed to the proud and newly incorporated city with apparently genuine, if sometimes perhaps overstated, warmth. One poem of greeting taken from the pages of the *Hondo Anvil Herald* perhaps adequately captures the sentiments of the time:

Welcome Soldiers

We welcome the soldiers to our town
and trust they will never meet with a frown,
just cheery smiles and a helping hand
while they train here to defend our land.

We are just a peaceful village small,
with nothing much to offer at all!
Just friendship true, good water and air,
and we trust that you will treat us fair.

You're Uncle Sam's best, so we've been told,
gentlemen true, not rude nor too bold.
so we're glad to have you come our way,
to protect us from harm—night and day.

The key to our city we give to you
with a hearty welcome to dwell here, too.
The doors of our churches are open wide,
you will find both joy and peace inside.

In this part of Texas, you will find
real happy people, the friendly kind.
"Deep in the heart of Texas," you see
the real southern hospitality.

While you are training up in the sky—
teaching our young soldier boys to fly,
we on the ground will utter a prayer
for your safe return from up in the air.

We trust you will never rue the day.[20]

In all likelihood, any big-city cynic who for some reason had acquired a fondness for the classic "Burma Shave" signs then popular throughout rural America must have thought that he had hit the mother lode with this piece of poetic sentiment.

The much-lauded young cadets fortunately had little time to either read or appreciate such sugary poetry. Their typical day started at 0600 hours and ended at 2200 hours with the sounding of taps. Training flights of up to five hours' duration, mostly in the Beechcraft AT-7 aircraft, took place at least two days a week. Interspersed were classroom sessions, drills, and the dreaded and highly unpopular daily hour of physical training, in weather conditions sometimes cold and wet, but much more often hot, dry, and dusty.[21]

Saturday afternoons and Sundays were free, and cadets often made the short mile-and-a-half journey into Hondo on their free time. Chief Justice Rehnquist, however, notes that "there wasn't much to do in Hondo," so he often made his way to other cities. He even recalls hitchhiking to Houston and Corpus Christi on occasion.[22] While it may be somewhat difficult to envision the austere-appearing chief justice of today thumbing a ride along a dusty Texas highway fifty-odd years ago, even as a uniformed youth, it is certainly neither an unpleasant nor unwelcome image that warmly comes to mind.

The chief justice also recalls going into town on a Friday night to watch the Hondo High School team play the team from nearby Fredericksburg. He can remember hearing the hometown fans loudly singing, "Hondo will shine tonight, Hondo will shine . . ." in celebration of the slightest on-field accomplishment of the local team.[23]

Aside from some occasional post-game revelry, Hondo's records do not indicate that a significant number of lawless or rowdy events occurred in the town during the war years. John Wentz, however, remembered that when there was at one point a rash of incidents involving soldiers and local citizenry, the base commander quickly threatened to place the entire city off-limits if such incidents did not immediately cease. The commander's threat was effective, and the relationship between airfield and community became far more peaceful virtually overnight.[24]

In most respects, Hondo actually seemed to live up to its published poem of welcome to the soldiers. Service clubs were established, and dances for the cadets were staged every Saturday night at the high school gymnasium. What must have been a particularly active USO was soon in operation in town. According to that organization's final tabulations at war's end, an astounding 878,768 people from the airfield had reportedly entered the facility from October 1942 before it closed in November, 1945.[25]

As there were some 1,150 days during the years of the USO

operation in Hondo, simple calculations would indicate that an average of 764 people visited the facility each day, on the perhaps shaky assumption that the USO was open each and every day during those years. At any rate, such a high level of reported attendance, give or take a few airmen each day, does at least suggest that the Hondo USO was an unusually popular place.

If not in town or hitchhiking along the road to other Texas cities, the cadets could enjoy a wide range of activities on the base in their all-too-rare spare time. Bowling alleys and a swimming pool helped pass the time between classes. Such Hollywood luminaries as Bette Davis and Red Skelton came to visit and entertain. A library with 2,000 volumes was available for literature lovers, and on occasion, musical groups would give concerts on the base. The *Hondo Anvil Herald* reported on May 21, 1943, that the American Symphony Orchestra had performed for an airfield audience, presenting works by Mozart and Bizet and featuring operatic arias by mezzo-soprano Miss Ellen Longone.[26]

Soldiers from the airfield also found a way to make travelers passing through town aware of the navigator school located nearby. With the permission of the chamber of commerce, amateur sign painters from the base struck out the word "drive" on Hondo's famous billboard to change the message to "don't navigate through it like hell."[27]

Though their leisure time was apparently well spent, the cadets' lives at Hondo were mainly about learning the art of navigation. The training included celestial navigation, dead reckoning, day position fixing, and other techniques. In an effort to acquaint the local citizenry with the main thrust of a trained aerial navigator's in-flight duty, an inquiring reporter from the paper went "behind the scenes," as he called it. "Navigation cadets are a cool-eyed bunch," the writer confided, "and 100 percent self-reliant." He continued, "Their job is similar to directing a blind truck driver freighting 10 tons of TNT at 60 miles an hour and willing to bet their lives they can keep the driver on the road."[28]

Perhaps inevitably, the intensive training schedule created a deadly potential for fatal aircraft accidents. From September 30, 1942, until October 18, 1945, Hondo Army Airfield suffered twenty-seven crashes resulting in nearly one hundred fatalities. A flying accident on October 2, 1942, killed eight airmen and all but destroyed the rural Hondo home of Henry F. Merriman. At a memorial service for the military victims held at the Horger Funeral Home in Hondo, nearly a thousand local citizens came to pay their respects.[29]

Despite such tragedies, training at the facility proceeded on schedule, and every eighteen weeks a class of newly winged navigators left Hondo for active duty in combat throughout the world. The school's initial performance had been such that base commander George B. Dany ordered a first-anniversary extravaganza to take place on July 3, 1943. The public was invited, and over 10,000 Texans turned out to see a formal review and a flyover of forty-five training aircraft involving a navigation competition that probably was not all that thrilling to casual observers on the ground. Perhaps even less exciting to most, a base-beautification project was also to be judged, with the lawn-cutting, grass-growing, and flower-gardening skills of the various barracks to be evaluated. The first prize of a cabinet radio was awarded to the best military landscapers by the president of the San Antonio Garden Club, Mr. Griswold Gillette.[30]

Happily for the throng of attendees, things became a bit livelier as the anniversary celebration progressed. A track meet was held, drill teams performed, and boxing matches and softball and baseball games were scheduled, with one complete inning of a baseball game played without the traditional advantage of using a ball.

For those hardy individuals still standing after these hectic events, a reception and three separate dances were staged, and the day finally ended at midnight with the crowning of Hondo Army Airfield's first-anniversary sweetheart. It was clearly a day to remember.[31]

As many people already know, it often becomes quite warm in Texas in the summertime. While the celebrants of the field's first-anniversary celebration must have sweltered in the midsummer heat without air-conditioning, the base commander on another occasion found himself ordered to supply cooling for other visitors to the airfield. A top-secret letter instructed then-Colonel G. B. Dany (later an Air Force major general) to arrange to have a 2,000-pound block of ice available on the airfield ramp for immediate loading onto an aircraft that was due to arrive on a certain date from Arizona. Moreover, the huge ice block had to be precisely ten feet long, three feet wide, and three feet high. The colonel obediently complied with this unusual order and only much later found out what had prompted it to be issued.

After the war, it was revealed that a persuasive scientist had personally convinced President Franklin D. Roosevelt of the efficacy of employing some Texas-dwelling free-tailed bats to carry incendiary bombs to Japan and cause them to detonate and thus destroy such paper-house cities as Tokyo, Kyoto, and Nagasaki, among others. The theory was that ice would cause the bats to hibernate while being carried in an airplane. Minuscule incendiary bombs would then be affixed by a clip to their tiny chests. When dropped from aircraft flying at low altitudes near Tokyo, for example, the bats would be released and would instantly emerge from hibernation on encountering the warm air. Presumably stunned at finding themselves in flight over a strange foreign city, they would hurriedly seek refuge in the eaves of many Japanese paper dwellings. In due time, the little firebombs would detonate automatically and, it was reasoned, Tokyo would become nothing but a gigantic pile of paper ashes and incinerated bats. Since the Hondo area was a seasonal home to such involuntary sacrificial bats, the professor was coming to the airfield to collect a batch of them and needed the ice to cool the creatures for an immediate flight back to Arizona to participate in a test-bombing exercise.

The bats were indeed collected after some considerable difficulty, adequately cooled by Colonel Dany's giant block of ice, and then flown from Hondo to Arizona, where a mock Japanese paper village had been constructed far out in the desert. The still-hibernating bats were then given their deadly cargo, taken aloft, and dropped over the village. Just as predicted, the bats promptly awoke, took shelter in the village, and detonated their bombs, along with themselves, and the whole paper town quickly burned to the ground.

Unfortunately, however, some of the bomb-bearing bats apparently failed to fully grasp their mission. Acting more like homing pigeons, they swiftly winged their way back to the nearby Arizona air base from which they had only just been transported. There the results were every bit as impressive as they had been out in the desert. Two hangars and ten United States aircraft were destroyed by the bat-borne bombs at a cost of some $2 million. As might be imagined, Colonel Dany did not receive any further requests either for giant blocks of ice or for an assortment of the tiny Texas bats.[32]

Even without the use of bat bombs, the Allied forces moved ever closer to a final victory in 1945. Following the defeat of Nazi Germany in May of that year, the mission of Hondo Army Airfield was converted from navigator training to schooling flight engineers. The last class of navigators graduated on July 21, 1945, and students of the engineer school, moving from Lowry Field at Denver, soon began arriving for a five-week cruise-control course.

The future engineers were in training to fly aboard B-29 bombers, but at the time the Army Air Force had none of the big planes to spare for training purposes. Perhaps this was just as well, since Hondo's runways were not really quite long enough to accommodate routine B-29 flight operations. Consequently, modified B-24 Liberator bombers were used as flying classrooms for the engineering students. In total, nearly 3,000 rated flight engineers graduated from the Hondo facility.

With the war winding down, August 1, 1945, was designated as National Air Force Day by its chief, Gen. Henry H. Arnold. Airfields throughout the nation held open houses to celebrate the service's thirty-eighth birthday and to recognize the contribution that airpower had made in achieving the victory apparently soon to be realized.

In Hondo, all businesses were closed for the day so that the citizens could visit the base and show their appreciation to the airmen who had been their next-door neighbors for more than three years. Once again, a formal military review opened the events of the day, followed by demonstrations and various athletic activities. A B-29 that had managed to land on the short runway and several B-24 bombers were on static display on the ramp, giving Hondoans their first opportunity to view inside the giant war planes.[33]

Just five days after the open house, a B-29 made a historic atomic bomb run over Hiroshima, Japan, and effectively brought World War II to its conclusion. The victory was saluted all across the nation, with Hondo and its airfield joining in the celebration.

With the war over, however, there was no longer a need for Hondo Army Airfield. Operations had been scaled back with the defeat of Germany, and now the base was scheduled to be closed at the end of 1945.

The field had done its job admirably. It had produced thousands of navigators and nearly 3,000 flight engineers, and it had provided good employment for throngs of civilians. In the process, Hondo's population had risen from 2,500 in 1940 to 12,000 by the end of the war. When the airfield closed, the city's population decreased rapidly, and by 1950, only 4,220 people remained.[34]

The base was officially closed on December 29, 1945. Nearly all the buildings and their contents were sold as surplus, and the property was put to limited civilian use. One barracks, once home to the contingent of Women's Army Corps (WACs) who served on the base, was moved intact into Hondo. Now located on the grounds of the Medina County Museum, plans have been made to completely renovate the derelict building and make it a key attraction of a proposed Hondo Army Airfield Museum.

By 1951, with the advent of the Korean War, however, the base was reactivated by the United States Air Force and pilot training was resumed. New buildings were constructed, and a golf course was added to the field's recreational facilities.

The base was again closed in June 1958, but the Air Force returned in 1973 to begin a pilot flight-screening program in conjunction with several private companies. That program was canceled many years later when the aircraft then being used in the training was found to be dangerously unsafe. Other buildings on the old field were leased to various business concerns, with City of Hondo agencies occupying still others.

Though vacant and derelict, many of the older buildings that remain standing serve to reflect how large and vital the base had been in its prime. The runways still welcome much smaller aircraft, of course, but the glory days of the sleek AT-7s, the lumbering B-24s, and the deadly B-29s are gone forever. Great, thick slabs of concrete and foundation footings remain to mark the sites of long-gone hangars, offices, and barracks, and crumbling asphalt roads lead to nothing.

A few aging veterans of World War II return to Hondo from time to time to walk about their old haunts or to look for their photographs in the class yearbooks that have been faithfully preserved at the popular Flight Line Cafe, located on the old runway.

Modern-day general aviation pilots listen, in what appears to be genuine awe, to the often-told war stories of an older generation, men now in their seventies and eighties who first came to Hondo as eager young cadets and who still proudly remember that what they learned there so long ago made it possible, after all, for them to help win a very big war.

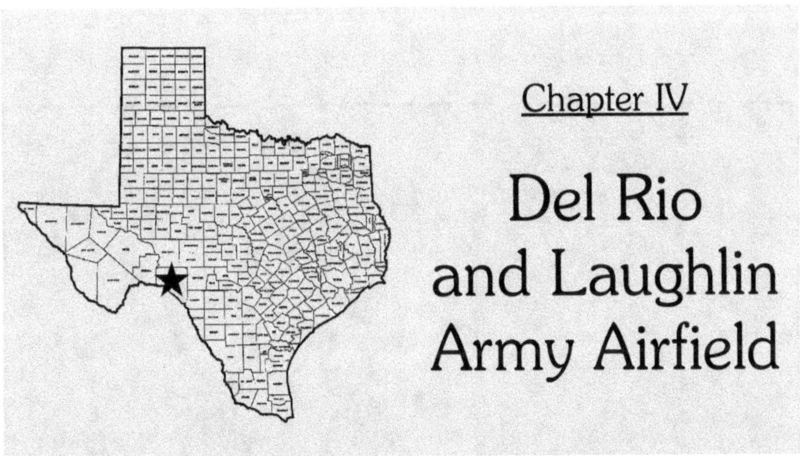

Chapter IV

Del Rio and Laughlin Army Airfield

There is evidence to suggest the presence of Indians in this area dating back 10,000 years.

Del Rio Chamber of Commerce Bulletin
1994

Unlike most cities in the western vastness of Texas, Del Rio appeared on some very early maps hundreds of years before either the stagecoach or the railroad reached the area. In 1590 the Spanish explorer Gaspar Castaño de Sosa was the first to visit what would much later become the city of Del Rio, and his route was soon followed by other Spanish conquistadors.[1]

In 1635 a group of Catholic friars crossed the Rio Grande from New Spain to establish a mission on its banks. Their purpose was to bring the white man's Christianity to the Native Americans who had inhabited the area for centuries. The site of the newly constructed mission was near an all-but-miraculous series of springs that gushed forth seemingly limitless quantities of fresh, cool water from deep beneath the harsh and apparently arid desert floor. The friars named the springs as well as their mission San Felipe Del Rio in honor of St. Phillip, upon whose day they had said their first mass at the site.

The mission flourished at first, but eventually the Native Americans grew increasingly resentful of the white invaders, and in

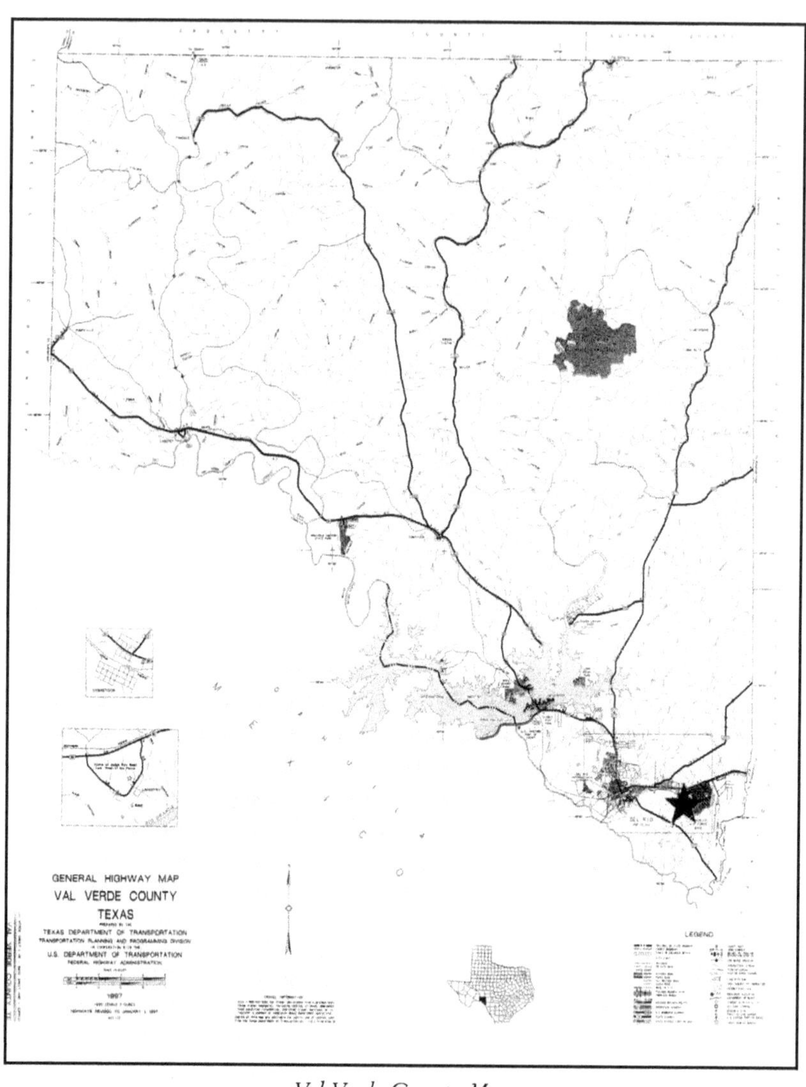

Val Verde County Map
This map of Val Verde County shows the location of Laughlin Army Airfield during the war years. An inset map of Texas shows the location of the county within the state.

time the churchmen were attacked and their mission destroyed. The Spanish, however, refused to be long denied access to the miraculous springs of San Felipe and the abundant fodder for Christian conversion to be found among the Indians. By 1808 another San Felipe Del Rio Mission had been established. Some twenty-five years later, a settlement bearing the same name had grown up around the mission proper.

The spring's excellent water, which flowed at the average rate of nearly 50,000 gallons per minute, proved to be an understandably irresistible lure to westbound travelers. In 1848, at the end of the Mexican War, the United States Cavalry often used the site as a welcome watering hole for its horses, and during Secretary of War Jefferson Davis's well-intentioned but ultimately futile camel experiment, parched dromedaries also refreshed themselves at this American oasis. Stagecoach routes soon made their way to the springs so that teams and passengers alike could partake of its waters before moving on to the west or northward toward Albuquerque.

Several entrepreneurial ranchers in the region soon recognized that San Felipe Springs was clearly the key to future development. A group of five cattlemen, led by James H. Taylor, began acquiring all the land adjacent to the springs in 1868. Within a year, the group had amassed more than 3,000 acres of land and had formed the San Felipe Agricultural, Manufacturing and Irrigation Company. The new organization planned and constructed the canal system that led to the development of the city of San Felipe Del Rio, just over a mile from the former Spanish mission of the same name.

Land in the new community was offered to settlers by the developers, and by 1883 the town was large enough to warrant a post office. Postal officials, however, removed the "San Felipe" from the town's name to avoid confusion with another town with a similar name, leaving only Del Rio to appear on maps of Texas thereafter.

In time, the railroads came to Del Rio, as did roadways that would eventually become federal highways. Despite the improved transportation facilities, the town grew slowly. By 1890, nearly twenty years after its formal founding, Del Rio could boast a population of only 2,000. Even as the seat of Val Verde County, the city had fewer than 12,000 people when the census was taken in 1930.[2]

Ten years later, as was true all across America and particularly true through rural West Texas, international events were taking shape that would soon bring great change. In 1941, with the coming of World War II, the remote little border town of Del Rio was unknowingly on the threshold of becoming a major strategic military location. The Army had been in and around the community for nearly a century, but never to the magnitude that this war was to introduce.

LAUGHLIN ARMY AIRFIELD

> *In short, the Army is not interested in Del Rio or Val Verde County for an Army Air Training School. There is no other reason, politically, economically or geographically . . .* ***there is something deeper seated than we can ascertain—and the Army doesn't want to even consider Del Rio as a site.***
>
> *Del Rio News-Herald*
> April 1, 1942

In just a few short weeks after his passionate editorial appeared in Del Rio's local paper, its editor was doubtless overjoyed to find that his paranoia had been for naught. As it developed, Del Rio was to have an air-training base of its very own, after all.

Perhaps it was the fact that the nearby cities of Eagle Pass and Hondo had just been awarded new Army airfields that caused the newspaperman such public distress. On the other hand, maybe it was the knowledge that Del Rio already had an established record as a military flying center that made the absence of a new wartime base so upsetting. After all, the editor's little city had been welcoming and nourishing Army fliers since 1915. In fact, the age of aviation had arrived in Del Rio four years earlier when one Galbraith Perry Rodgers landed near the town during the first transcontinental flight in American history. Rodgers's landing had been of such importance that one local priest closed his school for the day so that the students could see an aeroplane. Sergio Gonzalez, one of those who witnessed this historic event, recalled many years later that "everybody had a hard time with the animals [meaning buggy and wagon teams] when the plane landed and took off."[3]

By 1917 military aircraft were a familiar sight in Del Rio, having often landed there following reconnaissance missions during the Punitive Expedition directed against the wily Mexican revolutionary Francisco "Pancho" Villa. The performance of the aircraft, or more accurately, the absence of any measurably effective performance by the aircraft, served as the initial stimulus for the creation of the modern United States Air Force. Although it most surely never entered Villa's mind, he was the unlikely godfather of American airpower.

Irene Cardwell, a witness to the comings and goings of the pre–World War I aircraft used in pursuit of Pancho Villa, lived in a house near the edge of a rough field being used as a landing site. She recalled the officer in charge of the flight formation asking permission to tie his airplanes to the fence around her family's home so that they would not blow away during the night. When a rare desert rainstorm blew in, the then-young girl's father permitted the fliers to sleep on the porch.[4]

On July 19, 1919, an Army surveillance group was organized to patrol the United States–Mexico border from Brownsville, Texas, to Nogales, Arizona. Del Rio was a designated stopover spot for the patrolling DeHavilland DH-4B aircraft. One of the pilots of those flimsy aircraft on the border patrol was James H. "Jimmy" Doolittle, a future United States Air Force general and holder of the Medal of Honor for heroism during World War II. In later life, Doolittle fondly recalled his early flights along the border, even though flying and living conditions were primitive at best.

Doolittle, whom most historians identify as an aviator and not merely a pilot, is also remembered as an out-and-out daredevil in the air. According to local Del Rio legend, he once flew his DeHavilland through the Pecos River Canyon for the sole purpose of going under the Southern Pacific Railroad bridge that spanned it. A 1945 article in the *Del Rio News-Herald* noted that most local fliers insisted that such a feat would have been impossible, but, as the newspaper concluded, "Doolittle did it."[5] In his 1991 autobiography, the general admitted having broken standing orders to fly beneath the railway bridge, remembering that he "had to bank the wings nearly vertical to get between the upright piers [of the bridge]." Doolittle also ruefully recalled that one day shortly after the incident, "the biggest, toughest Texan" he had ever seen galloped up to him on the Army's flying outpost, angrily demanding to see the "SOB who flew under the Southern Pacific Bridge."

When it soon was made clear that the irate horseman was a telephone lineman who had been ordered to fix a phone line that had been accidentally severed by the miscreant pilot, the rarely meek Doolittle, who would someday boldly lead a legendary flight of B-25s over Tokyo, hurriedly promised to help find the culprit and quickly trotted off, out of harm's way.[6]

In the years between World Wars I and II, interest in civilian aviation increased greatly in the Val Verde County area, due to the immense distances involved in traveling throughout the region. Consequently, two landing strips were built near Del Rio to accommodate pilots, and flying activity continued to increase.

With the Japanese attack on Pearl Harbor, the United States put into full effect long-standing plans for creating a massive military air force. Unlike many other cities in Texas, however, Del Rio does not seem to have vigorously pursued the possibility of an Army airfield for several years prior to the war. As an April 2, 1942, *Del Rio News-Herald* article suggests, some early efforts had been made to convince the government to build a base near the city, but apparently the full-fledged campaign was initiated only after the war had actually commenced. Failing to get immediate governmental approval for an airfield, the community and its elected officials, and most certainly its newspaper, simply could not comprehend why the Army refused to seriously consider putting an air training facility near the town. For a time it was suspected that Del Rio's immediate proximity to the Mexican border was the reason, but the announcement of the plans to place a field at nearby Eagle Pass, also immediately on the Rio Grande, promptly dispelled that suspicion.[7]

After its self-pitying outburst of April 2, 1942, the *Del Rio News-Herald* soon had to eat a bit of journalistic crow when it announced that General Hubert Harmon, commander of the Army's Gulf Coast Training Corps, and his staff had arrived in the city to inspect the local airport as a possible airfield site. It is possible that the curious article of the preceding day had been published as a way to let General Harmon know that Del Rio was all but thoroughly fed up with the Army's apparent lack of interest in the city's potential as an air facility. If such was in fact the motivation for the somewhat whining editorial, the ploy failed when General Harmon concluded his brief inspection by stating that the site he had just surveyed would not be suitable for any training facilities. If the city and county leaders who had taken the officers on the airport tour were crestfallen at the general's parting comments, no published account remains.

However, in a stunning reversal of fortune, on May 15 the *News-Herald* was able to announce that an air school for Del Rio had at long last been approved. The welcome telegram from Congressman Charles L. South stated that the training school would "cost in excess of $3,000,000." That same day, Mayor Frank Walton received official notification of the War Department's decision from Senator W. Lee O'Daniel, while Judge W. F. Boggess received an identical telegram from Texas's other senator, Tom Connally. Mr. L. B. Duke, president of the Del Rio Chamber of Commerce, quite naturally reacted most positively to the good news, and then, with an eye toward long-range civilian-military relationships, proclaimed, evidently with a straight face, that "while we are highly gratified with the announcement, we who have worked on the proposition have received our thrill in the experience of working with the Army officers."[8]

According to the War Department's announcement, the school was to be located on a site some five miles east of town and would be operated as a bombardier-training facility. Apparently, General Harmon had not been as bluntly negative in his statement of April 3 as the newspaper editorial might have suggested. Accounts indicate that the general had in fact confided to his hosts that he would entertain proposals involving other potential sites in the immediate Del Rio area.

This statement triggered what must have been a feverish but surreptitious search for alternative property options by the Del Rioans, a hasty amassing of statistics, and the preparation of a formal proposal for General Harmon's consideration. The effort was promptly rewarded, as a mere three weeks elapsed between Harmon's initial visit and his final approval of the newly proposed training-facility site.

Members of the chamber of commerce's aviation committee had gone to General Harmon's headquarters in San Antonio on April 18 and convinced the senior officer that the proper location had been found for the flying facility. Within a week's time, Harmon and his staff, displaying a sudden enthusiasm for the Del

Rio project, visited the city two more times before making a final decision to move forward without any further delay.

The nearly 4,000 acres needed for the facility were acquired from Mr. B. S. Harrison at a non-negotiable price of $101,500, or some $25 per acre.[9] Mr. Harrison apparently had no problem in selling his land for the price the government had arbitrarily determined to be fair, but Gilbert Marshall, who held a two-year lease on the property, was not equally enthusiastic about vacating the site. For some unexplained reason, Marshall had been allowed to construct a substantial residence on the leased land, and he was reluctant to abandon his home, war or no war. The government promptly agreed to move the house, corrals, windmill, and barns to another location to assuage the dispossessed Marshall. Further, as a windmill is of little value without water to pump, the War Department even arranged for a well to be drilled at Mr. Marshall's new homesite.[10]

Just why the government was so remarkably munificent with the recalcitrant rancher was not divulged. In most similar instances, strong evidence exists that the Army usually just took what it needed, condemning existing structures in its war-fueled frenzy to build new bases without much if any regard for the wishes or welfare of those dispossessed.

At any rate, by early June 1942, the clearing of what had recently been rough grazing land had been completed and construction started. Though far from complete, the new base was officially activated on October 29, 1942, as the United States Army Air Forces Bombardier School, Del Rio, Texas.[11]

The pressing need for qualified multi-engine pilots, however, caused the War Department to change the mission of its newly constructed base before a single student bombardier ever arrived in Val Verde County. Within weeks of its activation, the field became somewhat ponderously rechristened "The U.S. Army Air Forces Transition Flying School, Medium Bombardment, near Del Rio, Texas." As *Tarfu*, the base newspaper, reported on March 12, 1943, with an almost audible sigh of relief, the name of the base was changed for a third time to a much simpler Laughlin Army Airfield.[12]

The Army had long resisted naming its flying facilities for heroic aviators, but one of the first exceptions was made for its new airfield at Del Rio. Lt. Jack T. Laughlin Jr. had been killed in action on a bombing mission over Java on January 29, 1942, the first Del Rioan to die in action in World War II. Maj. Gen. Gerald C. Brant, commanding general of the Air Force's Gulf Coast region, gave the dedicatory address honoring Lieutenant Laughlin on March 28, 1942. The lieutenant's widow and their small son joined hundreds of other local citizens to hear General Brant commend the War Department for permitting the local hero's name to be affixed to the base. The general also noted that Lieutenant Laughlin's military status as a reservist rather than a Regular Army officer made the base-naming exception an honor even more rare.[13]

Personnel and aircraft for the new Laughlin Airfield came from San Antonio's Kelly Field and from Fort Worth Army Airfield, where instructor training courses in the B-26 Marauder aircraft were already being conducted. The first of the B-26s made the three-hundred-mile flight from Fort Worth to Del Rio early in 1943, their crews reporting upon landing to Col. George W. Munday. The colonel had been commander at Laughlin since late December 1942 and would remain in that position until January 1944.[14]

The first planes to land at Laughlin were forced to touch down on the ramp, as the main runways were not yet completed. Other aircraft units soon flew to the field, including two glider-training squadrons.

The new school graduated highly skilled B-26 Marauder pilots every nine weeks, its graduates being pilots who had already earned their wings at various advanced training schools. They had spent nine weeks in pre-flight school, nine weeks in primary training, another nine weeks in basic school, and still another nine weeks in advanced training before coming to Laughlin for the final honing of their flying skills. The Del Rio facility was the first training school in the Army designed to teach those who already appeared to be the very best pilots to become even better. Following their graduation from Laughlin, the fliers were scheduled to go to operational-training units to meet their flight crews and become combat-ready. From there, the newly formed crews were dispatched to various theaters of combat operation worldwide.

Although the proficiency level of the incoming students appeared to be quite impressive, the formal B-26 training qualifications of some of their instructors seem to have been a bit illusory.

One instructor, Capt. Gerald L. Stephens, recalled that there were no established standards for training the flight instructors, nor was there much supervision from higher headquarters. Most of the fledgling instructors only had experience in single-engine aircraft, with seven to eight hundred hours of total flying time being the norm.[15]

Stephens said in an interview after the war that initially there were no formal procedures for checking out a new instructor. One second lieutenant, James K. Stepp, found a set of B-26 technical orders, read it thoroughly, and proceeded to teach himself to fly the often temperamental if not downright dangerous Marauder.[16] John P. McNeese accomplished the same feat by reading what he termed the *How to Fly the B-26 Manual* word for word before climbing into the aircraft and quickly learning to master it.[17]

Both McNeese and Stepp rapidly became effective teachers in the air, but Stepp apparently had a difficult time adapting to the military way of life. A test pilot for the Cessna Aircraft Company before the war, the lieutenant could not get the hang of Army protocol. He did not know whom, when, or even how to salute, for example, and often berated enlisted men who saluted him even when they did so properly. On one occasion, he was assigned the daunting duty of commanding one of the Army's traditional Saturday morning military reviews. Not knowing the first thing about giving commands to the large assembly of men, he asked a sergeant to stand next to him and provide him with the appropriate orders in a whisper so that he could bark commands to his soldiers.[18]

Another instructor, named Robert Ball, had at one time flown with the Royal Canadian Air Force, but he had been ignominiously dismissed from that service for piloting his plane through an open hangar. For some reason, the U.S. Army saw fit to overlook this misadventure and instantly assigned Ball to instructor status. Unfortunately, this assignment was soon terminated after the instructor persisted in flying to Fort Hood and buzzing the early-morning formations there at alarmingly low altitudes and causing the ground troops to scatter madly to safety.[19]

The tendency to depart from standard flight-safety policies seems to have been passed on from the instructors to their students. One favorite pastime at Laughlin was to fly as close to ranch windmills as possible, creating a prop wash that would cause the windmill's fan to rotate violently and, if all went well, actually fly off its mount. The pilot who caused his target fan to fly the greatest distance away from the windmill tower was declared the ace of the day.[20]

The buzzing of moving terrestrial objects was also considered great sport. Cows, goats, and as Robert Ball had discovered, even soldiers at Fort Hood, provided worthy targets for the exceptionally well-trained but often dangerously foolhardy pilots. The mounted cavalry at nearby Fort Clark also came in for its share of playful aerial attack. Laughlin's pilots would zoom over the mule-borne artillery trains at alarmingly low altitudes, causing troopers to leap from their mounts and prompting the animals themselves to gallop in panic into the brush and well beyond. Only a visit by the outraged Fort Clark commander to Laughlin's CO brought this intraservice rivalry to a halt.[21]

Automobiles, however, seemed to be the most compelling lure of all to Laughlin's high-spirited airmen. However, 2nd Lt. Ellsworth E. Lewman found on one occasion that low-level flight and subsequent automobile harassment could be costly to fame, fortune, and military career. His fundamental error lay in unknowingly singling out as his prey the official car of his training officer. As Lewman swooped over the officer's vehicle at a reported four-foot clearance, the sharp-eyed occupant of the car could easily read the capricious pilot's aircraft tail number. At his promptly convened court-martial, Lieutenant Lewman was fined $600, a relatively staggering amount of money in the early 1940s.[22]

The sheer amount of flight activity at Laughlin, perhaps in conjunction with the seemingly high degree of reckless flying, caused many accidents to occur. In the 962 days that the advanced school was in operation between February 1943 and the closing of the base in 1945, there were twenty-six major accidents and three forced landings. In all, seventy-four airmen lost their lives and twenty-nine Laughlin-based aircraft were destroyed during the war years.[23]

Early in those years, the B-26 had gained a bad reputation among pilots, earning the aircraft such unwanted nicknames as "Widow Maker" and "Flying Prostitute." According to some accounts, the unfortunate reputation of the Marauder was essentially a domestic one gained in stateside training mishaps. In combat and in the hands of more seasoned pilots, the aircraft performed admirably. Some of the training incidents also seemed to stem from inexperienced ground crews and non-standardized loading techniques. This combination of negative factors could well have been at the core of Laughlin's tragic accident record.

In combat, however, the Marauder's performance was commendable. The planes flew the first medium-bomber mission of the war against the Japanese over Rabaul, New Guinea, on April 5, 1942, participated in the fight for air supremacy over the Normandy beaches on June 6, 1944, and amassed a total of nearly 130,000 sorties in the European theater alone. Although 911 of the Marauders were lost in combat, the lobbying efforts of pilots in tactical units kept the plane in production throughout the war, overriding continuous urging by the Army's high command that the B-26 program be discontinued.[24]

When they were not flying or caring for the always-challenging Marauder, the officers and men assigned to Laughlin found ways to cope with the often equally challenging and unique way of life in wartime West Texas. Men from the eastern part of the United States were particularly taken aback at the differences between their homes on the other side of the Mississippi and their new military habitat on the Rio Grande.

One such airman was Allard E. Stevens, who found Del Rio to be "almost like the old western towns in the movies," with plank sidewalks and raucous saloons. Stevens was particularly struck by the restroom facilities in one of those saloons. There were two doors placed in the rear wall of the bar, clearly marked "His" and "Hers." Likely to the dismay of nearly everyone both inside and outside the saloon, the two doors opened directly onto an alleyway, with only a short partition dividing the "his" side from the "her" side and nothing whatsoever protecting the shocked bar patrons from the unwelcome gaze of casual passersby.[25]

Sgt. Paul O. Russell recalled that home life in Del Rio was particularly challenging. As was the case in almost all communities with a new military facility close by, housing was a major problem. "Everything habitable in or near town was put to use for housing," Russell remembered after the war. Even chicken coops and buses became the dwelling places for the airmen and their families. One such bus was occupied by Russell, even though the bedroom and the bath were located nearby in the bus owner's house. Using the vehicle as a living room and kitchen, the Russell family considered themselves quite fortunate, and it cost only $75 per month.[26]

Housing conditions on the base were almost as bad as the makeshift accommodations in town. Most of the housing units at the field had been hastily and inexpensively constructed of black fiberboard. The heat generated by the relentless subtropical Rio Grande sun would stay in the poorly built barracks until well past midnight. Many of the men preferred to sleep outside rather than try to endure the oven-like quarters.[27]

One of the significant major advantages of wartime duty at Laughlin Army Airfield was the proximity of Villa Acuña, located just across the Rio Grande in Mexico. In this small, sun-baked community, bored soldiers could readily find all manner of delights and diversions. They could also just as easily find trouble, and their superior officers reminded them of this most vigorously and repeatedly. Although Del Rio's relationship with its sister city was amicable enough, border-crossing regulations were stringently enforced.

One of Del Rio's best-known residents, Dr. John Brinkley, had done much to make the name Villa Acuña widely known to men coming to Texas from other parts of the nation. The good doctor had established his powerful radio station, with the call letters XERA, in Villa Acuña to take advantage of Mexico's apparent lack of official concern over broadcasting power limits. In the United States, stations were restricted to an output of no more than 50,000 watts, but the Mexican-based XERA blasted forth at a rumored one million watts, making it "the world's most powerful broadcasting station," according to Brinkley himself. Some Del Rioans claimed they were receiving Brinkley's highly questionable radio hints for good health through their telephones, while ranchers testified that their barbed-wire fences were picking up the high-wattage broadcasts. Many others believed that the doctor's messages were somehow emanating from the fillings in their teeth. Perhaps more plausible reports also claimed that XERA's strong signal often interfered directly with Laughlin's own radio communications.[28]

Although his curious medical recommendations and advice, which often involved goat-gland transplant surgery, were often dismissed as pure quackery by more traditional physicians,

Brinkley's broadcasts did much to promote the virtues of Del Rio in general and made listeners many thousands of miles north of the border aware of the existence of the little town of Villa Acuña throughout the late 1930s and early 1940s.

It is quite possible that at least some of the pleasure-seeking American soldiers who crossed the international bridge to enter Villa Acuña had visions of the romantic village on the banks of the "silvery Rio Grande" so often rhapsodized by John Brinkley. If so, they were soon disabused of such lyrical conceptions. The town was, as Allard O. Stevens saw it, "usually hot and always dusty, dirty and very economically depressed."[29] Soldiers could see women washing clothes in the waters of the Rio Grande, which was in reality anything but silvery, despite Brinkley's promises. Flies were everywhere, particularly in the open-air meat markets, yet prices of that fly-blown meat were cheap enough in the many cafes and restaurants, with a filet mignon selling for well under a dollar. Although no ruling came from Laughlin's headquarters about the eating of Mexican beef, an early order was issued forbidding the drinking of water on the other side of the river. According to most accounts, Mexican water was seldom if ever the beverage of choice anyway among pleasure-seeking soldiers on a pass in Villa Acuña.

On one visit across the river, for example, Sgt. Frank Levene reportedly sampled various beverages other than the illegal water while out on the town. According to *Tarfu,* Laughlin's official newspaper, the usually silent sergeant consumed only one Cuba Libre and one beer before proceeding to be awarded the dubious title of "hog-calling champion of Villa Acuña."[30]

By late 1943, too many soldiers were thought to be participating altogether too freely in the temptations of border-town society. Villa Acuña's red-light district, known as "The Stockade," was put off-limits by Laughlin's authorities, with Mexican police instructed to arrest any soldier who attempted to enter the district. Similarly, any airman found to be drunk and disorderly anywhere in the village was to be apprehended and turned over to one of the military police squads that patrolled the streets.

To further protect its personnel, Laughlin officials ordered regular inspections by Army medical officers of all Villa Acuña cafes and cantinas. Those that failed to meet stringent sanitary standards were closed with the cooperation of the village government. When it was further discovered that many waiters kept one order book to be presented to the diners and another totally different book to be turned in to the cafe's cashier, strict price ceilings were implemented and prominently posted. Non-complying Acuña restaurants were summarily closed by the U.S. Army Air Force, even though it lacked the actual legal authority to do so.[31]

To further minimize the potential for trouble across the border, the base for a time required all of its personnel to be out of Mexico by no later than 10:00 P.M. on weeknights and 1:00 A.M. on Sunday. While this regulation undoubtedly put a damper on many social activities, the soldiers and their Mexican hosts found ways to make the most of the hours before the curfew fell. Several cantinas, for example, established Wednesday afternoons as "recipe day." Bartenders experimented with new potable concoctions, and novice barmen tried their hand at mixing old favorites. In either case, the experimental products were given free to eager soldiers visiting from across the river.[32]

Although there were obvious problems between the base authorities and Villa Acuña's more notorious dens of iniquity, official relations were for the most part cooperative and amicable. The airfield's soldiers occasionally marched through the village streets in formal parades, much to the delight of the townspeople. In late September 1944, Laughlin's 706th Band staged a concert for an audience of more than four thousand assembled in the village plaza. If the Mexicans had come hoping to hear traditional American martial airs, they must have been disappointed when the band played such perhaps predictably thematic hits as "Lady of Spain," "La Golondrina," and "Rio Rita." The concert concluded with a rousing version of "La Cucaracha" and a speech of thanks by Acuña mayor Graciano Patino.[33]

Occasionally, official celebrations and events on the north side of the Rio Grande were expanded to include visitors from the other side. In July 1945, Texas Governor Coke R. Stevenson came to Del Rio to participate in a bond rally. He was joined on the podium, which was the bed of a pickup truck, by Benecio López Padilla, governor of the Mexican state of Coahuila.[34]

Back on the air base, the deadly serious business of training advanced pilots for combat went on day and night. *Tarfu* could only obliquely allude to the rigorous schedule of flight instruction. Journalistic evidence of the gravity and danger involved in Laughlin's mission surfaced only in rare mentions of accidents or deadly crashes. The main thrust of the paper, however, seems to have been idle gossip, reporting of base athletic events, and, like most military publications of the time, the circulation of unbelievably tasteless jokes and puns.

A small but modest assortment of the knee-slapping humor of the early 1940s is perhaps in order here. From the August 20, 1943, edition comes:

> She: "Do you think you're Santa Claus?"
> He: "No, why?"
> She: "Then leave my stockings alone!"[35]

On October 5, 1943, the newspaper printed this one:

> "I got to thinking of the wickedness of the world last night," said the deacon, "and prayed for you, young lady."
>
> "Next time, Deacon," she retorted "you'd better phone."[36]

Finally, the December 31, 1943, *Tarfu* ended the year with this gem:

> GI: "Can I take you home?"
> Gal: "Sure, where do you live?"[37]

A little humor clearly went a long way fifty-seven years ago.

Despite such pardonable examples of wartime humor, *Tarfu* often offered interesting journalistic items to its readers. On one occasion, for example, the paper gave an account of a drill during which tear gas was set off in the operating room of the base hospital to test the attack readiness of the hospital staff. Most of the doctors and nurses found their gas masks in fairly short order, the paper relates, but one poor patient, already anesthetized for his operation, was all but overlooked in the confusion of the drill.[38]

Another test of Laughlin's security levels occurred in late May 1944. Two soldiers, Cpl. Carleton A. Coon and Cpl. John Hilliard, were outfitted in Nazi paratrooper uniforms and ordered to walk around the airfield to see how many soldiers would react to their appearance. Curiously, not many reacted at all. One civilian employee thought the men were baseball players, their swastika armbands notwithstanding, while others chatted amiably with the strangely uniformed men, laughing at their put-on German accents. No one bothered to stop the duo as they strolled onto the flight line and climbed on board a B-26. The "Nazis" casually made their way about the base for several hours, prompting only one officer to call the base security guard to report what he termed "suspicious looking soldiers." All others who saw the two men wearing enemy uniforms either ignored them or assumed that they were merely visiting Allied personnel. "Must be Canadians," said one, while his comrade was sure they were Australians. The entire charade was nearly too much for one observer, who later told a representative of the newspaper that the two looked like men from Mars as far as he could tell.[39]

Despite such amusing if curious diversions, the deadly business of war continued at Laughlin until the final victory was won and World War II came to an end. Thousands of pilots had sharpened their skills at Del Rio's base and had gone on to play an important role in attaining victory.

On August 27, 1945, just days after Japan conceded defeat, a damaging fire struck Laughlin Field. The principal maintenance hangar was destroyed in the blaze, and five B-26s were lost. Early estimates put the fire cost at several million dollars, nearly what the base itself had cost to construct only three years earlier. Fortunately, no one died in the blaze.[40]

The loss of one of the field's principal buildings served to exacerbate the fears of prominent Del Rioans that the base would soon be closed. Within three weeks following the fire, their fears were confirmed when an announcement came from the headquarters of the Army Air Forces Training Command stating that Laughlin was to be among nine fields to be closed on or before September 30, 1945, just twenty-three days later.

Local businessmen took the news "philosophically," as the *Del Rio News-Herald* put it, with most believing that the loss of the hangar had only expedited the closing of the field now that peace had come. Mayor Frank Walton was in favor of sending a message of protest to the War Department, but he resigned himself to doubting if it would prevent the closing. At least, said the mayor, "it will show we are interested in maintaining it if at all possible."[41]

Obviously, the War Department and its successor, the Department of Defense, never completely forgot Del Rio's keen interest in having a military airfield nearby. The old World War II base did close as scheduled, to be sure, with many of its buildings razed and its vast acreage once again used for the grazing of livestock. Yet world conditions would soon create a need for a new Laughlin Field, where flying conditions were nearly always superior and where the community had proven its desire to warmly embrace and support a major military facility.

When it became apparent in the early 1950s that victory in World War II was not going to bring anything resembling lasting peace, the United States began to rebuild its military forces, which had recently been all but dismantled. Many cities across the nation soon realized that their World War II air bases, although closed, might have a chance at a new life.

The Del Rio Chamber of Commerce moved swiftly to let the government know how warmly it would welcome the return of Laughlin Field to an active status. Armed with statistics and updated meteorological data that proved the ideal flying conditions in their region, chamber officials journeyed to Washington to present their case. Their well-prepared report showed that minimum flight conditions in the vicinity of the immediate base area existed less than 6 percent of the time, and that inclement weather in general had never been a factor in Laughlin's flight operations during the World War II period. The chamber executives, in short, proved that they were ready and able to make the return of Laughlin a successful venture, and Air Force officials obligingly soon let it be known that they were willing to bring the historic and honored flying field back to active duty.

As a result of that mutual commitment, Col. William T. Samways assumed command of a re-commissioned and hurriedly rebuilt Laughlin Air Force Base on May 1, 1952. The base was activated into the Air Training Command and further assigned to the Flying Training Air Force. The 3645th Pilot Training Wing was promptly established on the field with its mission to provide basic single-engine training.

Within five months, the mission was changed to provide

instruction in the F-84 and T-33 aircraft for jet fighter operations. For the first time in its long history, Laughlin entered the era of jet-propelled flight.

In April 1957 Laughlin became a Strategic Air Command base and home to the B-57 Canberra and the top-secret U2 reconnaissance aircraft. It was from Laughlin AFB that a U2 overflew Cuba to note the build-up of Soviet missiles on that island nation in 1962. The only American casualty of the Cuban missile crisis that soon followed was Maj. Rudolph Anderson, a Laughlin-based U-2 pilot who was shot down while on a surveillance mission.

The mission of the base has changed many times since its rebirth in 1952, but its primary objective since 1962 has been to train top-quality military pilots for combat operations. Since then, nearly 10,000 undergraduates have been awarded their silver wings in recognition of their attainment of the Air Force's highest standards.

Laughlin's contribution to the community has multiplied with the passing of time. In addition to the vital involvement of its personnel in Del Rio's community life, the base's financial contribution to the city's economic well-being is immense. According to figures released by the Air Force, Laughlin's 1998 fiscal impact on the Del Rio–Val Verde region was in excess of $156 million. Nearly 5,000 people are employed on the base, and thousands of others provide service to it. In a county with 11,142 employees in total, Laughlin AFB is clearly a key factor in the area's overall economy.[42]

The Laughlin Heritage Foundation, a non-profit organization composed of civilians and military personnel, actively works to ensure that the rich legacy of the base is not allowed to fade. Through its efforts, the foundation has helped forge an unusually strong alliance between the community and the air base.

From its colorful history, replete with Mexican bandits, barnstorming pilots, and daredevil aviators, Laughlin has emerged as both a vital link in the nation's security and a stabilizing mainstay in the regional economy. Del Rio and Laughlin AFB are enduring proof that military and civilian interests can coexist in harmony.

Old Glory comes down during a retreat formation at Pampa Army Airfield, circa 1944.

— Courtesy Freedom Museum USA, Pampa, Texas

Inspecting officers salute the colors at Pampa Field.
— Courtesy White Deer Land Museum, Pampa, Texas

An informal sing-along in the Pampa Service Club.
— Courtesy White Deer Land Museum, Pampa, Texas

The regionally famous Pampa Field Dance Band, circa 1943.
— Courtesy White Deer Land Museum, Pampa, Texas

A social function at the Pampa Officers' Club. Note the optional long gloves.
— Courtesy White Deer Land Museum, Pampa, Texas

Pampa Field's chapel, one of the few buildings that would survive into the twenty-first century.
— Courtesy Freedom Museum USA, Pampa, Texas

A jaunty cadre unit of WACs arrives at Pampa.
— Courtesy Freedom Museum USA, Pampa, Texas

A formation of B-25 bombers in flight over the Texas Panhandle.

— Courtesy Freedom Museum USA, Pampa, Texas

Training aircraft sweep over a formal review at Pampa.
— Courtesy White Deer Land Museum, Pampa, Texas

A massed review at Pampa Field. Reports indicate that nearly 2,000 men participated in this 1944 formation.

— Courtesy White Deer Land Museum, Pampa, Texas

A formation of another kind. Here, a few of the thousands of cattle that moo where B-25s once roared. The last surviving WWII hangar at Pampa Field looms behind the herd.

— Author's photograph

A compass rose has survived on the feedlot that was once an airbase. B-25s and other planes were brought here periodically for compass alignment. The eight principal directional segments can still be seen.

— Author's photograph

All that remains of Pampa Field's distinctive water tower.

— Author's photograph

This little-used gate was once the busy entranceway to Pampa Field.
— Author's photograph

This concrete guardhouse once detained base personnel who returned to Pampa Field in no condition to make it to their barracks.
— Author's photograph

The chapel building was moved into Pampa from the base and is still in use as a church.

— Author's photograph

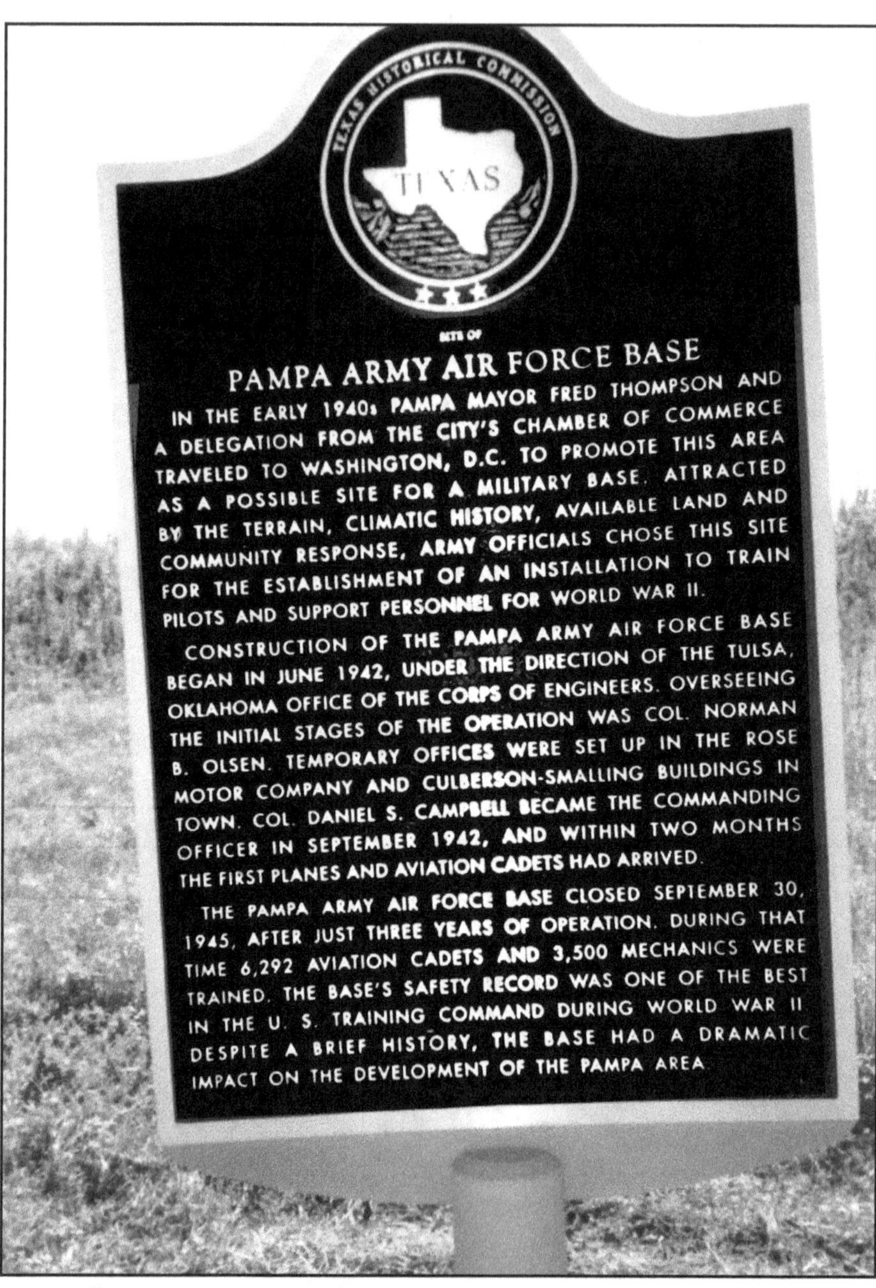

An all-too-rare Texas Historical Commission marker gives a fine capsule history of an important old airfield.

— Author's photograph

Hondo's nationally famous sign, with the word "navigate" roughed in prior to being added for the duration. Soldiers Vernon Casey, Bernard Goette, and a casual fellow identified only as "Mac" contemplate their tasks.

— Courtesy Medina County Museum, Hondo, Texas

The Hondo sign as it looks today, without the word "navigate" anywhere to be seen, but with "please" added.

— Author's photograph

Mildred Van Fleet poses by the Hondo Navigation School sign, circa 1943.

— Courtesy Medina County Museum, Hondo, Texas

A double-decker vehicle transported soldiers to and from town. Hondo's train station is in the background. The building now houses the Medina County Museum.

— Courtesy Medina County Museum, Hondo, Texas

SERVICE CLUB

A jeep equipped with a makeshift public address system is used to announce comic Red Skelton's appearance at Hondo. The name of Red's co-star was mysteriously expunged on the original photograph.

— Courtesy Medina County Museum, Hondo, Texas

Three optimistic military gardeners cultivate their zinnias in Hondo's sunbaked soil.
— Courtesy Medina County Museum, Hondo, Texas

The Hondo Airfield Cadet Drum and Bugle Corps poses in front of the base's typical tarpaper buildings, October 1942.
— Courtesy Medina County Museum, Hondo, Texas

Hondo's 743rd WAC Squadron marches smartly in an October 1943 re-enlistment parade.
— Courtesy Medina County Museum, Hondo, Texas

A view of a derelict World War II hangar still standing at Hondo in late 1999.
— Author's photograph

Another glimpse of a rapidly deteriorating old hangar.
— Author's photograph

Another deteriorated World War II building at today's field.
— Author's photograph

All that remains of the WWII WAC barracks. The building was moved to the grounds of the Medina County Museum to await restoration.
— Author's photograph

The exterior and interior of Laughlin's Officers' Club, 1943.
— Courtesy Whitehead Memorial Museum, Del Rio, Texas

An evening in the Laughlin NCO Club, 1943.
Note the waiter in his undershirt in the top photograph.
— Courtesy Whitehead Memorial Museum, Del Rio, Texas

Soldiers relax in one of Laughlin's day rooms and in the library, 1943.
— Courtesy Whitehead Memorial Museum, Del Rio, Texas

Texas Governor Coke Stevenson is joined by his Mexican counterpart, Benecio Lopez Padillo, of Coahuila, to celebrate a War Bond drive. No red carpet for these two, just feed sacks in a pickup truck.

— Courtesy Whitehead Memorial Museum, Del Rio, Texas

The Del Rio Junior Chamber of Commerce arranged this colorful 1944 event to commemorate the successful conclusion of a bond drive. After his hanging, "Herr Hitler" was placed in the coffin and paraded throughout town.

— Courtesy Whitehead Memorial Museum, Del Rio, Texas

An early photograph of Laughlin as a base belonging to an independent U.S. Air Force, circa 1947.
— Courtesy Whitehead Memorial Museum, Del Rio, Texas

An aerial view of postwar Laughlin AFB, circa 1955.

— Courtesy 47 FTW History Office, Laughlin AFB, Texas

Modern-day Laughlin AFB, a vital air base on the Rio Grande.
— Courtesy 47 FTW History Office, Laughlin AFB, Texas

Midland County Map
This map of Midland County shows the location of Midland Army Airfield during the war years. An inset map of Texas shows the location of the county within the state.

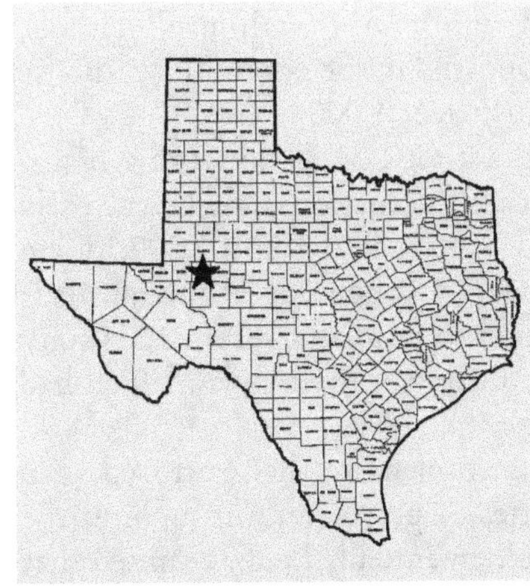

Chapter V

Midland and Midland Army Airfield

There was just absolutely nothing to look at out there. One old-timer I knew called that whole Midland-Odessa part of Texas the "Flat Brown," and I kind of think he was being overly generous.

Thomas F. Bellingham
Dallas, Texas

Midland, the self-crowned Queen City of the South Plains, came into being in June 1881 as Midway Station, the putative halfway point between Dallas and El Paso on the Texas & Pacific Railway. The site of the tiny watering stop that eventually became a queenly city is in fact only 289 miles east of El Paso and 327 miles west of Dallas, but apparently to railroad crews laying track westward over a century ago, a mere 38 miles one way or the other did not disqualify the station from being deemed the midway point along the route. In 1884 the "station" part of the name was dropped in order to obtain approval for a post office, and the town became officially known as Midland, Texas.[1]

Soon after the post office was opened and the railroad was operating on its recently laid track, a real estate syndicate purchased a large parcel of land at the site and began to promote settlement. In just a short time, more than one hundred families moved into the locality, and in March 1885 Midland became the seat of government for the newly created Midland County. A courthouse, schools, churches, and a newspaper soon appeared in the community, and by 1900 the population had reached just over 1,000.

A center for major ranching activity, Midland's growth was impeded by drought and cattle market fluctuations, and by the early 1920s, the town's population had declined to some 1,800, down from its 1915 peak of over 2,500 people. When one of the railroads serving the community discontinued its Midland run in 1921, city fathers could foresee only a bleak future for their town, which had at least briefly seemed so promising.[2]

Fortunately, that promise was soon more than restored with the discovery of enormous quantities of petroleum throughout the surrounding Permian Basin. It would eventually be determined that the region held a full 25 percent of America's proved oil reserves. Midland was strategically located to become the logistical center for the many major oil companies that rushed into the region, thus setting the stage for the petroleum-driven boom-and-bust cycles that would long define the city's history.

After the first discovery well had been successfully drilled, the economy of the region soared. Nearly forty oil companies had opened offices in Midland by 1929, and new buildings were rapidly being constructed to accommodate the thousands of newcomers who were flooding into the city. By 1930 Midland's population had more than doubled, reaching nearly 6,000 permanent residents. As the community and the entire Permian Basin would soon come to realize, however, there was little that was truly permanent in the petroleum business. The coming of the Great Depression in the early 1930s drastically reduced the demand for oil, and rival new East Texas fields were quick to satisfy what little demand there was. By 1932 Midland's first bust had followed its first boom, establishing a pattern that would recur for the rest of the century. Nearly one of every three workers in the city was suddenly unemployed, and real estate values plummeted, taking the town's tax base down with it. Many citizens were forced to go on county welfare rolls in order to simply survive, and those too proud to do so moved away from the region to seek employment elsewhere.

Once again, however, the always fickle fortunes of a petroleum-based economy smiled on the beleaguered community. A federal tariff on foreign oil combined with a state-ordered regulation of production to bring stability and new exploration to the Permian Basin. In the late 1930s, the economy was booming once more. The city's population was again approaching the 10,000 level, and construction projects were back in full swing.

Unlike the boom of the 1920s, however, the resurgence of the late 1930s and early 1940s would endure for an unusually lengthy period of time. America's entry into World War II created and then ensured a rapidly accelerating demand for Midland-area oil.

Fortunately for the community, the war brought much more than a resurging petroleum industry. In 1941, after months of tireless effort on the part of civic leaders, the War Department announced that Midland had been selected as the site for a major flight-training facility. The combination of an unlimited demand for its oil and the infusion of millions of federal dollars would create an extended period of economic affluence that Midlanders still fondly remember to this day, even though the boom-and-bust pattern has been repeated many times in the intervening years.

WORLD'S LARGEST BOMBARDIER SCHOOL

The bombardier was a child of World War II. His life expectancy was short . . . his specialty was born, flourished and died all within one decade.

Bruce Callander
Air Force Times
April 9, 1984

A decision in early 1941 to build what was to become the world's largest bombardier school at Midland was not easily reached by federal officials. Prominent businessmen and community civic leaders had been actively promoting the idea in the nation's capital for well over a year before War Department authorities accepted their proposal.

The focus of Midland's plan was Sloan Airport, located not quite ten miles west of the city. Samuel Sloan had built his tiny airfield in 1927 on a 220-acre tract that he had leased from area rancher Clarence Scharbauer. Upon Sloan's death in a plane crash in 1929, his brother purchased the land and operated the field for ten years before selling it to the city of Midland in 1939 for less than $15,000.[3]

As soon as city officials had legal title to the small facility, they set about seeking federal support to expand it into a more significant municipal airport. More important was the desire of the town's leaders to see the airport become a major military air installation.

U.S. Congressman R. Ewing Thomason enthusiastically joined the air-base campaign that had been launched by his Midland constituents, and by June 1940, he was able to report to them that the War Department had promised to give "careful consideration to the possibility of establishing an Army air training school at Midland."[4]

A month later, a group of Army officers landed at Midland to inspect the facility. General F. L. Martin, leader of the inspection party, pronounced the field to be not only in excellent condition but also in a strategic location that "fitted in perfectly with the national defense picture."[5]

While Midland's airport backers were no doubt highly encouraged by the general's unofficial appraisal of their project, they were probably equally bemused when it was announced shortly after General Martin's visit that Congressman Thomason, their lead man in Washington, had simultaneously been promoting another military installation for the city. The congressman, apparently not yet a true convert to the efficacy of modern airpower, had also been soliciting the support of the War Department to establish a cavalry remount station near the city. Army officials, themselves apparently not wholehearted advocates of either airpower or internal-combustion engines, sent a team of cavalry experts to Midland to investigate the potential for the major horse operation envisioned by Thomason. According to newspaper reports, government wranglers did buy twenty-two cavalry mounts in the area as a test, but ultimately decided against a permanent remount depot.[6]

Evidently unruffled at the rejection of his cavalry plan, Congressman Thomason promptly redoubled his efforts for an air base, this time with outstanding success. In October 1940, President Franklin D. Roosevelt announced that over $150,000 had been allocated to the WPA for improvements to Midland's airport. Another $150,000 was budgeted for further improvements some six months later. Clearly, the campaign was bearing some obvious fruit, but no official word of an impending training base was soon received.[7]

Hopes began to rise in April 1941 with the Midland visit of Maj. Gen. Gerald C. Brant, who was the commander of the Gulf Coast Air Corps Training Center and the man who would have overall responsibility for the new base if it were ever approved. The general told a hastily called mass meeting of Midlanders that prospects for a major training base were quite strong indeed. Brant ended the meeting on a high note when he stated that "a school may be in full operation in the fall."[8] All Midland seemed euphoric at this news, conjectural and unofficial though it might have been.

Brant's optimism soon proved to be valid, however, and on June 13, 1941, the local *Reporter-Telegram* blared forth from its front page, "Midland Gets Air School."[9]

After years of campaigning and frustration with governmental ponderousness, the official announcement of the air base was like a cork popping from a bottle. A veritable flood of activity began that very day as plans, long dormant, were hurriedly put into motion.

The airport itself was suddenly determined to be much too small, so additional acreage was rapidly acquired, bringing the tract to over one thousand acres in size. Before the war ended, the airfield had expanded to several thousand acres. The entire property, including hangars, existing runways, and raw land, was to be leased to the federal government for the customary one dollar per year. Like other Texas cities with airfields to lend to the War Department, Midland was obviously not getting into the air-training-base business to make money from leasing its real estate.

On July 17, 1941, ground was broken for the new facility. Within 90 days, more than 3,000 workers swarmed over the site building new hangars and barracks and a 6,000-foot runway, and erecting a 500,000-gallon water tank, even though one of the heaviest rainfalls in Midland's history delayed all construction for weeks.[10]

Work on the field was in full swing on October 9, 1941, when Lt. Col. Isaiah Davies, the newly appointed commander of Midland Army Airfield, arrived at the Texas base. Davies had enlisted as a private in the U.S. Cavalry in 1914 and had earned his officer's commission and his silver aviator's wings during World War I. He had served under the command of the legendary Gen. Billy Mitchell and had participated in the test-bombing of the German ship *Ostfried-*

land that had been a milestone in Mitchell's ongoing campaign to promote military airpower in the United States. Although he lacked the college education usually expected of air officers, the fifty-one-year old Davies was by all accounts an outstanding commander, and in less than one year at Midland, he was promoted to the rank of brigadier general. A photograph in the *Reporter-Telegram* shows a diminutive but dapper Davies, still a lieutenant colonel, alighting from his aircraft to be greeted by Midland's Mayor M. C. Ulmer, symbolically astride a large buckskin Texas cow pony.

An early 1942 article in the *Midland Reporter-Telegram* describes Davies in words seldom used to characterize general officers. According to the newspaper, a cadet was asked by his visiting mother to identify a particularly dignified and energetic officer whom she had spotted. "Mom," replied her son, "he is General Davies. Note the stars on his shoulders," the young man went on. "He twinkles as brightly as those stars, Mom . . . he just twinkles and twinkles and twinkles." The boy's mother doubtlessly was pleased that her son was under the command of such a sparkling leader of men.[11]

Just two months following the new commander's arrival, the United States entered the war immediately following the Japanese attack on Pearl Harbor. Construction work on the nearly completed facility was accelerated as the first of the bombardier candidates began to arrive at Midland. When the base was first announced, there were only two hundred bombardiers in the entire Air Corps. During the early war years, nearly 13,000 bombardiers would be trained in the state of Texas alone.

At first, most of the cadets arriving at Midland were washed-out pilot candidates who were still eager to fly as crew members. As the war progressed and the need for qualified bombardiers increased, the Army actively recruited officers and cadets to go directly to such training centers as Midland. These trainees received six weeks of pre-flight instruction elsewhere before starting the twelve-week advanced school at Midland Army Airfield.

Prior to the arrival of the first class of cadets at the just-completed air base, Colonel Davies invited the local citizenry to an open house so that they could see firsthand what the much-heralded but heretofore top-secret facility was like. According to the *Midland Reporter-Telegram*, more than 15,000 West Texans swarmed through the main gate. Even though much of the base was declared off-limits to the visitors, they were apparently impressed by what they were permitted to see. Once the actual training got underway, civilian access to most areas on the base would become highly restricted.[12]

On February 6, 1942, just a week following the open house, the first class of 119 cadets arrived to begin a twelve-week course of instruction. After a month of ground school, the cadets were taken aloft to learn how to actually use the Norden bombsight in flight. Before ever seeing the highly classified bombsight, each cadet swore a solemn oath to protect the instrument with his life, if need be, and never divulge the secrets of its operation to anyone, friend or foe alike. With armed sentries present, each bombardier-to-be raised his right hand, and gazing at a bombsight displayed like some pagan idol in front of him, grimly intoned:

> In the presence of almighty God, I do solemnly swear and affirm that I will accept the sacred trust placed in me by my Commander in Chief, the President of the United States of America, by whose direction I have been chosen for bombardier training. I pledge myself to live and act according to the code of honor of the Bombardiers of the Army Air Forces. I solemnly swear I will keep inviolate the secrecy of any and all confidential information revealed to me, and, in full knowledge that I am a guardian of one of my country's most priceless military assets, do further swear to protect the secrecy of the American Bombsight, if need be, with life itself.[13]

The Army was so concerned that the secrets of the Norden might fall into enemy hands, no operational manual was ever printed to inform would-be bombardiers how to use one. Students learned from diagrams drawn on easily erased blackboards and from seasoned instructors. No notes could be taken out of the training classrooms, forcing the cadets to memorize all operational details of the secret bombsight.

One former bombardier, writing long after the Norden had passed from top-secret to obsolete, described the instrument as a combination of a telescope and an early form of a computer. Like all such instruments, its performance could only mirror the accuracy of the data put into it by the bombardier. Further, if weather conditions were below standard limits, the bombsight was useless and the mission a failure. If the bombardier were correct in his assumptions about wind speed and direction, the weight of the bombs, the airspeed of aircraft, et cetera, the Norden bombsight could be a formidable and accurate weapons-launcher. It was the task of schools such as Midland to train its students to achieve that necessarily high level of competence and to terminate the training of those who were found unsuitable for further instruction and eventual combat duty.[14]

The training commenced with a ground simulator that was primitive at best. It consisted of a scaffolding on wheels that rolled across a hangar floor as the student pursued a moving box that represented the target. A marker suspended from the self-propelled scaffold made a large dot on top of the box, if the cadets were able to make marker and box come together at all. How any students were able to satisfactorily pass this difficult phase of training remains a mystery to many former bombardiers.

Those who did manage to move on to the in-flight part of their instruction often found working with the Norden bombsight to be highly challenging, at least at the outset. To operate the sight, the student found it necessary to straddle it, with his hands manipulating its many knobs and levers in an awkward if not contorted position, his eye pressed firmly against what the Army capriciously called a "soft rubber" sighting piece. Perhaps when the bombsight left the factory, its eyepiece may have been soft, but just a few days in the blistering Texas sun took most of the softness away. The cover of the May 18, 1942, issue of *Life* magazine showed a Midland bombardier after a training mission, his right eye swollen and puffy and ringed with a circle of black that made him resemble a pugilist more than an aircrew member. Judging by surviving photos of black-eyed bombardiers, it seems likely that considerable additional blackening was often added for dramatic effect.

After completing his calculations and steering the AT-11 training aircraft to his target, the cadet at last had the satisfaction of actually dropping some bombs. They were 100-pound devices filled with sand and just enough black powder to create a puff of smoke to mark where the bomb had hit. Midland's school had twenty-three bombing ranges located on ranches throughout the Permian Basin. Some of the ranges had targets drawn on the ground surface in shapes approximating battleships, bridges, truck convoys, and even oil refineries.

In a January 13, 1991, article in Midland's *Reporter-Telegram,* Professor J. Tillapaugh of the University of Texas of the Permian Basin related that many of these World War II target shapes are still visible in an eight-county area surrounding the old Midland base. The West Texas practice area utilized by the training school was larger than the state of New Jersey, according to the professor. Large six-by-eight-foot warning signs advised passersby of the danger of entering the practice ranges, which were in use both day and night.[15]

While the signs apparently kept curious trespassers away from the practice ranges, the bombs themselves were sometimes accidentally misdirected. No humans were reportedly injured by such mishaps, but livestock sometimes fell victim to the 100-pound projectiles, much to the consternation of some area ranchers. Fire caused by the marking powder in the bombs quite often ravaged the dry prairies, creating even further outrage among the cattlemen. One errant bomb spared both livestock and prairie but totally destroyed a country store that was fortunately closed at the time of impact. After the war, many of the blue practice bombs, devoid of their fuses, were used as yard decorations in Midland and Odessa.[16]

Given the frequency with which the practice bombs were being dropped from the Midland-based AT-11s, it is a wonder that more collateral damage was not caused. It is estimated that more than a thousand bombs were released by the cadets during a typical training day. In total, a reported 1,245,107 bombs were dropped on Midland's ranges during the war years. One report announced that the number of bombs striking the area on any given day exceeded the amount dropped on London during the 1940 blitz.[17]

Of the first class of 119 cadets to enter the school in February 1942, all but sixteen graduated three months later. The 13-percent attrition rate for the class rather curiously became the norm for the many classes to follow at Midland. Of the 103 who graduated with the first class, several of the new bombardiers with better performance records were retained as instructors, while most of the others were ordered to crew training centers. From there, the crews would be assigned to combat units throughout the world. New classes continued to arrive at Midland on a regular basis every three weeks as planned, even though the incoming classes were enlarged as the need for bombardiers accelerated. In total, 6,627 cadets went through the school, flying a total of 861,510 hours in the three years the field was in operation.[18]

Although the many cadets assigned to the bombardier school had little opportunity to visit either Midland or nearby Odessa, the community reached out warmly to the instructors and other permanently assigned personnel. The servicemen who could get passes to leave the base were welcomed into Midland homes and churches. Social events for officers were frequently staged at many of the city's better homes, and the newspapers regularly published reports of the marriages of local girls to military men stationed on the base.

One instructor, Henry Goulet, remembers that when he went into town, civilians invariably asked, "Hi, soldier! How do you like Midland?" During one of the Permian Basin's infamous sandstorms, he was tempted to reply, "I might as well have stayed in North Africa." The friendliness of the people made a lasting impression on Goulet, as it did on so many soldiers. He married a local girl and returned to Midland after the war to become a permanent resident.[19]

Colonel Davies, so soon to become a brigadier general, proved to be a master at base public relations. A frequent speaker at Midland civic clubs, Davies did much to promote goodwill between the base and the local citizenry. Perhaps even those unlucky cattlemen whose livestock had been the first casualties brought about by Davies's bombardiers were somewhat mollified by the commander's charm.

Undoubtedly one of Davies's more unique public relations programs was his Future Bombardiers of America organization. With its membership open to boys aged from eight to sixteen, the club encouraged interest in the bombardier program and gave its members unusually free access to the base. Each young man took an oath of secrecy not unlike the one sworn by his adult counterpart and even got to meet real cadets at social events. Davies clearly realized that with the youth of Midland as members of his team, the city's parents would soon become enthusiastic supporters of the base and its mission.[20]

There can be little question about Midland's hospitality toward air base personnel. In the city's downtown area, a service club was soon in operation, where soldiers could get refreshment and meet local civilian volunteers.

The nearby city of Odessa also warmly welcomed the servicemen, gaining a reputation for having much more in the way of Texas honky-tonk entertainment than its more conservative sister city to the east, making it immensely popular with servicemen. Both towns honored graduating cadets with farewell banquets, and each also sponsored traditional barbecues for students and permanently assigned personnel. When one group of cadets complained that they had seen no evidence of Texas's legendary cowboy culture, rancher Clarence Scharbauer sent twenty of his cowhands in full round-up regalia to the base on horseback.

Odessa's relationship with the base was by all accounts every bit as cordial as was Midland's. A keen rivalry had long existed between the two cities, however, and Odessa's newspaper, the *American,* seemingly found it difficult to identify the big base as Midland Army Airfield. References to the base appeared in the paper frequently, but such terms as "our airfield," "the big bombardier school," or even "Sloan Field," were almost always employed to avoid using the name of the archrival city located just twenty miles to the east.[21]

Clearly, many airmen found much to their liking in Odessa. One historian notes that the city's girls were keen to entertain any soldiers who came west to the oil town. "With their eyelashes curled upward and the latest New York fashion fads on their minds," wrote the historian, "the gals set out to entertain the soldiers and make them feel at home."[22]

One airman found himself so well entertained that he made Odessa his lifelong home after the war. Sam McClelland came to the Midland base as a corporal in 1942 and found "there was just not much going on, but the people were friendly." On the Fourth of July, the newly arrived soldier went to Odessa on what he describes as being a "hot and salty day." Learning that there was a USO dance in progress at the American Legion Hall, McClelland made his way up "a long dusty road" to the hall. Once inside, he wasted little time. Spying an attractive girl dancing with another soldier from the base, he cut in and asked the girl, "Why don't I come see you for a chicken dinner at your house?" Perhaps overwhelmed at the corporal's direct approach, she quickly issued the invitation he sought. Less than a year later on June 5, 1943, the couple was married, and they have lived in Odessa since that time.[23]

On July 4, 1942, in another of General Davies's more inspired public relations projects, the citizens of the Permian Basin were invited to witness the destruction of a small-scale mock-up of Tokyo that had been erected some ten miles south of the base. Material for the mock city had been contributed by Midlanders, and for weeks prior to the Independence Day event, air base workers had labored in the desert to fabricate Japanese-style houses, factories, and office buildings out of the used lumber and cardboard so generously provided by the townsfolk.

On the day of the demonstration, national media representatives arrived in Midland to cover the event, and a cameraman from RKO Studios arrived to film the destruction of the mock Tokyo for use in a movie appropriately titled *Bombardier*, which was then in production in Hollywood. All residents of the Permian Basin were invited to watch this demonstration of what trained bombardiers hoped to soon be doing to the real paper city of Tokyo, Japan.

An estimated crowd of 20,000 West Texans followed the well-marked route to the bomb site to gain a good view of the destruction, but from a relatively safe distance. As it developed, General Davies had underestimated the response to his ambitious stunt just as completely as his staff had failed to anticipate the need for restroom facilities or drinking water for the spectators. As thousands of cars moved toward the site along hastily constructed unpaved tracks across the scorched desert, an immense traffic jam soon formed. When many of the 1942 and older-model unair-conditioned vehicles soon became overheated and stalled, the congestion grew even worse.

While only a few of the would-be spectators got close enough to watch the bombs actually strike the toy city, the results were apparently quite spectacular. Some seventy aircraft approached the target at an altitude of less than five hundred feet to drop nearly fifteen hundred bombs for several hours until darkness fell and the Texas-style Tokyo was reduced to nothing but glowing ashes and blowing dust. An official photograph shows an apparently elated Isaiah Davies watching the last flames subside. Perhaps the general is also reflecting on the school's motto, which was "Hell from Heaven."

By this time, most of the wheezing automobiles had been turned around by their drivers, having seen little but distant formations of AT-11s and lots of smoke. Aerial flares were dropped over the homeward-bound vehicles to illuminate their way across the desert through the dust that swirled in great clouds from Midland to Odessa and beyond. General Davies, who had witnessed the bombers' glorious raid from his own aircraft before landing for an on-site observation deemed this Fourth of July one to remember. Even the normally subdued *New York Times* was enthusiastic about the successful bomb run in the Texas desert, but General Davies's superiors at Army Air Force headquarters took a dim view of the proceedings, the details of which had apparently been kept from them in advance. From on high came a sternly worded directive that henceforth, bombing practice would be restricted to standard targets and to be conducted without fanfare, without Hollywood cameramen, and most certainly without the general public invited to be on-site observers.[24]

Overlooking its occasional forays into what may have been ill-advised but successful public relations stunts, the Midland base became increasingly important in the Army's overall plans for combat-crew training. By 1943 the airfield had become the headquarters for other bombardier schools that had just opened at Childress, San Angelo, and nearby Big Spring. As an alarming number of experienced bombardiers lost their lives in combat, and as more and more aircrews were needed to man the rapidly expanding American air armada, the facility at Midland was unable to supply enough trained bombardiers to meet a totally underestimated demand.

Competition was keen among the training schools under Midland's supervisor. Col. John W. White left his position at Midland to assume command at the new bombardier school at Childress, Texas. There he put into action what came to be called "The All-American Precision Bombing Olympics." The event, held annually at the various bases in the Training Command, pitted top cadet bombardiers from each school against one another in demonstrations of bombing proficiency. Included in the four-day-long competition were tests of skip-bombing, circular error evaluation, and considerable socializing, which presumably was not evaluated. The winning team was awarded a trophy that was soon proudly on display at the team's home field.[25]

As the tide of war slowly turned in favor of the Allied forces, the demand for trained flight crews tapered off from its peak. Accordingly, the numbers of cadets assigned to Midland and its sister bases diminished after late 1943. For a time, the Midland facility was used to provide refresher courses for experienced combat bombardiers and to train even more instructors, although there were fewer students to teach.

The late-war development of the lead-combat crew concept also reduced the demand for highly trained bombardiers and navigators. The lead aircraft would act as the point plane in a flight formation, with other craft simply following it into the combat area and over the target. When the better-qualified lead bombardier would signal that his bombs were away, the other aircraft would then drop their weapons at a pre-set interval designed to maximize the destructive effect of the bombs dropped by the lead planes. Quite understandably, some well-trained and equally skilled "follow" bombardiers resented this copycat approach to the performance of their duties.

As the training regimen at Midland slackened, so did the morale of the personnel stationed there. With victory in the war in sight and a growing perception of not being as vitally needed as before, cadets, officers, and enlisted men alike began to lose interest in their work and find fault with the Army Air Force in general and with Midland in particular.

In an effort to boost morale, mess-hall service was reevaluated and apparently improved. A second officers' club was opened for the exclusive use of bachelors, a step taken to either shield the married officers' families from possible embarrassing incidents or to provide the ostensibly less conservative unmarried personnel with a place to unwind without undue criticism and censure.

Base headquarters sponsored a series of questionnaires designed to measure the depth of the obviously growing discontent and to determine how to quell it in a positive way. The answers received on the questionnaire forms must have come as something of a shock to those senior commanders who were convinced that theirs was an all-but-ideal installation. More than nine out of ten respondents found off-base facilities either poor or totally unsatisfactory, and a large percentage decried the lack of adequate housing. The responses reflected the strong impression that as far as bombardiers were concerned, the war was as good as over and their time and the taxpayers' money were being wasted on a base whose mission had suddenly become obsolete. One comment on a completed form must have particularly stung those in command. "War is a brutal, horrible farce," wrote one combat-weary bombardier back at Midland for an unneeded refresher course, "and so is the Army."[26] Another officer, however, sounded a chord that must have been music to the ears of the city leaders who had labored so long to get an air base. "Meeting the friendly people in and around Midland," he wrote, "helped my morale considerably."[27]

Improved morale and friendly people notwithstanding, it soon became apparent that the days of Midland Army Airfield were numbered. By the time World War II finally ended in September 1945, all bombardier training at other Texas bases had been discontinued and consolidated at Midland. On February 6, 1946, the fourth anniversary of the first class to arrive at the field, the final group of cadets to graduate received their commissions and wings. Three days later, all training ceased at the base that had produced nearly 8,000 bombardiers in those four years.[28]

No formal announcement of the closing of the base was forthcoming from the War Department, and local chamber of commerce and Army Air Force officials engaged in what became a routine pastime of reassuring the public and the media that the base still had a bright future, even in peacetime. Despite those misleading claims to the contrary, the base was placed on an inactive status in late June 1946, and six months later, the property was declared to be surplus. In time, the site reverted to the city, and its buildings were converted to other usage or moved away. The runways and hangars were retained of course, and in time a new Midland International Airport was born where tiny Sloan Field had once been in limited operation.[29]

Midland itself survived the loss of its "Bombardier College" just as gamely as it has survived many other economic disappointments in the long years since. Toughened by adversity and still demonstrating a remarkable civic ability to restructure repeated busts into sustained periods of prosperity, the Queen City of the South Plains still reigns supreme in her kingdom on the "Flat Brown."

The airport that grew where the great air base once flourished is an active one, due in part to the presence of the headquarters of the Confederate Air Force (CAF) and its outstanding collection of World War II aircraft on display on airport property. Founded in 1951, the CAF is dedicated to the mission of preserving, in flying order, at least one of each model of aircraft that saw service in the war. Over 10,000 members worldwide support the effort of this unique organization.

Not much remains of the giant military air base that made such a contribution to America's war in the air more than fifty years ago. The 500,000-gallon water tower remains intact and in operation, as do a few rebuilt sheds and a hangar. The concrete base that once supported the old field's flagpole is still discernible in the grass close by the water tower, and the taxiways and runways still serve commercial and privately owned aircraft. Perhaps the most enduring of all mementos of the long-dead military base, however, can be found in Midland International Airport's official FAA designation code, "MAF," preserving for all time the heritage of Midland Army Field.

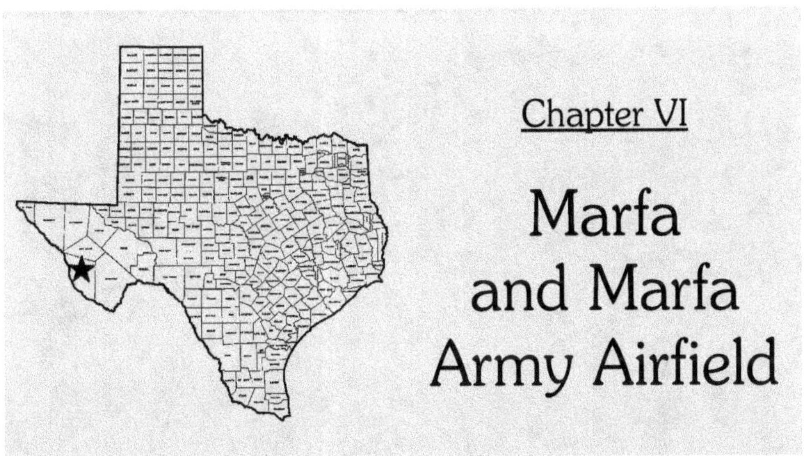

Chapter VI

Marfa and Marfa Army Airfield

We used to stop in Marfa on our way to Fort Stockton back when I was just a little kid. There wasn't hardly anything to do around there, but boy, did it ever get cool at night, even in the summertime.

Elliott Pringle
El Paso, Texas

Travelers such as Mr. Pringle have been passing through Marfa for centuries. Apache, Comanche, cavalrymen, railroaders, smugglers, rumrunners, and just ordinary tourists have visited the little community on what is now known as the Marfa Plateau. Situated in far West Texas at the junction of two historic trails that eventually became important arterial highways, Marfa's elevation is just short of a mile above sea level, which accounts for the cool summer evenings much too rare elsewhere in the state.

Significant settlement of the town did not take place until 1883, when the Galveston, Harrisburg and San Antonio Railway laid its miles of track parallel to what is now U.S. Highway 90, providing a vital rail link between Del Rio and El Paso to the west. According to most accounts, the freighting depot and water stop established by the GH&SA was given the unusual name Marfa by the wife of one of the railroad's executives, who just happened to be

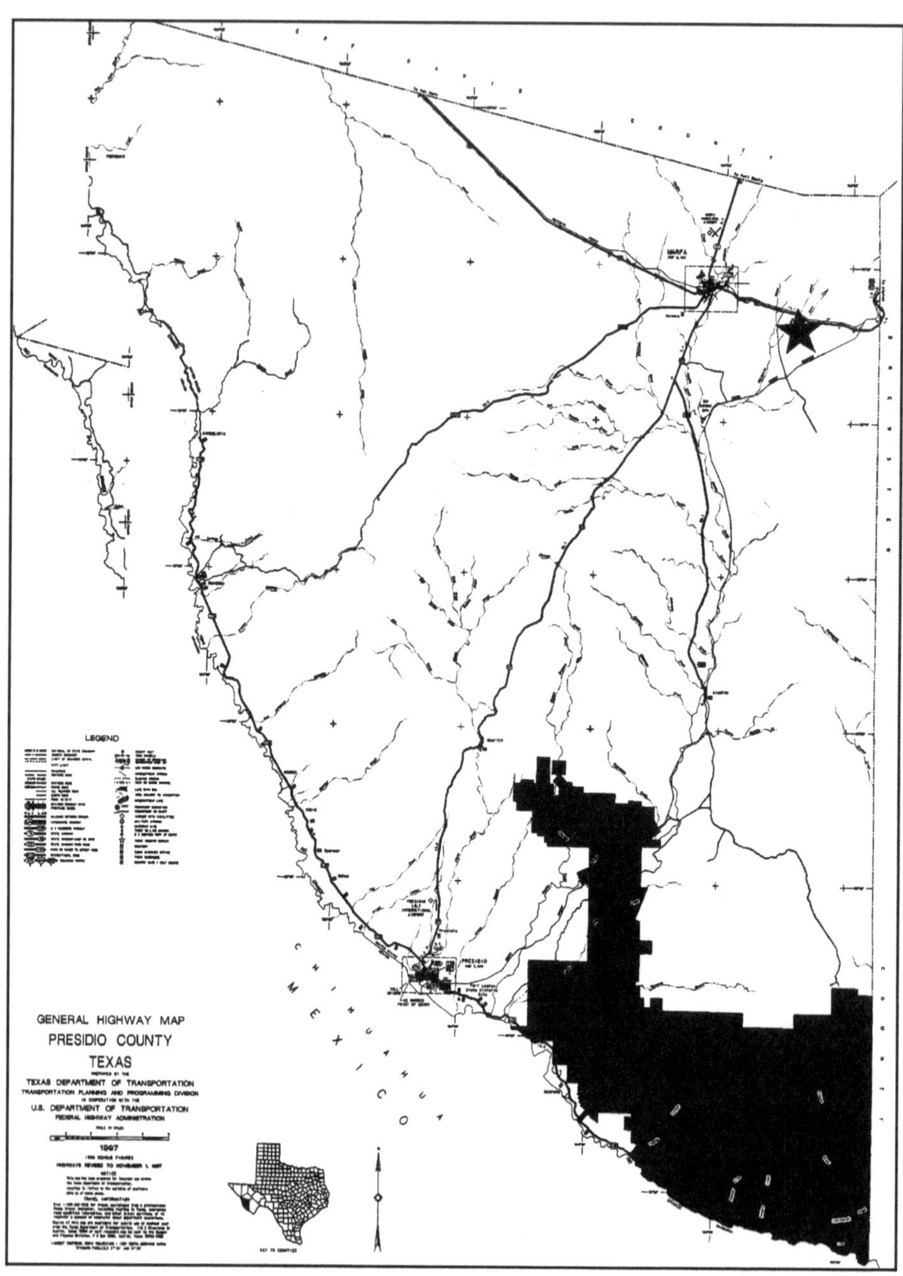

Presidio County Map
This map of Presidio County shows the location of Marfa Army Airfield during the war years. An inset map of Texas shows the location of the county within the state.

reading Fyodor Dostoyevsky's *The Brothers Karamazov* at the same time as the site was selected.[1]

Within two years of its founding, the little Texas town with a Russian name was selected to become the seat of Presidio County and boasted a population of nearly five hundred. In addition to a magnificent new three-story courthouse, which is still in use, the town had a post office, several saloons, and a small number of churches. The sheer remoteness of the county seat seemed to be a deterrent to any dramatic increase in population, and by 1900 only a thousand claimed Marfa as their home. The town did not experience much growth until the early part of the twentieth century when the United States Army came to the region in force for the first but by no means the last time.[2]

In 1911 elements of Army cavalry units first arrived in Marfa, taking full advantage of the area's abundant forage grass, moderate temperatures, and convenient railroad access to establish a camp from which to patrol the nearby Rio Grande. Disturbances along that often-turbulent border with Mexico had become more frequent during the Mexican Revolution. When the disturbances grew increasingly confrontational, a permanent facility, identified first as Camp Arthur and then renamed Camp Marfa, was established just south of the town. Cavalry troops ranged out of the new camp on regular patrols, and in time aeroplanes were added to the Army's expanding surveillance program.[3]

Eventually, fourteen additional military observation posts were placed along the border, all under the jurisdiction of Camp Marfa. Despite the many outposts and the often ineffective surveillance flights, the Mexican Revolutionary leader Pancho Villa tested the U.S. Army's reconnaissance efforts to the fullest. In 1914, when Villa's troops captured Ojinaga, just across the Rio Grande from Presidio, thousands of Mexican citizens and soldiers surrendered to American officials, and Camp Marfa was transformed virtually overnight into a gigantic refugee center.

By 1918, even though the border situation had become relatively peaceful, the Army determined that its installation at Marfa was far too vital to be abandoned. What had previously been only a primitive, tent-filled outpost was shortly developed into a modern military installation, complete with a ninety-six-bed hospital, a radio station, a theater, and wooden barracks for the cavalrymen. In

1930 Camp Marfa was renamed Fort D. A. Russell, in honor of an Army officer who had served with some distinction in the Mexican War. Russell had died in action as a brigadier general in the Union Army during America's Civil War.[4]

The fort's expansion had a positive effect on the city of Marfa, and the town's population soon grew to nearly 4,000. During the years of the Great Depression, Fort D. A. Russell annually contributed nearly a half-million dollars to Marfa's struggling economy. On February 2, 1933, despite previous governmental assurances to the contrary, the fort was closed, presumably for all time. Events just beginning to take shape elsewhere in the world, however, would soon cause the Army to return to Marfa to a degree never envisioned by the city's leaders.[5]

MARFA ARMY AIRFIELD

They took us in and assimilated us into their society. We were foreigners in a vague sense and they accepted us fully.

C. M. "Fritz" Kahl
Former MAAF Flight Instructor
Mayor of Marfa, 1999

Although Fort D. A. Russell was reactivated in 1935 and later developed into an officer-training school in preparation for the war that many authorities correctly predicted was soon to come, Marfa's largest military facility was not announced until that worldwide war was well underway. It was the superb flying weather recalled by many former D. A. Russell reconnaissance fliers that was a key factor in the government's decision to open a gigantic Army flight school east of the town. The area's excellent rail transportation facilities also made Marfa a prime location for a major military installation, as the cavalry had discovered more than a quarter-century earlier. The continuing warm support of Fort D. A. Russell by Marfans was also an important factor in building the new facility.

All that was needed was an available tract of land that could accommodate lengthy runways, hangars, and barracks for thousands of men. In the vast open spaces surrounding Marfa, it seemed quite likely to government officials that such a site could be easily located.

On March 27, 1942, Maj. Norman L. Callish of the Army Air Force came to Marfa to locate such a parcel of land. Accompanied by city officials, the major inspected numerous potential sites but left town apparently without making any decision. In less than two weeks, however, Callish returned with several other officers to continue his search and soon identified a 2,750-acre site less than eight miles east of town on Highway 90 as his choice. Following a series of hurried surveys by military engineers, the parcel was formally deemed suitable, and negotiations for its purchase were commenced at once.

Mr. Thomas G. Hendrick of Abilene, Texas, the owner of the land, agreed to sell it to the City of Marfa for $6.50 per acre, or $17,875. To ensure the funding for the purchase, the cities of nearby Alpine and not-so-nearby Presidio joined Marfa in agreeing to buy the land with the proceeds from a tri-city bond election designed to yield some $30,000. The bond issue was approved in Marfa by a vote of 80 to 1, and by equally impressive margins in Alpine and Presidio. The initial plan was to then lease the entire parcel to the War Department for the customary one dollar a year. The United States government, however, had financial plans of its own and announced its intention to purchase the land outright. This governmental decision, no doubt accepted warmly by the three cities involved in the prior negotiations, also included an agreement to sell the parcel back to Mr. Hendrick for the original purchase price should the Army ever decide to abandon the soon-to-be built facility.[6]

This was clearly a win-win arrangement for all parties concerned, and on May 22, 1942, Marfa's local newspaper ran a banner headline announcing the government's decision to build and operate the flying school. The paper's front page reproduced the identical telegrams from Texas's two United States senators that stated that the facility would cost less than $3 million and that construction would be supervised by the Army Corps of Engineers' Albuquerque office. According to the newspaper account, the entire construction phase of the airfield would require only ninety days.[7]

A week later, the newspaper further disclosed that all negotiations with the landowner had been finalized, with Mr. Hendrick consenting to an easement across the four-and-a-half sections of land to bring power to the airfield. The costs of bringing in the power lines and the laying of pipelines were estimated at $21,000, or more than the cost of the land itself, the paper announced.[8]

In the same edition of the newspaper, the Marfa Chamber of Commerce issued a plea that would be repeated throughout the existence of the airfield. "Help! Help! Help!," implored chamber secretary A. E. Ligon, "New Marfans need places of residence."[9]

Tiny Marfa, faced with an impending surge of construction workers that would soon be followed by servicemen and their families, was never able to find enough residences to satisfy the constantly growing demand. Newspaper editorials from 1942 through mid-1945 continued to literally beg for listings on any type of housing. The truth was that adequate housing simply did not exist in Marfa or in surrounding towns. Houses could not be built rapidly enough to keep up with the incoming flood of humanity.

As evidence of the magnitude of that flood, records indicate that Marfa's population grew by nearly 50 percent during the wartime years. There was a 47 percent increase in the number of telephones in use, and sales volume at the post office increased by 92 percent in the period from 1942 to 1944. This figure did not reflect some additional 3,000 free letters that were mailed daily by servicemen.[10] Even though their city was growing and its resources were being sorely tested, Marfans proved themselves totally committed to the war effort in general and to the welfare of their new Air Force neighbors.

To test the city's level of wartime preparedness, a blackout drill was arranged for late April 1942. The publisher of *The Big Bend Sentinel,* Marfa's weekly newspaper, was appointed an official observer for the event and assigned an observation post atop the tower of the Presidio County Courthouse, directly across the street from the paper's offices. At 9:30 P.M., the appointed hour for the mandatory extinguishing of all lights, the publisher was pleased to note that Marfa was suddenly plunged into total darkness, as ordered by civilian defense officials. There was, however, one literally glaring exception. In the sea of darkness that the city had suddenly become, a solitary light burned brightly for all to see, friend and possibly airborne foe alike. Much to the chagrin of the publisher, he realized that the offending ray of light was streaming from his newspaper's own offices. After running down the hundred or so narrow and darkened stairs of the courthouse tower, the publisher quickly reached his office, only to discover that the brightly burning bulb was one that had been thought for years to be burned out. For some unfathomable reason, the long-dormant bulb had begun to glow again at precisely the minute the blackout was scheduled, making it perhaps another mysterious Marfa light.[11]

Despite the embarrassment caused the publisher by the suddenly revitalized light bulb, the overall drill was declared a success. The first blackout exercise held in January 1942 had been less successful, mainly because Army personnel had permitted automobiles, headlights ablaze, to stream into the city during the drill, effectively pinpointing the precise location of Marfa, Texas, to any incoming Axis aircraft that might have selected the town as its target for the night.[12]

Enemy fliers would probably not have known that there were other lights in the area that could not have been extinguished by any government order, blackout drill or no blackout drill. Since 1883, in an area east of town and adjacent to the proposed site of the new airfield, witnesses had been viewing and wondering about what had become known as the Marfa Lights. Almost every evening just after sunset, a dancing, pulsating, and colorful light-show extravaganza was often readily apparent to dedicated viewers who looked eagerly in a southeasterly direction. Some others, however, stared in vain night after night, failing to catch even a glimpse of the capricious lights.

The phenomenon was first officially recorded by cowboy Robert Reed Ellison while riding the range at night. His immediate reaction was that he was seeing the lights of Apache watch fires, and he hastened into Marfa to warn the townspeople of the possibility of an impending attack. Local residents, however, assured him that the darting illuminations had in fact been visible for years. Many old-timers had investigated the lights, seeking their source, but no one had ever found ashes or burning embers to prove that any sort of fire had caused the phenomenon to occur.

Mrs. W. T. Giddings, a longtime area resident, had her own opinions about the source of the lights. She was convinced that the Marfa Lights were in some way supernatural and ghostly, but friendly nevertheless. Mrs. Giddings was fond of relating how her father had become lost in a blizzard many years before, and how the helpful lights had led him to a cave where he found shelter from the storm. During World War I, other more pragmatic observers had convinced themselves that the lights were in fact of human origin and signaled an invasion by enemy forces crossing the Rio Grande from Mexico. Pilots in search aircraft, however, could find neither evidence of any invaders nor, indeed, any other visible source for the lights.

Over the years, explanations of the phenomenon have been as varied and unpredictable as the Marfa Lights themselves. To some, they are a form of St. Elmo's Fire, and to others an atmospheric condition caused by an interaction of warm and cold layers of air that somehow bends and reflects distant light. To some more imaginative modern-day observers, the Marfa Lights are clear-cut evidence of space-dwelling aliens attempting to signal earthlings.[13]

In addition to the long-running debate about what causes the lights, many wonder why the phenomenon occurs only where it does. According to Fritz Kahl, the same sort of light spectacle may be seen in other locales throughout the region. "The Marfa Lights viewing area on Highway 90," says the mayor, "is located where it is simply because that particular display is convenient for motorists. Other similar displays," notes Mayor Kahl, "take place in more remote areas, away from the view of the general public." It is fascinating to note that the official Marfa Light viewing area referred to by the mayor is within fifty feet of what was once the main entry gate to Marfa Army Airfield.[14]

When that gate and the air base behind it were nearing completion, interested Marfans were invited to attend a special chamber of commerce meeting to better understand the problems that the airfield might create for the community. On August 3, 1942, forty civic-minded Marfans attended the session to hear reports of how other cities had dealt with those various social and logistical problems. Speakers from Austin, Odessa, and Midland addressed such concerns as sanitation, traffic, utilities, school overcrowding, and, of course, housing. According to published reports of the meeting, few if any solutions were forthcoming, but at least the local citizens were formally apprised that some vexing difficulties might lie just ahead when the new field was opened.

On the brighter side of the forecasts offered during the evening event were welcome predictions that Marfa retailers could expect to realize a breathtaking increase in sales volume when the base was activated. Mr. Paul Nelson, manager of Midland's J.C. Penney Company store, reported that stores in his city had experienced sales increases ranging from 50 to 100 percent in the first year Midland's Army Airfield had been open. His welcome remarks reportedly brought cheers from the assemblage.[15]

Even while the local citizenry rejoiced at the prospect of impending good financial fortune, the editor of *The Big Bend Sentinel* saw fit to take them to task. Accusing the people of Marfa of "not fulfilling their patriotic obligation by not opening their homes to military tenants," the editor reiterated the cry of "Help! Help! Help!" in solving the growing housing crisis in the rapidly expanding city. Fritz Kahl remembers that the frantic search for housing was by no means limited to Marfa itself. Alpine, Fort Davis, and even the nearby state park-operated Indian Lodge were all struggling to find accommodations of any sort for the thousands of servicemen and their families who were descending upon the area.[16]

Marfa's El Paisano Hotel did somehow find a way to provide a suitable residence for Col. Gerald O. Hoyle, the airfield's project officer and subsequently its first commanding officer. A thirteen-year veteran of the Army Air Force, Hoyle had been involved in the building and opening of other air-training facilities located in California and New Mexico.

From his temporary headquarters in the Marfa National Bank Building, Colonel Hoyle announced that the new training facility had been officially activated as of August 17, 1942, although construction was still continuing and flying classes had yet to convene. The purpose of the school, it was announced, would be the training of pilots in multi-engine aircraft, with the Cessna AT-17 as the principal plane to be used. Former flight instructor Kahl recalls how the AT-17 was initially underestimated by the pilots. "We thought we had to nursemaid them," remembers Kahl, "we didn't understand how sturdy those wood-and-fabric airplanes were." Later, B25s and P-38s were assigned to the base.[17]

Even though the reliable planes had been ordered and an experienced officer placed in command, Marfa Army Airfield was still being built on what one almost lyrical newspaper account referred to as "lush prairie." Most cattlemen in the area, then as now, would find it a far stretch of the imagination to identify as lush any grazing land that provided mainly creosote bush and prickly pear for forage.

However, the chosen site was reasonably flat and likely even better suited for AT17s than for herds of Hereford cattle.[18]

In September 1942, nearly five months after the airfield project had been announced, Army Air Force officers flew into Marfa to interview civilians for the 250 permanent on-base jobs that would soon become available. In early October, Colonel Hoyle told the newspaper that the facility would soon be ready to receive its first class of aviation cadets, and in November the War Department announced that all "essential construction" had been completed at a cost exceeding $6 million, more than double the original estimate put forth only six months earlier.[19]

On November 25, the first of many AT-17s arrived at the field, along with a cadre of servicemen who would provide ongoing support for the student pilots soon to arrive. In total, more than 5,000 permanent personnel would eventually be required to accomplish the airfield's training mission.[20]

With the arrival of so many newcomers at last a reality, *The Big Bend Sentinel* launched a drive to ensure that their welcome would be at least nearly as warm as Marfa's summer days. An editorial, headlined "Correct Welcome for New Residents Most Essential Now," admonished readers that the general reputation of the community was at stake when it came to being courteous and fair to the newcomers. Although rent and price ceilings had been imposed on the entire region, the paper pointed out that it was imperative that "no undesirable advantage" be taken of the new arrivals. By all accounts, the citizens of Marfa heeded the advice of the *Sentinel.* Servicemen were welcomed in places of business and were invited into homes and churches. One longtime resident remembers soldiers as guests in her family's home on Christmas Day 1942. "We sat around and talked, sharing memories of past Christmases and hearing how the holiday was celebrated in other states," she recalls, "and we all laughed at each other's funny sounding accents."[21]

Just a few weeks before Christmas 1942, the base headquarters was moved from the Marfa Bank building to the new airfield, officers moved into the bachelor officers' quarters, and the enlisted men perhaps reluctantly left their in-town residence at the Toltec Motel in favor of tarpaper-covered open-bay barracks on the field. Only nine months after the base had been announced, other significant buildings on the nearly completed facility included a hospital, a theater, officers' and enlisted men's service clubs, a gymnasium, a chapel, and numerous athletic fields. A clothing store was built, designed to resemble a traditional building that had once flourished at nearby historic Fort Davis. According to one report, the store was of "department store proportions." Of primary importance on the new field, of course, were the gigantic hangars and the immense grid-like arrangement of concrete ramps, taxiways, and runways.[22]

At one peak time during the base's existence, nearly 500 aircraft were assigned to it. To accommodate such a sizable fleet, the field had four hangars, the largest being 32,000 square feet in size. There were five runways, four of which were 7,500 feet in length and 150 feet wide. In addition to the main facility, four auxiliary fields had been constructed within a 30-mile radius of the main airfield.[23]

Flight training at the massive installation finally got underway on December 7, 1942, the first anniversary of the Japanese attack on Pearl Harbor. One hundred and eighty pilot candidates comprised the first training group, which bore the official designation of Class 43-B.

When the first class graduated on February 6, 1943, the speaker at the ceremonies was Capt. Maurice S. Horgan, a combat veteran with the famed 19th Bombardment Group then stationed at Pyote Army Airfield. In his address, Captain Horgan very likely deflated more than a few soaring egos when he reminded the new second lieutenants that they were now merely "pilots with basic tools." The battle-seasoned flyer further challenged his audience by saying, "Although you know how to fly, you are just beginning the work [of becoming combat aviators]." Base commander Hoyle then perhaps restored some of the graduating class's earlier exhilaration when he announced that in Seattle a Boeing B-17 heavy bomber had just been dedicated in honor of Marfa's Class 43-B. The unlikely donor of the funds to buy the huge warbird was the Furniture Club of Detroit, Michigan. Following the speeches, a review, and the awarding of their silver wings, the graduates and their families enjoyed a festive banquet given in their honor at Marfa's First Christian Church.[24]

Each month following the graduation of Class 43-B, another cadet unit completed its training schedule. The graduation events in time became major social activities, with parades, flight demonstrations, base open houses, and banquets, and usually culminated in a dance honoring the new pilots. In the roughly three-and-a-half years that the flight-training base was in operation at Marfa, nearly 8,000 young men received their wings.[25]

Unfortunately, such an intensive training regimen almost inevitably led to tragic accidents. Even though the Marfa facility held the second-best accident-to-hours-flown rate in the Air Force, eight cadets were killed in training mishaps.

The first fatal incident occurred on March 29, 1943, at the flight school's southern auxiliary field. According to contemporary reports, an AT-17 aircraft simply nosed over into a rapid descent and crashed, instantly killing the instructor, Lt. William M. Hoover, and seriously injuring his student, Cadet George H. Hallin. Another instructor, Lt. Howard L. Yeager, a former football star with the New York Giants, performed heroically in his efforts to rescue the victims from the burning aircraft. When he was unable to unfasten the unconscious cadet's seat belt, Yeager simply ripped the seat from the floor of the plane and carried Cadet Hallin to safety, still strapped to his seat. The ex-Giant received the Soldier's Medal for his heroism, but unfortunately Hallin eventually succumbed to his injuries.[26]

Other fatal accidents soon followed. On August 30, 1943, an area rancher found a crashed aircraft that had been missing for more than two weeks. The bodies of Lt. Willard Wilson and Lt. Robert Renald, the two pilots of the craft, were removed from the crash site on Chinati Peak, located fifty miles southwest of Marfa. The cause of this third fatal accident in as many months was not immediately apparent.[27]

Despite such tragic occurrences, flight training at the base continued at a grueling pace. Construction work was also always in progress, and new housing units and additional classroom space were in constant demand as the field's pilot-training program escalated.

A seemingly never-ending flood of newcomers continued to stream into the Marfa area, putting even greater pressure on the already overtaxed housing situation. Despite an increased number of quarters being built on the base, hundreds of officers, enlisted men, and their families continued to seek rental units in Marfa and in neighboring communities. A rental survey, conducted in mid-1943, showed that military personnel living off-base were spending a total of $187,000 for rental housing each year in Alpine and only $50,000 per year in Marfa. In early 1943, there were reportedly 157 officers residing off the post, as were 277 enlisted men and more than 400 civilian employees. The total complement of personnel assigned to the base at the time was 3,131, comprised of 269 officers, 2,258 enlisted men, and 604 civilians. Clearly, the officer corps preferred to live in Alpine or Marfa, while the enlisted men apparently could only rarely afford to live off the field. The officers paid an average of $43 per month from their comparatively larger salaries for the privilege of living in town, and the enlisted men paid an average of $31 in monthly rental fees.[28]

Military personnel, whether living in Marfa or just visiting, often found it difficult to understand why there were no street signs to be found at any intersection in town. The newspaper promptly launched a campaign to erect the sorely needed signs. The paper's yearlong effort eventually proved successful, but by then local citizen W. T. Webb had already found a way to give newcomers satisfactory directions months before the long-sought signs were in place. Webb had miniature Marfa maps printed on pocket-sized cards, and when someone asked him how to locate an address, out came a map card that was then appropriately marked and given to the visitor.[29]

Two Marfa airfield cadets apparently could have used better maps of Mexico when they became lost on a routine flight along the Mexican border on October 6, 1943. Out of fuel, they landed their UC78 in a dry lake bed and made their way some 150 miles to the village of Ahumada, in the state of Chihuahua. The two were reported missing for nearly four days, while their unexplained absence caused much concern both on base and in town.[30]

According to most accounts, Marfans virtually adopted the servicemen at the airfield just as they previously had the soldiers at nearby Fort D.A. Russell for many years. They read of missing aircraft, fatal accidents, and lost lives with genuine sympathy and warmly welcomed all military personnel to become part of the community. An article in *The Big Bend Sentinel* on December 12, 1943, for example, relayed an open invitation to any four soldiers to share the Christmas dinner of Mr. and Mrs. V. E. Smith. Other Marfa residents were encouraged by the newspaper to invite servicemen to take part in family Christmas observances. The USOs in both

Marfa and Alpine planned Yuletide festivities for those not fortunate enough to be entertained in local homes. Carol singing and taffy pulling were among the diversions offered the soldiers, but of particular interest seemed to have been the huge quantities of food donated to the USO by local citizens. Area businesses provided gift boxes for the festivities, with some parcels containing certificates for free long-distance calls to homes all across the nation.[31]

Many of the soldiers who sought perhaps more exciting social diversions used the Christmas holidays or weekend passes to cross the border into Mexico. The many activities not readily available to servicemen visiting Marfa or Alpine often lured men across the Rio Grande. Army curfews mandated that visiting soldiers not tarry too long on the Mexican side of the river, but many personnel were reportedly not easily discouraged from crossing the border as often as their military duties would permit.[32]

By May 1944, with the war well into its third year, activity at the airfield continued its accelerated pace. Col. Donald B. Phillips told the Marfa Rotary Club that more civilian employees were desperately needed to help sustain the successful record of achievement at the field. The colonel noted that every effort was being made to improve working and living conditions on the nearly two-year-old facility. Colonel Phillips also said that despite rumors to the contrary, he was unaware of any plans to close the flying school, pointing out that the war was far from being won.

In early September 1944, however, Dan E. Root, the regional inspector of the Texas Liquor Control Board, apparently believed the end of the war imminent. Consequently, he requested that area liquor stores refrain from selling any alcoholic beverages for a forty-eight-hour period following the cessation of hostilities. Although the inspector did not have the authority to force the stores to comply with his request, he was pleased to report that most outlets had volunteered to close for at least one day when the end of the war was finally announced.[33]

With the actual end of the war not yet in sight, despite the premature concerns of the Liquor Control Board, training at the airfield was expanded to include multi-engine pilot candidates from other nations. A detachment of Chinese officers arrived in late 1944 to begin training. As the members of the group had only a limited knowledge of English, all teaching and in-flight instructions were monitored by interpreters to ensure understanding of and adherence to safety procedures. The foreign students followed the same training regimen as their American counterparts, except for extra classroom hours studying English. The first group of Chinese pilots graduated on November 21, 1944.

In addition to foreign students, Marfa Army Airfield was a temporary home to various well-known celebrities from time to time. Actor Robert Sterling was assigned to the field, and Marfans were seemingly starstruck when his actress wife, the glamorous Ann Sothern, came to visit him, staying at the El Paisano Hotel. Fritz Kahl remembers encountering a Marfa-based serviceman who would gain fame a few years later in Hollywood. As Kahl recollects, base chaplain H.H.D. Landeck opened his chapel each day at noon so that airfield personnel could enjoy hearing the remarkable singing voice of a singularly overweight military policeman named Alfred Arnold Coccozza. Word of Coccozza's talent soon spread throughout the entire area, and Kahl claims that the singer "would sing anywhere at the drop of a hat." The singing policeman appeared off-base at local churches, women's clubs, and virtually anyplace else people gathered. Long after the war, Mr. Kahl went into a motion picture theater and recognized the face on the screen and the voice on the soundtrack as being those of one Alfred Arnold Coccozza, now known to his countless fans as Mario Lanza.[34]

According to a respected film biography reference sourcebook, Coccozza/Lanza's professional musical career was just being launched when it was interrupted by military service. He had gained an audition with famed conductor Serge Koussevitsky in 1942 that had netted the twenty-one-year-old singer a scholarship and a contract with Columbia Records for a concert tour. Instead, Coccozza, as the Army knew him, found himself on a compulsory tour of Marfa, Texas, and its airfield.[35]

At the field's sister installation, old Fort D.A. Russell, located on the other side of town, activity had been fairly static throughout the war compared to the bustling flying school. The pace at the one-time horse cavalry post was markedly enlivened, however, in early 1944 when 195 German prisoners of war arrived soon after being captured in North Africa. The men, veterans of Field Marshal Erwin Rommel's *Afrika Korps,* caused quite a stir in Marfa as might be expected. "They were good-looking blond boys," recalled one-time local resident Myrtle Shepherd. "My YWCA and Baptist women's groups would make them cookies." Schoolchildren would wave at the prisoners as they were marched around the fort, but no German-speaking locals could be found to effectively communicate with the captured enemy soldiers.[36]

On one occasion, the parade of Rommel's ex-troopers created a near riot in Marfa. As the prisoners marched past a saloon, a patron whose son had been killed in action in the European theater rushed from his barstool to hurl a beer bottle at the passing formation. After this incident, the prisoners' march route was changed.[37]

Perhaps motivated by this less-than-cordial welcome, three of the prisoners escaped on April 2, 1944, and remained free and on the move for several days before being taken prisoner once again. One of the escapees, Raymond Moler, stated after his recapture that the group's plan had been to cross the Mexican border and make their way on to South America and then, somehow, back to Germany. Apparently lacking either a compass or a reliable sense of direction, the escapees were eventually apprehended some 130 miles northwest of Marfa near the town of Sierra Blanca, Texas. Had they headed south from Fort D.A. Russell and traveled the same distance in the same number of days, the men would have been nearly seventy miles into Mexico and would perhaps have stood at least an even chance of continuing their planned journey to South America and beyond.[38]

As was often the case with German POWs toward the end of the war, however, many were quite content to stay in American prison camps rather than attempt to escape and make their way back to Germany to rejoin an obviously collapsing Nazi war effort. The prisoners at Marfa were given fairly light maintenance duties around their camp and, considering the cookies given them by the kindhearted ladies of the city, life in the Texas camp must have seemed far superior to a likely death on the frigid Russian front.

In time, Fort D.A. Russell, prisoners and all, became an adjunct of Marfa Army Airfield. The old cavalry barracks on the post provided at least a partial solution to the continuing housing crisis created by the steadily expanding air base.

Despite the ongoing construction activity on the field and denials from senior Army officials of rampant rumors that both the airfield and the fort would soon be inactivated, the shocking news of an order to place both installations on a stand-by basis was received in Marfa in late April 1945. The very same edition of *The Big Spring Sentinel* that carried the story of the plans to close the two installations within a short three weeks' time also reported, without editorial comment, assurances to the contrary that had recently been uttered by the base commander, Col. Harry R. Baxter. The colonel, addressing a Rotary Club luncheon on May 1, stated that he had not been advised of any plans to put the airfield on standby. Apparently, no one had informed Colonel Baxter that H. A. Coffield, Marfa's mayor, had actually been notified a week earlier by federal authorities that both Baxter's airfield command and Fort D.A. Russell were scheduled to cease operations by the end of May.[39]

On May 11, 1945, Maj. Gen. Ralph P. Cousins, commanding officer of the Army's Western Flying Training Command, finally sent a letter officially confirming that Marfa's airfield would be "temporarily inactivated after May 25." The general went on to praise the residents of the area for their cooperation in helping the base achieve its training goal. "A large portion of the success of the field," asserted the general, "may be attributed to the fine helpful spirit of residents of the Big Bend area." [40]

On May 23 the final class of Marfa-trained multi-engine pilots received their silver wings during ceremonies on the base. Following the graduation of Class 45-C, all other pilot candidates, including the Chinese fliers, were assigned to training facilities elsewhere in anticipation of the deactivation of Marfa's airfield. Most of the aircraft were flown to distant military installations, and all local flying activity ceased. The base, with only a skeleton maintenance crew remaining, was officially closed to all but aircraft declaring an emergency.[41]

The stunning realization of how enormous the economic impact of the closing of both military installations would be had just begun to set in when the War Department, with its legendary unpredictability, suddenly announced that the airfield was to be reopened almost immediately. By June 30, only five weeks after it was closed, the airfield was back in operation as part of the Troop Carrier Command, with the new name "818 Air Base." [42]

Area merchants, landlords, and civic officials all breathed a mighty collective sigh of relief when it was further stated that about 2,200 military personnel would soon be arriving to serve on the field. When the actual number of servicemen assigned to the base proved to be less than half the original estimate, Marfans were nonetheless overjoyed to realize that their field was still a vital part of America's war effort.

Civic spirits were sent soaring once again when a subsequent War Department announcement divulged that in fact 4,000 servicemen would be coming to the reopened air base. A few days later, it was further disclosed that the recently shuttered Fort D. A. Russell was also scheduled to be reactivated.

A celebratory open house staged at the airfield on August 1, 1945, found a huge crowd of enthusiastic area residents on the base basking in the belief that the airfield would soon be even bigger and better than ever before. They inspected the newly arrived troop-carrier aircraft, enjoyed food and beverages, watched athletic events, and openly rejoiced that their very own airfield had come back to life.[43]

Unfortunately, the joy was short-lived. Just one week later, the dropping of the atomic bomb on Hiroshima and the swift capitulation of Japan brought an end to World War II. Suddenly, Marfa Army Airfield *aka* 818 Air Base was no longer needed, and news of another and most likely final deactivation of the facility was formally announced. Perhaps to assuage the feelings of local residents, the period of deactivation was scheduled to last from December 1945 to January 1947, but most observers recognized that the air base, shuttered once again, would most likely never be returned to an active status.

The closing of the airfield was swift and, as many had feared, final. By December 20 most facilities on the base were abandoned, all flying was discontinued, and within a few days, only two pilots remained on the field.

Perhaps the feeling of loss was even greater among Marfans than it was in some other cities that were also experiencing the loss of their military installations. The earlier closing announcement had been a blow, to be sure, but the quick reconsideration and reactivation had filled the local residents with an almost overwhelming joy of survival. When the second blow was landed, however, the months-long roller coaster ride of great expectations followed by shattering disillusionment came to an abrupt and painful halt.

As might be expected, civic spirit plummeted. Each citizen in the community intuitively seemed to sense what local historian Cecilia Thompson later put into words. "The glory days of military activity were over," she wrote. "Marfa would never be the same again." [44]

The economy of the region plummeted right along with people's spirits. According to Mayor Kahl, the town "fell on its face." The population began to shrink, businesses closed, and the two military facilities, one long proud of its old Army traditions and the other once teeming with aircraft, began a rapid descent into disrepair, destruction, and decay.[45]

Old Fort D.A. Russell, although inactivated even before the war had ended, was able to withstand the onslaught of time and desolation better than its much younger cross-town sister, Marfa Army Airfield. Many of its buildings, being of a sturdier pre–World War II construction, were able to survive into the twenty-first century and to gain new life as home of the Chinati Foundation.

Across town and eight miles to the east, Marfa's airfield quickly reverted to grazing land, its pastures no more lush than before. Some of the buildings were sold and moved to Alpine. The chapel where chubby MP Coccozza used to sing had been transported intact over Paisano Pass to serve Alpine worshipers, while one of the huge hangars was somehow hauled over the same narrow and winding roadway to become a school gymnasium. Both buildings are still in use almost sixty years after their postwar relocation.

The city of Marfa itself suffered a downslide following the war, although a particularly bright spot in its postwar history centered around movie director George A. Stevens's decision to film scenes of a major motion picture on the Marfa Plateau, based on Edna Ferber's controversial novel *Giant*. The movie brought many famous stars and national attention to Marfa when it was filmed there in 1955. Longtime residents still seem to glow with pride as they relate tales of James Dean shooting jackrabbits on the town's main street following a day of work before the cameras. The aloofness but undeniable attractiveness of actor Rock Hudson also continues to trigger fond memories, and descriptions of wild parties unlike anything previously witnessed by Marfans often creep into daily conversations.

Perhaps the most favored subject among those *Giant* aficionados still left in town is, of course, actress Elizabeth Taylor. Her impact on the little city was clearly electric. She was often seen visiting with the locals, pursuing her well-known quest for memorable bowls of chili, and in general thoroughly captivating the traditionally starstruck Marfans. Many years later, one old gentleman, a regional resident for many years, agreed to do a magazine interview about his life in the wilderness of the Big Bend. Perhaps hoping to elicit colorful comments about old airfields, glorious sunsets, towering mountains, or mysterious dancing lights, the reporter asked the weather-worn old cowboy to describe the most beautiful thing he had ever seen. Without a moment's hesitation, and with his eyes suddenly alive, the octogenarian replied, "Elizabeth Taylor at twenty-two."[46]

Nearly all physical evidence of the making of *Giant* has melted into the region's desert landscape. Modern-day tourists ask to see the big house that graced the film's Riata Ranch, only to be informed that it was just a one-dimensional facade. Perhaps disappointed, the visitors' attention then usually turns to the famous Marfa Lights. They are promptly directed to a parking area some eight miles east of town where an official state historical marker describes the phenomenon in some detail. Many of the visitors then patiently wait until dark to see for themselves this dazzling array that has frightened cowboys, triggered heated scientific debates, and ignited the fantasies of UFO advocates for decades.

As they wait for nature's light show to begin, few if any ever ask or even seem to know about the mammoth air base that once sprawled across the desert immediately in front of their eyes. Just yards on down the highway toward Alpine, persistent observers can discern a wall that once framed the airfield's main gate. When the light is just right, old base roadways can be faintly seen, going nowhere but still marking the spaces where long-destroyed buildings once stood. There is no historical marker to tell the story of the once-mighty airfield. Virtually nothing remains of the sprawling facility where long ago, thousands lived, and where too many died in the service of their country. Yet, every bit as ghostly as the mysterious flickering lights that fascinate hordes of onlookers each year, the spirit of Marfa Army Airfield lingers out there somewhere, hovering forever over the creosote and sagebrush of the West Texas desert.

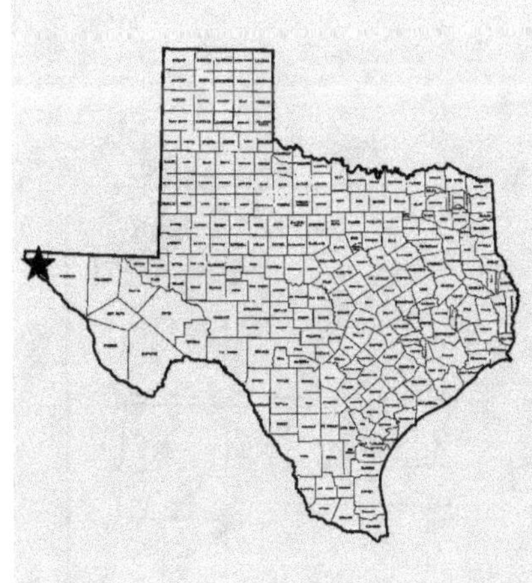

Chapter VII

El Paso and Biggs Army Airfield

Poor Mexico! So far from God and so close to the United States.

Attributed to
Gen. Porfirio Díaz
President of Mexico
1877–1911

As its longest-serving *presidente*, Porfirio Díaz likely had very good reason to consider his country's distance from God. The general was also painfully aware that what had historically been a vital part of Mexico had been absorbed by the Colossus of the North only thirty years before he had assumed power. Governed first by Spanish administrators and then by Mexico City, the vast territory now controlled by the United States included Texas, New Mexico, Arizona, and California, all of which had long been part of the Mexican domain until 1848.

The first Spanish explorers had reached the sprawling region probably as early as 1535, with the legendary Francisco Vázquez de Coronado arriving just five years later. The first confirmed exploration of the river that the Spaniards called the Rio Bravo took place in 1581 when the Rodríguez-Sánchez Expedition made its way through a chasm between two mountain ranges that opened directly onto that river. Traveling northward from the heart of Mexico, the explorers gave the pass they had discovered the appropriate name El

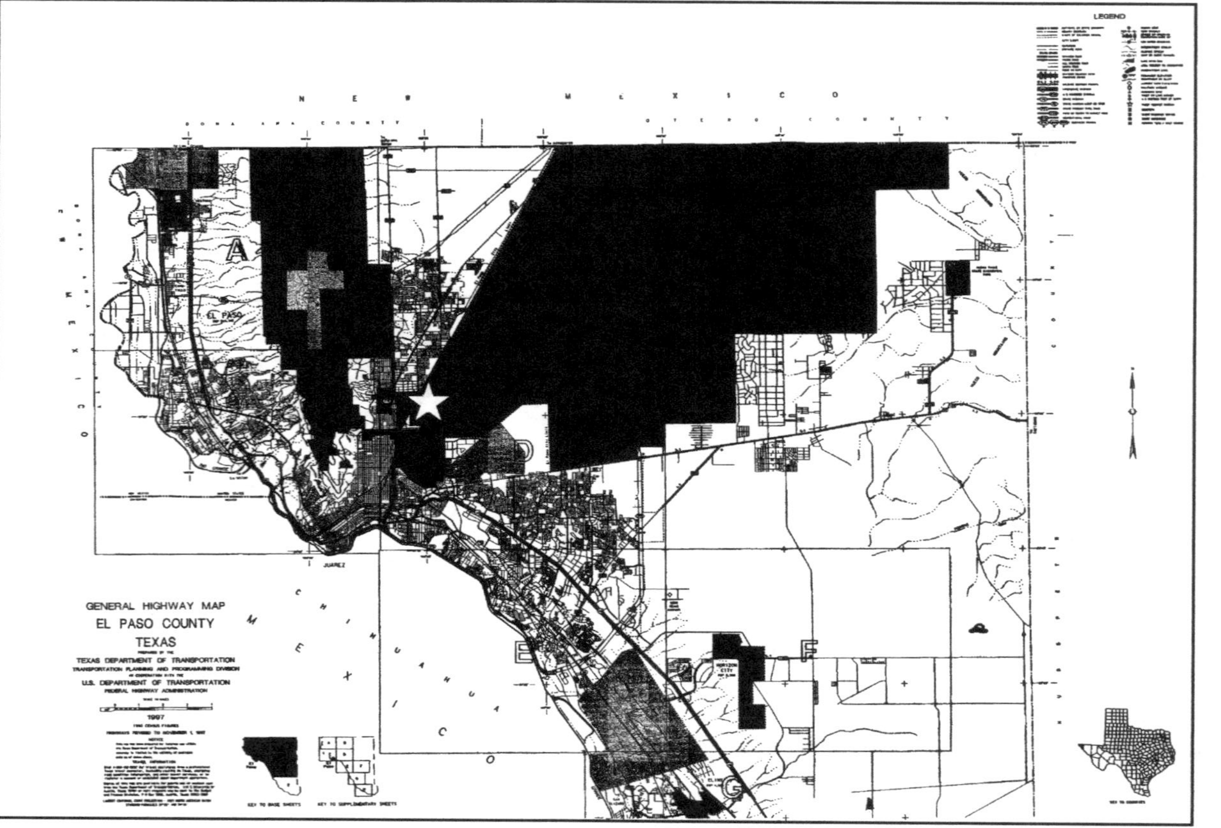

El Paso County Map

This map of El Paso County shows the location of Biggs Army Airfield during the war years. An inset map of Texas shows the location of the county within the state.

Paso del Norte. Spain's sporadic and somewhat tenuous claim to the entire region was not to be firmly fixed until 1598 and the arrival of the adventurer Juan de Oñate, who is given credit for superimposing onto the huge southwestern corner of North America a Hispanic culture that still endures.[1]

On the southern banks of the river some called the Rio Grande, near the Spanish Pass of the North, small settlements with such sibilant names as Socorro, San Lorenzo, Senecú, San Elizaro, El Paso del Norte, and Ysleta were established. Catholic missions were soon in full operation dutifully bringing Christianity to the Native American people who had lived in the immediate area for centuries. In 1682, in the chapel of the Ysleta Mission, the first mass was sung in what someday would become the state of Texas.[2]

Under the guidance of the missionaries, the early inhabitants built networks of canals and *acequias* in an effort to harness the waters of the Rio Grande for agricultural purposes. The efforts met with at least temporary success, and vineyards and vegetable farms flourished until the river, turned angry by the rapid melting of snowcover far upstream or locally heavy springtime deluges, or both, suddenly rampaged out of its banks. Not only were crops and livestock destroyed, but whole villages were washed away, and many human lives were lost as well. In *Great River*, Paul Horgan's classic biography of the Rio Grande, the author describes one particularly violent flooding that caused the river's width to grow from five to five hundred feet in a terrifyingly brief span of time, washing away decades of man's taming efforts in a giant wall of water.[3] Once each spring's riparian crisis had passed, however, a flurry of rebuilding and replanting by survivors again challenged the seasonal power of the river, often only to be destroyed once again the following year.

Over time, the persistent, if battered, settlers grew to respect the might of the Rio Grande enough to build and plant at a distance at least relatively safe from the average annual flood. As the communities finally stabilized and began to expand, commercial enterprises soon followed. When Mexico gained her independence from Spain in 1821, a major trade route was established between Santa Fe in the north and Chihuahua to the south, crossing the Rio Grande at El Paso del Norte.

Although the river was not in fact a political boundary, since both Santa Fe and Chihuahua were clearly in Mexican territory, some of the North American traders who freighted their goods down from the northern terminus tended to stop at least temporarily on the northern banks of the Rio Grande in the shelter of the mountains before moving on to the south. Such tradesmen as James W. Magoffin and Hugh Stephenson, who had pioneered the Chihuahuan extension of the trade route just as they had the Santa Fe Trail years before, frequently camped on the river's northern banks.

Although the capricious natural force of the Rio Grande dominated the history of the first three centuries of settlement at El Paso del Norte, the powerful forces of politics and war combined to bring a permanent and far more potent change to the entire region in the mid-1800s. President James Polk's Mexican War, arguably provoked by the United States in 1846 but most surely concluded victoriously by the U.S. Army in 1848, easily wrested from Mexico the little settlements on the Rio Grande, forever ending any substantial Mexican claims to what had already become the American state of Texas.

The Rio Grande became at once an international border, with Mexico to the south and the United States on the north. With its wartime victory and the resulting Gadsden Purchase, the United States had found the ultimate vent to its claim of Manifest Destiny and an avenue to the riches of the Pacific shore. The extent of those riches was greater than even Mr. Polk could have dared dream, as the 1849 discovery of gold in California would soon demonstrate. The north-south focus at El Paso del Norte soon became an east-west focus when would-be prospectors and ordinary settlers alike streamed through the border settlements heading westward.

New communities soon emerged on the northern bank of the Rio Grande, on what was now indisputably the American side of the river. Chihuahuan/Santa Fe traders Magoffin and Stephenson built towns of their own; so did others, including one Benjamin Franklin Coons, who gave his middle name not only to his village but to the mountains that loomed behind it.

By 1854 an Army post had been formally established at Fort Bliss near Franklin, and by 1859 another entrepreneur had laid out a town next to Mr. Coons's village of Franklin. In naming it El Paso, he created immense confusion with the three-hundred-year-old town of El Paso del Norte, located immediately across the Rio

Grande in Mexico. Not until 1888 would the original Spanish El Paso acquire its new and current name, Ciudad Juarez.[4]

FORT BLISS AND ITS FLYING FIELD

Fort Bliss is unique among Army posts. It has been captured by Confederates, laughed at by bandits, been home to America's first military air operations, and is now El Paso's biggest employer and the Army's biggest installation.

Edward C. Hurley
El Paso, Texas

There were several sound reasons to establish a major Army outpost in the newly founded village of El Paso, Texas, following the Mexican War. The just-proclaimed international border along the Rio Grande had to be defended, the young and wild little town needed a good deal of policing, and the flood of pioneers headed west required protection from Indians. Probably more important than anything else, the projected route of the new transcontinental railroad needed to be staked out and the route patrolled. By 1854 what had been a series of Army camps had grown into a fairly sizable and, as El Paso's history shows, permanent military installation, albeit one that would move five times before its final location was fixed in 1893.[5]

On March 31, 1861, the Union Army fort was surrendered to elements of the Confederate Army, commanded by Lt. Col. John Robert Baylor. The abortive Confederate invasion of New Mexico was launched at El Paso, but by late 1862 the installation was once again in Union hands.

In 1865, with its own civil strife at last resolved, the United States turned its undivided attention to westward expansion and the final realization of Polk's dreams of Manifest Destiny. Whether some of those dreams actually included expansion across the Rio Grande into Mexico itself has long been a matter of historical conjecture, but at the very least, the large United States military presence on the northern banks of the river that had become an international boundary could hardly have gone unnoticed by European and Mexican authorities. The direct support by the United States of the efforts of President Benito Juarez to expel French forces from

Mexican soil raised much international speculation about the true extent of America's interest in her neighbor across the Rio Grande.

When Mexico's further internal conflicts splashed northward across the river, however, the U.S. Army found itself at last cast in a major role, with El Paso's Fort Bliss at the very center of the action. The Mexican Revolution triggered a series of international and internal events that put the troubled nation in jeopardy and its relations with its powerful neighbor to the north at the breaking point. Although President Woodrow Wilson earnestly sought diplomatic ways to stave off what appeared to be growing anarchy in Mexico, apparent foreign violation of the Monroe Doctrine and ominous threats to American life and treasure made a direct armed clash with Mexico more imminent.

Despite the fact that Mexican presidents and Mexican generals were falling and new ones rising at an all but comic-opera pace during this time, one colorful individual rose out of the turbulence to emerge as the symbol of all that was irreverent and threatening in a Mexico in chaos. He was a short but massive man, usually silent but nearly always violent, with a demonstrated fondness for killing other men that made even the most lurid fiction seem pale in comparison. His given name was Doroteo Arango, but he had assumed the *nom de guerre* of Pancho Villa, or more to his liking, General-in-Chief Pancho Villa.[6]

Ironically, it was this horseback revolutionary, a self-appointed commander with no formal military training, who in many ways brought about the birth of America's air force. His actions along and occasionally across the Rio Grande made it necessary to create an aeronautical flying field at what was originally intended to be solely a cavalry post at Fort Bliss. While the events of the upcoming World War I would have surely forced the United States to enter into the age of military aviation, Villa's ability to strike on American soil only to disappear into the wilderness of northern Mexico gave the United States air advocates a sharp slap in the face that abruptly awakened them to the fact that the Army's fledgling air arm was under-manned, poorly equipped, and ill-maintained. Remedial action swiftly followed, giving America a military air advantage that it would put to good use in the skies over France in a few short years.

Villa always seemed to taunt the United States, daring to launch attacks that would at the least embarrass and inconvenience, if not enrage, the Goliath to the north. His infamous raid on Columbus, New Mexico, in early March 1916 killed seventeen Americans, galvanized northern resolve to seek revenge, and launched a yearlong, fruitless invasion of Mexico by U.S. forces attempting to find the Mexican raider and in some way punish him for daring to attack the United States of America. The general-in-chief, however, not only evaded capture and punishment, but continued to cross the border to strike other little villages, without any significant further damage except to the larger country's already wounded national pride.

Brig. Gen. John J. Pershing, the supreme commander of America's so-called "Punitive Expedition" into Mexico, eventually realized that automobiles were not going to locate Villa, and the cavalry only proved that it was much easier to get lost on horseback in the rugged terrain of Northern Mexico than it was to find one revolutionary firebrand. An El Paso newspaper rather mockingly noted that the entire undertaking was similar to "turning a jackrabbit loose in Oklahoma and sending the El Paso police to find him."[7] Perhaps Pershing felt much the same way, as he finally turned to aircraft in a desperate attempt to at last find Villa, his own jackrabbit.

The results of America's first foray into air combat operations were all but laughable. Of the eight Fort Bliss–based biplanes involved in the search, six soon crashed, and the other two were for sundry reasons totally unable to fly. Meanwhile, a mocking Pancho Villa remained well-hidden in the harsh mountains of Mexico. Nonetheless, it was, as one historian puts it, "the first trial of arms" for the American air force, and the results of that trial, though damning, gave forceful impetus to the nation's future in the sky. As for Pershing, he simply declared the entire charade to have been a victory, returned to Fort Bliss, and then proceeded to rocket to fame as the supreme commander of the American Expeditionary Forces in World War I. This second time around, its lessons learned on the Rio Grande, Pershing's air arm served him well.[8]

After the war in Europe, Fort Bliss continued to expand while making the transition from a cavalry post to an artillery installation. The fort grew from its original few thousand acres into a giant complex stretching across a million acres and measuring seventy-five miles in length to more than fifty-five miles in width.[9]

In 1919, at the very heart of the rapidly expanding military reservation, the Army created a formal flying field to supplant the primitive landing strip that had been employed during the search for the elusive General Villa. In 1925 the field was named Biggs Army Airfield in honor of Lt. James B. "Buster" Biggs, a native El Pasoan who was killed in a plane crash near Beltrain, France, at the very end of World War I.[10]

The war in which young Buster Biggs gave his life stimulated America's interest in aviation, and aircraft were soon a common sight in the skies over El Paso. Lighter-than-air dirigibles were joined by DeHavilland DH-4s in routine patrol flights along the border.

The Army often staged public exhibitions to demonstrate its growing proficiency in flight operations and to gain civilian support for aviation in general. One such event was staged at the Fort Bliss flying field on February 25, 1923. Various stunts and daring aerobatic feats were performed by pilots of the 12th Aero Squadron, which was based at the field. Nearly a thousand onlookers watched in amazement as the planes looped, dived, and spun over their heads. Clearly, military aviation had come a long way since the embarrassing days of the Punitive Expedition just seven years earlier. At least these planes could get into the air and manage not to crash with embarrassing regularity.

One stunt performed that day, however, was not well-received by either the spectators or the press. When it was announced that a ninety-year-old woman was going to parachute from an open-cockpit DH-4 to prove just how safe parachute jumping could be, the crowd hurried to the demonstration site. They saw the quite elderly parachutist being helped into the plane's cockpit and then cheered her as the pilot taxied his aircraft in front of the grandstand so that all could clearly see his passenger, ready for the flight in her helmet and traditional long, flowing scarf.

As the fascinated spectators looked on, the pilot brought the plane to an abrupt halt just before taking off and clambered out of the cockpit to make a last-minute check of his craft's right landing gear. To the horror of all, the plane began to move and gain speed, finally lifting off with the wildly gesturing old lady alone on board and the pilot standing on the runway apparently in a state of shock.

The DeHavilland continued to climb erratically and proceeded to make some highly unorthodox in-flight maneuvers before it finally leveled off at an altitude of approximately five hundred feet.

Suddenly, a parachute was seen trailing from the plane, supporting the figure of the old aviatrix, who appeared to be making good on her advertised jump from the airplane, albeit now a plane without a pilot.

To the further horror of the crowd, however, the parachute failed to open fully, and both chute and erstwhile female pilot hit the hard ground with a terrific thud that could be heard yards away in the grandstand. Spectators joined with Army medical personnel in rushing to the ominously still figure that lay beneath the shroud of the partially opened parachute. Much to their dismay, the crowd found the figure to be merely a dummy dressed as an old woman, with the parachute tied to it in such a way to ensure that it could not possibly open.

One irate medical officer vowed that he would court-martial the individuals responsible for this cruel hoax, and the civilians in the crowd grew increasingly indignant, even as the apparently pilotless plane made a perfect landing on the runway in front of them. Out of the cockpit jumped a laughing Capt. Claire L. Chennault, the flying field's aviation engineering officer, still attired in his long granny dress, wig, and sensible shoes. Chennault somehow escaped the threatened court-martial for his role in the prank and went on to establish the famous Flying Tigers in China prior to World War II. He eventually rose to the rank of major general in the U.S. Army Air Force during the war.[11]

Other famous military fliers visited Biggs Field in the years between the two world wars. Capt. Eddie Rickenbacker, one of the Army's foremost aces of the first war, came to the field to meet with Brig. Gen. Billy Mitchell, America's early champion of airpower. Other future generals, including Henry H. "Hap" Arnold and Jimmy Doolittle, flew into Biggs Field on several occasions.[12]

Apart from air shows, visiting aviators, and parachuting pseudograndmothers, Biggs Field was little more than a refueling stop for transient aircraft in the years immediately before World War II. An old balloon hangar and a few tarpaper shacks were the only indication that the dirt landing strip was anything other than a clearing in the desert brush.

When the landing field was obscured by blowing sand and dust, which was often a problem, pilots were instructed to put their aircraft down nearby on what was officially the Fort Bliss reviewing field. Even though airplanes were clearly coming in for landing at relatively high speeds, commanders of marching formations frequently refused to give the orders necessary to clear the review area. In the face of such obstinance, the fliers were compelled to attempt to land on the nearly invisible sand covered strip.[13]

As events in Asia and Europe in the late 1930s indicated that the United States might soon be involved in war, obviously needed improvements to Biggs were set in motion. A new radio tower was built, a communications building was constructed, and powerful radio equipment was installed. In 1940 a larger maintenance hangar was built and Army National Guard personnel were assigned to the rapidly expanding air facility. Aircraft being ferried from West Coast assembly plants to East Coast bases regularly stopped at Biggs for refueling or repair if required. On average, more than 3,000 planes stopped at Biggs annually in the late 1930s.

Early in 1941, with America's entry into the war virtually inevitable, expansion at the old flying field was accelerated. Four sections of land were surveyed for Air Corps use, and construction was started on the first paved runways on the base. A $10 million expansion program was soon underway, to include new hangars, barracks, maintenance shops, clubs, chapels, and swimming pools. Dusty old Biggs Field, for years a home only to dirigibles and border-patrol aircraft, by mid-1942 had become a completely new and modern Army air installation.[14]

As the construction work neared completion, the new base came under the command of the 2nd Air Force, which had the responsibility for all heavy-bombardment training in the United States. The headquarters of the 20th Bombardment Command also transferred to the field, bringing with it the training programs for B-17 Flying Fortress combat crews. Other aircraft were soon assigned to the new base, including medium bombers, fighters, and observation planes. Additionally, the airfield played host on a round-the-clock basis to thousands of other Army aircraft that were constantly crisscrossing the nation.[15]

The huge base soon boasted three paved runways instead of a single dirt strip. The longest of these was 9,500 feet, while the other two were each 7,000 feet in length. In total area, the field had grown from 208 to 3,156 acres.[16]

Four hangars now took the place of the one rickety old balloon hangar that had long been the field's only permanent building. The largest hangar was nearly 50,000 square feet in size, and others were nearly as large. Thousands of aircraft used the expanded facilities as the training program intensified. In November 1942, even more planes and personnel were assigned to the El Paso facility when the 16th Bombardment Wing transferred from Wendover Field in Utah. Biggs had come a long way since 1939, when only one officer, twelve enlisted men, and one airplane were assigned to it. Just three years later, nearly 8,000 men were assigned to the base.[17]

The great increase in flying activity and in air training exacted a heavy toll on the expanded facility's personnel and aircraft. The looming Franklin Mountains located just a few miles west of the field claimed the lives of many crewmen as the training intensified. One aircraft underestimated the height of the mountain ridge by only two precious feet, resulting in a crash that took three lives. Other aircraft, either assigned to the field or in transit, went down in the Franklins or in the rugged mountains of nearby New Mexico.[18]

When they were not facing the hazards of flying, personnel from Biggs Field relaxed at the many recreational facilities on the base itself or at adjacent Fort Bliss. There was much to see and do off the military installations as well, in nearby El Paso or across the Rio Grande in Ciudad Juarez. The *Air Officers Guide* of the era offers only a subtle suggestion that off-duty hours spent in Mexico could be recreationally rewarding. "Just across the border," advised the text in muted understatement, "the city of Juarez offers varied and unusual entertainment facilities." It is often suggested by some old-time Biggs veterans that cross-country flights were planned to include a convenient layover at the field so that war-weary aviators could sample the many delights and diversions awaiting them across the Rio Grande.[19]

While the airmen came and went from the giant base northeast of their town, El Paso's civilians contended with the war on the home front. Rationing made life confusing, if not downright difficult, and shortages of gasoline and certain foodstuffs often created hardships for those not in uniform.

Alicia Gonzalez, however, who was eleven years old when the war started, recalled that in many respects, her life actually improved. "World War II changed our lives forever," she declared in an oral-history project. She remembered that her neighborhood in the barrio began to change for the better as new employment opportunities came about. As the defense industries continued to flourish, many young girls found jobs in downtown El Paso stores selling merchandise to servicemen and their families. Those same girls represented the most noticeable wartime change for Alicia Gonzalez. Earning a salary for the first time in their lives, the young woman started "buying pretty dresses, wearing beautiful high-heel shoes, and many were wearing new hats to church on Sunday."[20]

As all of the wartime jobs available in El Paso required American citizenship, many Mexican nationals began studying English and attending citizenship classes. Even much older would-be Americans enrolled in night school. Ms. Gonzalez also fondly recalled that her family's standard of living changed dramatically because of the war. When rationing limited the acquisition of certain commodities, her family now had money enough to cross over to Ciudad Juarez, where virtually everything was available in non-rationed quantities and at much lower prices. The family's wood stove was soon replaced by one that used gas, and the old ice box soon gave way to a new electric refrigerator.

There was a bit of restriction still involved with the new refrigerator, however. It had a coin box attached to it that required feeding each time the door was opened. Every week the appliance store would send a collector to the house to harvest the coins and the collected sum was used to defray the amount still owed on the new appliance. Once its door had been opened frequently enough to generate adequate coinage, the refrigerator would be paid off and the coin box rather ceremoniously removed.

Life in Alicia Gonzalez's barrio was by no means restricted to putting nickels and dimes into the refrigerator's coin box. She remembers that many of the older girls from her neighborhood, likely dressed in their newly acquired finery, would often go to the depot to see the troop trains pull in on their way to the West Coast. Some girls would give the soldiers their names and addresses on slips of paper in hopes of receiving correspondence from the South Pacific theater of war. Apparently, many of those hopes materialized, as Ms. Gonzalez can remember attending weddings in the church, with grooms looking "so handsome in their uniforms." When the war ended in 1945, many of the residents of the old barrio had been able to move to better neighborhoods, and others had become United States citizens. Many returning soldiers had taken advantage of the GI Bill to enroll in colleges and universities. There had been tragic casualties caused by the war, to be sure, and too many gold stars were to be seen in neighborhood windows, but for Alicia Gonzalez and her friends, the war had provided an open door to a better way of life and a brighter future.[21]

Elisa Martinez was also a young child when the war started, and her most haunting memory of life in El Paso at the time is one of fear. Her family recognized the importance of Fort Bliss and Biggs Field and dreaded the day that the city would be attacked by enemy planes. Air-raid drills would be announced by wailing sirens, and brilliant searchlights would then crisscross the sky, sometimes touching the dark face of the brooding Franklin Mountains. Ms. Martinez also remembers that people prayed much more than they had before the war. She went to the church with her grandmother every evening to pray for peace.[22]

Ysidro Cervantes probably prayed for peace, too. A teenager when the war started, he watched his brother and his cousins go off to fight. In time, he also joined the Navy and saw action in the South Pacific. Once in uniform, however, Mr. Cervantes was delighted to find that doors long closed to minorities began to swing open. He discovered, too, that a sense of pride came with wearing the American uniform. "We were Americans first," he recalls, "and were now sharing in the civic culture through our participation in the war."

Cervantes notes that the war also brought prosperity to El Paso, the city growing right along with Fort Bliss. Perhaps most significant among his memories is the realization that El Paso "came together as a united community during the war." As in other cities, the military presence, born of urgency, had at last blurred the long-established barriers of social misunderstanding and mistrust.[23]

George Saucier was also in high school in El Paso during the war years, and he can recall how local families opened their homes to the servicemen stationed at Biggs Field and Fort Bliss. Each Sunday after church, Mr. Saucier's mother would invite soldiers to the family home for chicken dinner. Then there would be games or drives into the countryside to help the military men forget their loneliness and the dangers of war.

The Sunday dinners were commonplace throughout the city, and according to Saucier, the end result was often similar to the handing out of names and addresses at the train station. At their families' chicken dinners, many girls met young men who would become their husbands after the war. Perhaps Mr. Saucier accurately describes the war years in El Paso when he recalls that "it was a time of uniting . . . and there was a spirit of goodwill [and] sharing."[24]

At Biggs Field, however, the training for combat continued unabated through 1945. The runways were extended to accommodate the new B-29 bombers that had replaced the B-17 as the Air Force's prime weapon. Because of the increased demand for space, Fort Bliss gave additional acreage for airfield use, increasing the total area of Biggs to nearly 4,000 acres.[25]

When the war ended in mid-1945, El Paso was spared the devastating base-closure traumas that seriously impacted many other towns and cities in Texas and across the nation. Bomber training at Biggs Field was discontinued, but the smaller aircraft of the 19th Tactical Air Command's 20th Fighter Group soon filled the skies along the Rio Grande.

In 1947 the bombers returned once again, to operate from further-lengthened runways as part of the newly created United States Air Force's Strategic Air Command (SAC). Fort Bliss was ordered to give up more of its land to provide space for housing the families of Air Force personnel, and the name of the old facility was changed once again, this time to Biggs Air Force Base.

As a SAC base, Biggs was home to that strike force's formidable aircraft, including B-36s, B-47s, and B-52s. The new arrivals were not immune to the hazards of flight, however, and planes continued to crash in the mountains and in the desert. One B-47 went down on a vacant lot in a residential area in El Paso, and a B-52, named *Ciudad Juarez,* was inadvertently shot down by an aircraft of the New Mexico National Guard. Three SAC crewmen lost their lives in the tragic mishap.[26]

In 1951 the Air Force allocated an additional $8 million for improvements at its El Paso base. The monies were expended for new maintenance facilities, improved runway lighting, and state-of-the-art refueling facilities. Biggs Air Force Base, it seemed, was now well-equipped to become a permanent and effective installation of the Strategic Air Command.[27]

Unfortunately, appearances can be deceiving, when the permanence of Air Force bases is concerned. In late 1964, rumors began to circulate throughout the community that mighty Biggs would soon be closed, despite the millions of dollars that had only recently been spent to expand and improve it. Stung by the rumors, El Paso's Mayor Williams journeyed to SAC headquarters at Offutt Air Force Base to seek confirmation or denial of the reported closing. Likely much to his disappointment, he was advised that the base would indeed soon be closed, and the B-52s and their supporting aerial refueling tankers moved to Abilene's Dyess AFB.

Shortly after his return to El Paso, however, the mayor received a reassuring letter from SAC's commander stating that it had been further determined that Biggs would now remain active "at least until 1970."[28] The SAC promise proved hollow just two short months later when the last B-52 took off for its new home as originally planned and Biggs Air Force Base fell silent.[29]

The last B-52 to leave the field bore the proud name *Ciudad Juarez II*, in honor of the bomber so tragically destroyed by friendly fire from a New Mexican Air Guard plane a few years earlier. The official wing historian could not resist noting that this *Ciudad Juarez* was "perhaps careful to avoid flying over New Mexico."[30]

Even with the sudden departure of the Strategic Air Command, El Paso was again spared the traumatic effects of the closing of a major military installation. The Air Force base merely reverted to Army control and became once again a part of Fort Bliss, with its old name of Biggs Army Airfield proudly restored.

The social and economic impact of Fort Bliss and its airfield on its host city is immense. At the end of the twentieth century, 25 percent of the city's permanent population worked at the installation, and one of every five dollars injected into El Paso's economy was directly generated by Fort Bliss and Biggs Army Airfield. Thousands of military retirees also contribute millions of dollars to the local economy. It is estimated that the overall financial impact of Fort Bliss on the community exceeds $1.5 billion annually.[31]

From a small garrison initially assigned to protect settlers from Indians, the fort has come a long way since its early days. Its history is as colorful as the region it serves, a history greatly enhanced by the vital role played by an old Army airfield that became an Air Force base only to emerge once again as a modern Army field. From observation balloons to the ill-fated pursuit of Mexican renegades to valiant service in wars both hot and cold, Biggs, by any of its many names, has truly served the nation well.

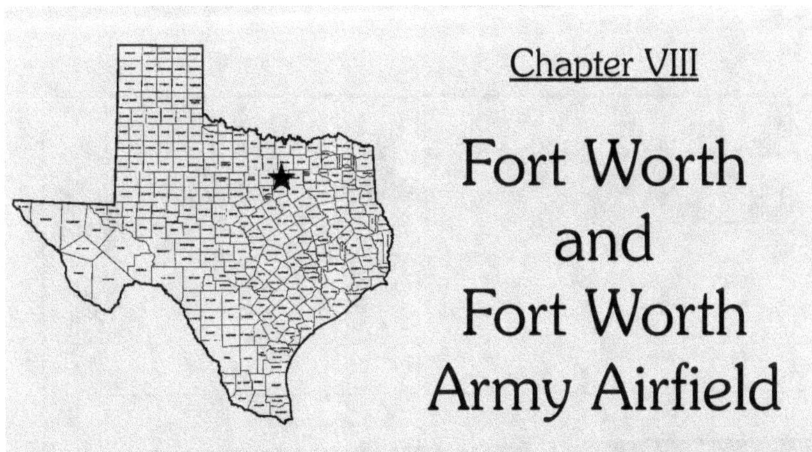

Chapter VIII

Fort Worth and Fort Worth Army Airfield

> Out where the skies are a trifle bluer,
> Out where the friendship's a little truer,
> That's where the West begins.
>
> Arthur Chapman
> *The Denver Times*

In the highly creative mind of newspaper publisher Amon G. Carter, the man the nation knew as "Mr. Fort Worth," the West unquestionably began in his city, even though reporter Arthur Chapman most likely had the city of Denver in mind when he wrote his "Ode to the West." To regional wags who delighted in fueling the traditional rivalry between Carter's cowtown and another bustling metropolis located just thirty miles away, if Fort Worth was where the West began, then surely Dallas was where the East petered out.

As its name clearly implied, Fort Worth, be it the true gateway to the West or not, began its existence as a military installation on June 6, 1849. Acting on the recommendation of some frontier scouts who had once bivouacked in the area, Maj. Ripley A. Arnold established an Army camp at the confluence of two forks of the Trinity River. Arnold named the new outpost Camp Worth by way of tribute to Mexican War hero Maj. Gen. William Jenkins Worth, who had died while on active duty in San Antonio some three years earlier.[1]

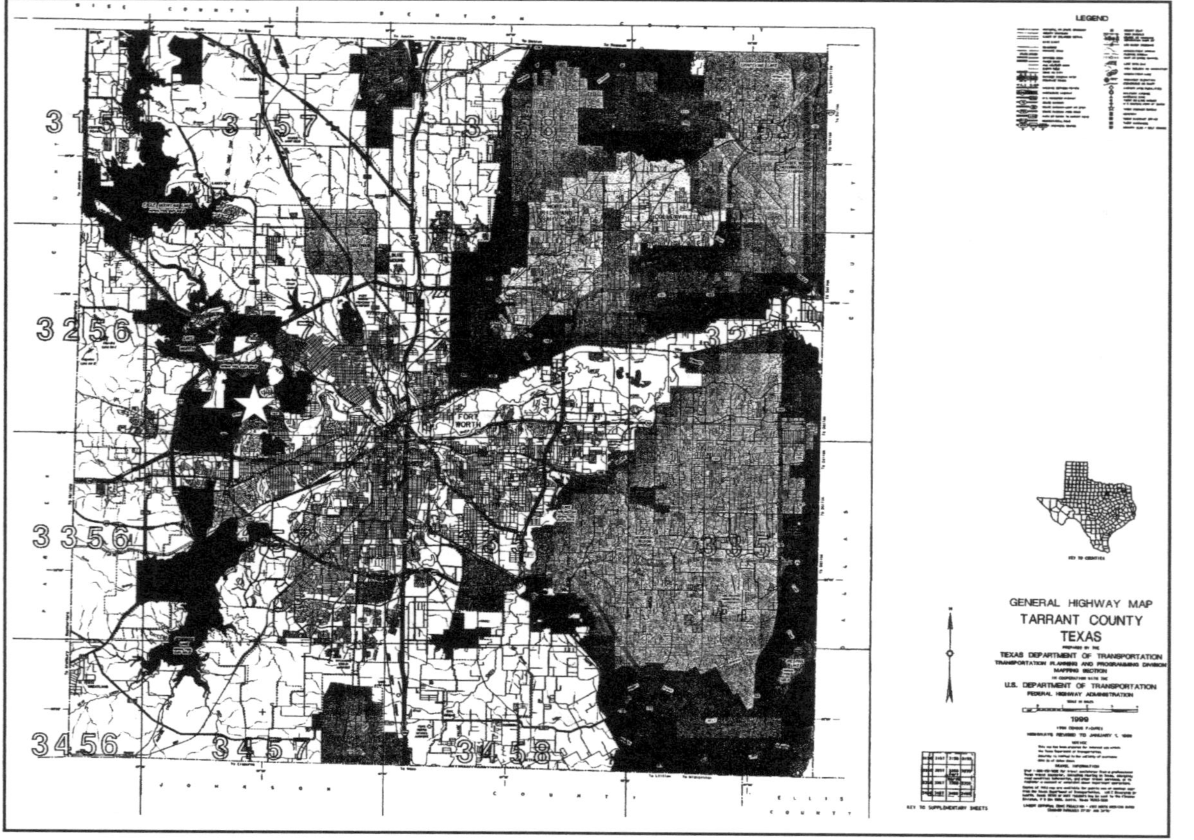

Tarrant County Map
This map of Tarrant County shows the location of Fort Worth Army Airfield during the war years. An inset map of Texas shows the location of the county within the state.

The mission of the camp, which was redesignated as a fort shortly after its establishment, was to serve as a link in a chain of military fortifications created to protect the frontier of the new state of Texas. Although no actual palisade-like fort was ever constructed on the banks of the Trinity, the mere presence of the Army dragoons was enough to discourage any serious Indian incursions in the immediate area. One halfhearted attempt by a small group of Taovaya Indians to harass the tiny encampment was cut short by a single shot from a dragoon howitzer, the only artillery piece in Fort Worth's token arsenal.[2]

By early autumn 1853, the frontier had moved farther westward, creating a need for a new chain of guardian outposts. As a result, the so-called fort on the Trinity River was abandoned, and its garrison marched some eighty miles to the northwest to take up its duties at the newly established Fort Belknap. As soon as the troopers had trudged away up the trail to their new assignment, local settlers took possession of the deserted campsite.

In a matter of months, a town began to flourish where a military installation had briefly existed. By 1854 there was a school, a handful of general stores, and the usual smattering of saloons. By 1856 two stagecoach lines were serving the community, and the future of Fort Worth seemed promising enough to prompt its citizens to seek a county-seat status for their rapidly growing city. Unfortunately, the nearby village of Birdville had held the distinction of being the seat of Tarrant County government since 1849. Nevertheless, an election was soon arranged to formally determine which of the two communities was best-suited to become the permanent county seat.

It was customary in those days to provide thirsty prospective voters with a drink or two of whiskey before the polls opened, and both Fort Worth and Birdville backers arrived early on election day well-supplied with enough barrels of liquor to adequately lubricate the democratic process. Fort Worth's supporters, however, managed to secretly siphon off the contents of Birdville's barrel, giving Fort Worth an instant two-to-nothing liquor advantage over the incumbent county seat. Not surprisingly, the election then followed an easily predictable course, and the one-time Army outpost on the Trinity became the county seat of Tarrant County. It was not until 1860, however, that the decision to move the county seat became official. By that time, the long-anticipated American Civil War was about to become a terrible reality. The effects of the war were devastating to the new county seat, and by the end of the conflict the population had dwindled to less than two hundred hardy individuals.[3]

Recovery was slow but steady, and by 1872 the community had incorporated. Within three more years, the first of several railroads had reached Fort Worth, virtually ensuring it a successful future. The coming of the railroads soon established the city as a major shipping point for Texas's burgeoning cattle industry. Other related business activities caused the community to expand rapidly, and by 1920 the population exceeded 100,000.

During World War I, several sizable military installations had operated in what had once been a tiny frontier Army outpost, causing the area population to grow. The surge in the state's petroleum industry at roughly the same time also contributed to the growth of the city, and within ten years following the end of the war, Fort Worth's population stood at nearly 165,000, reflecting a growth of over 50 percent since the previous census of 1920.[4]

The stifling Great Depression of the early 1930s, which all but devastated the economy of much of Texas, had a lesser impact on Fort Worth than on nearly all other cities. For the most part, this fortunate situation was due to the combined promotional wizardry and political acumen of the same Amon G. Carter who liked to pretend that the West began in his city. He also believed wholeheartedly that his Fort Worth deserved more than its fair share of federal funding for a vast array of civic improvements. Carter's powerful influence in Washington, D.C., generated a steady flow of federal funds that shielded Fort Worth from much of the Depression's economic chaos and put in place a pattern that would prove highly beneficial in the war years that were soon to follow.

MILITARY AVIATION COMES TO FORT WORTH

West Texas is bound on the north by Colorado and Oklahoma, on the west by New Mexico, on the south by Mexico and on the east by Amon Carter.

Amarillo Globe
1936

The editorial writer of Amarillo's morning newspaper may have been somewhat geographically uncertain about Texas's northern neighbors, but he was right on target about the boundary to the east. As publisher of the powerful *Fort Worth Star-Telegram*, Amon Carter made and unmade political careers, squeezed federal dollars out of an all-but-empty United States treasury, successfully lobbied for major industries to flock to his town, and provided a permanent financial foundation for his fellow West Texans. In the early 1940s, it was estimated that at least half of the workforce of Fort Worth was employed by corporations Carter had brought to the city.[5]

After pressuring Franklin D. Roosevelt's administration into earmarking scarce federal monies for the building of a major auditorium and a giant coliseum in Fort Worth, plus a massive renovation and expansion of the city's public schools during the height of the Depression, Carter was in fine fettle as World War II approached. In close cooperation with the city's many petroleum-rich financiers, he began a determined campaign to bring a major defense facility to Fort Worth even before the United States became involved in the conflict.

As early as 1939, Carter had personally discussed with Roosevelt the growing prospects of America entering the war. At the forefront of those discussions, at least in Amon Carter's view, was the absolute necessity for one of the already-announced government-financed aircraft factories to be constructed in Fort Worth as soon as possible. With little to no difficulty, he was named chairman of the chamber of commerce committee that was charged with the immediate responsibility of convincing both the federal government and key aircraft manufacturing companies that Fort Worth was by far the best location in the nation for such a plant.[6]

The unique government/private industry scheme as designed by the Roosevelt administration called for the War Department to build the manufacturing facility, which would then be operated by a private aircraft corporation. Moreover, it had also been determined by Army Air Force leadership that it would be expedient to locate a training base adjacent to most aircraft production plants, on the sound theory that "complete flight crews could be produced" at the same rate that aircraft became available for them to fly.[7]

The twin lures of a major defense plant and a large military base sent Carter into a frenzy of activity. When Consolidated

Aircraft Corporation's president, Maj. R. H. Fleet, expressed interest in operating a facility in Fort Worth, Carter and his committee put together an elaborate formal proposal that included tax-abatement offers, promises of an unlimited pool of skilled workers, city-improved transportation facilities, and much more. Brig. Gen. Jacob E. Fickel arrived in the city in May 1940 to inspect potential sites for both the plant and the air base, and the chamber's committee made sure that the officer received a red-carpet welcome.

When the effects of the cordial hospitality had given way to hard decisions, Carter and his associates convinced Consolidated that Fort Worth's site on the west side of the city was indeed where the War Department should build its defense plant, but unfortunately, the War Department, in the person of Maj. Gen. George H. Brett, was of a differing opinion. Perhaps somewhat shielded from Carter's often bombastic and forceful persuasion, Brett believed Tulsa, Oklahoma, to be the best site for both plant and base. An exchange of telegrams between Consolidated's Fleet and the Army's Brett clearly indicated that the corporation had taken the attractive bait offered by Carter. "We think Fort Worth site is ideal," wired Fleet, but "Fort Worth not under consideration in present project," countered Brett. Finally, on December 19, 1940, Consolidated's president tried a bit of levity to perhaps soften the stern general. "Your telegram reminds me of Henry Ford statement that customer could choose any color he desired just so he chose black." Unbending, Brett fired back, "Choose any color you wish but you are still going to get black."[8]

To Fleet, Carter, and the Fort Worth business community, Brett's black unmistakably meant Tulsa. The Army's decision threw the seldom-denied Amon Carter into a rage. He quickly dispatched a scathing telegram to Roosevelt in which he declared that the selection of Tulsa over Fort Worth for the combined plant and air base was just short of being a "crime against national defense." FDR could only weakly counter that since the decision in favor of Tulsa was an Army matter, his presidential hands were tied.[9]

By no means convinced, Carter launched a communications campaign that inundated congressmen, senators, old friends, other military leaders, and virtually anyone else in Washington who might have any influence with the president. Within two short weeks, FDR realized that Amon Carter was not to be denied, and on

January 4, 1941, it was publicly announced that *both* Tulsa and Fort Worth would be getting new Consolidated aircraft plants.[10]

Three days later, Army Air Force officers arrived in Fort Worth to officially endorse the plan to build an air facility immediately adjacent to the manufacturing plant site. When the city eventually had difficulty finding sufficient funds with which to build the airport, it simply deeded the land to the federal government, which agreed to construct the facility. Within a year, that installation on the shores of Lake Worth would become Fort Worth Army Airfield.[11]

The government's decision obviously brought great joy to Amon Carter. Gracious, if not downright smug in his victory, he sent a folksy telegram to the president of the United States. "Bless your heart," intoned the wired message, "Thanks for your timely and friendly help." In all likelihood casting an eye toward the possibility of even greater governmental largesse, Carter asked Senator Morris Sheppard to arrange to have FDR's son, a lowly Air Force captain at the time, appointed the "military overseer" of the plant's construction phase.[12]

Even with the Consolidated plant now committed to a Fort Worth location, Carter was not satisfied. When he learned that the plant in Tulsa was to be identical in all aspects to the one soon to be built in Texas, he again worked his influential magic with Roosevelt. To satisfy Carter's claim that his plant absolutely had to be the biggest such facility in the world, or at least bigger than the one slated for Tulsa, FDR instructed the Army to add an additional twenty-nine feet to the Fort Worth plant. At a cost of some $30 million, it thus became by only thirty feet the largest aircraft-manufacturing facility in the world at the time it was opened, employing more than 30,000 Texans, old-timers and newcomers alike.[13]

At the groundbreaking ceremonies staged to signal the beginning of the plant's construction in 1942, Carter and Maj. Gen. Gerald C. Brant wielded the traditional shovels to turn the first earth on the site. Although contemporary reports indicate that rain fell in torrents throughout the entire ceremony, a photograph shows that the weather failed to dampen Carter's ebullience. The general's uniform, however, clearly shows that it was a very wet April day in west Fort Worth.

As the giant plant was being constructed, the Army began

acquiring adjacent additional land for what was to become Fort Worth Army Airfield, even though finding a suitable and durable name for the proposed air base proved to be a troublesome task. At first, it was known quaintly enough as "the airstrip next to the bomber plant," but when that title seemed less than impressive to many observers, the name of the facility became Lake Worth Industrial Airport. This civilian-sounding title soon gave way to the more obviously military Army Air Force Combat Crew School, but by July 1942 the base was known as both Tarrant Field and Tarrant Aerodrome. A few weeks later, the base was officially named Fort Worth Army Airfield.[14]

The sudden entry of the United States into World War II in December 1941 caused work on the Consolidated plant to accelerate dramatically, and by February 1942 production of the company's famed B-24 bombers was underway, even though the plant itself was still under construction.

The search for a suitable name for the newly built bombers triggered a minor internal employee-relations problem. Consolidated's management arranged for a corporation-wide contest to be held, with all submissions of likely bomber nicknames to be anonymous. Only a number identified the author of each suggested name. The name "Liberator" was chosen as the winning entry, and eyebrows were raised when it was revealed that the name had been submitted, anonymously of course, by none other than the wife of company president Maj. R. H. Fleet. Despite some lingering questions about how the name had been selected, the B-24s that rolled off Consolidated production lines onto the ramps of Fort Worth Army Airfield next door were forever known as Liberators.[15]

The airfield itself was activated on July 29, 1942, but not officially completed until the end of December of that year. More than 200 buildings mounted on short concrete piers stood on what had previously been open fields that sloped gently down to the boggy banks of Lake Worth. The published construction cost of the field had been almost $6.5 million, but expansion of the facility began almost the day after it was declared complete. The original plans had called for housing to accommodate 400 officers and more than 3,500 enlisted men, but additional living quarters were needed within weeks of the opening of the field. At the peak of the construction process, some 3,200 workers were on the site.[16]

The first class of student officers arrived for transition training in the brand-new Liberators on October 14, 1942. The major maintenance difficulties that soon arose were exacerbated by a shortage of mechanics qualified to service the B-24s. Despite the many problems, however, flight training was conducted on a twenty-four-hour-per-day basis.

Training in the B-24 involved the development of crew coordination among the eight-member team that flew on each aircraft. In addition to the pilot and the copilot, the crew included a navigator, a bombardier, an engineer, and three gunners. All of the men who came to Fort Worth Airfield had graduated from their respective specialty schools and were assigned to the field as a training crew. According to the *Fort Worth Star-Telegram* of October 12, 1942, each team was scheduled to "eat, sleep, study, and train together 24 hours a day and even learn each other's minds and reactions."[17]

According to other published reports, the eating-together part of crew training was also a twenty-four-hour-per-day routine. Reporter Ann Perlman believed herself to be the first female to eat in the "strictly stag" mess hall that on December 10, 1942, was so new that she could still smell the paint. Going through the noon chow line, Ms. Perlman, who usually preferred cottage cheese and pineapple for her luncheons, watched in alarm as the first KP steward placed a one-inch-thick slab of roast beef on her plate, followed by "at least a thousand calories worth of mashed potatoes." The next server ladled a small mountain of peas next to the potatoes and then smothered the entire plate with a thick sea of gravy. By her own admission ready to "wave the white flag" in surrender, Perlman could only look on in dismay as "salad, bread and butter, and punch finished the orgy."[18]

The mess hall was open all day and all night, although breakfast was served only until 10:00 A.M., lunch until 3:00, and supper service ended at 8:00, with coffee and sandwiches available around the clock. The food offered at every meal was plain, nourishing, and as Ms. Perlman learned, plentiful. According to Mess Sergeant C. Lehr, the "most foreign dish" he taught his crew to prepare at the Fort Worth base was Spanish rice.[19]

The men on the base were summoned to their noon meal by the clanging of "Old Bronze," a then-fifty-two-year-old bell that had previously seen service on locomotives of the Wichita Valley

Railway Company. The bell had taken part in two wars before being placed in use at the Fort Worth facility. In 1898 it had been on a railroad engine that carried troops from Texas to Florida in the Spanish American War. In 1917 the bell had clanged its way across America on a locomotive carrying soldiers bound for World War I duty in Europe. In addition to its noontime tolling, the bell was also rung every hour on the hour from 6 A.M. until 10 P.M., by order of base commander Col. James S. Stowell.[20]

If "Old Bronze" were not enough to keep the field's airmen aware of the passage of time, Colonel Stowell also employed an Army howitzer to start off each day. Every morning at 6 A.M., as the colors were raised over the field, the mighty cannon, in concert with the clanging bell, roared to mark the beginning of another day of training. At 4:45 P.M., the artillery piece was fired again to signal the end of the workday. Unfortunately, the many civilian residents of nearby communities who had no particular interest in the base training schedule were also treated to the early-morning blast of the howitzer. In time, as the intensity of training accelerated, the cannon's daily roar was likely lost in the constant, thunderous roll of the B-24 engines that echoed across Lake Worth both day and night.[21]

Despite the combined din of cannon, bell, and aircraft engines, the citizenry of Fort Worth warmly embraced the military establishment that had become their neighbor. Newspaper accounts from the era bear constant witness to the highly imaginative ways the people of Fort Worth invented to show their appreciation to the airmen. On October 25, 1942, for example, the *Star-Telegram* reported that the Fort Worth Inter-Sorority Council had raised $150 to buy a portable public-address system for the base. Lt. V. M. Clark, the field's special-services officer, thanked the young ladies for the gift, saying that the new system would be used for "all theatricals, entertainments, and meetings" held in the field's none-too-imaginatively named War Department Theater.[22]

In another entertainment effort, the community mounted a drive for musical instruments to be donated to men at the airfield. Mrs. Nelson Scurlock, who headed the drive, reported that pianos had been donated by the University Place Music Club, the Optimist Club, the Utopian Club, the University Place Study Club, and the Harmony Club. Despite this outpouring of generosity, Mrs.

Scurlock stated that three to four additional pianos "would find nimble fingers to play them at the field."[23]

Other musical instruments also found their way to the day rooms on the base. Mr. W. D. Sanders donated a violin that bore the date 1813, while a complete set of drums, cymbals, and a triangle came from Mount Carmel Academy. According to the newspaper account, the instruments were "leftovers from an old orchestra no longer in existence at the academy." More cymbals came from Mrs. J. W. Chenault, while Mrs. Leo Phillips surrendered a flute and a mandolin to brighten the off-duty hours of some musicians who had temporarily become soldiers.[24]

Apparently, many of the airfield's musicians brought their instruments with them. The Fort Worth Army Airfield Band transferred to the new facility en masse from Majors Field, near Greenville. Its musical director, M/Sgt. Harry Bluestone, had been the concertmaster for Paramount Pictures in Hollywood before the war came. Pvt. Homer Mensch brought his string bass with him when he enlisted in the Army following a promising career under the baton of such legendary musical giants as Arturo Toscanini, Leopold Stokowski, and Serge Koussevitzky.[25]

Pfc. Maurice Wilk, a violinist from New York, had previously served as concertmaster of the Brooklyn Symphony, which had as its frequent guest conductor Sir Thomas Beecham. S/Sgt. Emil Cadkin, one of the band's three full-time arrangers, had once studied under Arnold Schoenberg and had worked with such composers as Max Steiner and Erich Korngold in Hollywood before entering the service. Clearly, the Fort Worth Airfield musical organization was no assemblage of amateurs. Their music was of such professional caliber, in fact, that the Army Air Forces Radio Show, featuring the band, was broadcast at 6:30 P.M. each Monday on a nationwide hook-up from Fort Worth's Will Rogers Memorial Auditorium. The show was open to the public, and the audience took pride in the high quality of the performances presented by their airfield's professional musicians.[26]

Another military musical event that proved popular was a two-day staging of "This Is the Air Corps, Mr. Bones," which was billed as a "musical minstrel show." Lt. Joseph Rivkin, who before the war had been a casting director for Hal Roach Studios in Hollywood, found many talented performers to star in the production. Among them was Cpl. Aaron Spelling of Dallas, who had been on his way to Hollywood to pursue an acting career when the war came. Spelling did, of course, eventually make it to California, where he became a highly successful television producer. In total, sixty singers, dancers, and actors appeared in the September 14–15, 1943, extravaganza, written and produced by Lieutenant Rivkin, who also starred as "a very un-military Mr. Bones." Sponsored by the Fort Worth Junior Chamber of Commerce, all proceeds from the two performances were given to the airfield's enlisted men's recreation fund.[27]

Those military personnel not particularly musically inclined easily found other activities to occupy their off-duty hours on the base. A theater, service clubs, day rooms, and a gymnasium served as centers for recreation and amusement. Physical training was a daily requirement for all personnel, including officers. It is likely that at least part of this daily regimen included golf lessons, particularly since one of the trainers was a well-known Fort Worth golf professional named Ben Hogan. As word spread of Hogan's uncanny ability to transform all but the truly hopeless duffer into a par golfer, he was eventually transferred to the Army Air Force Training Command Headquarters located downtown, apparently to work his magic on the colonels and generals who had offices there.[28]

Hogan's new golf-pro assignment was to what in early 1944 was billed as the largest single educational institution in the world. From its headquarters in the twelve-story Texas and Pacific Railway building in downtown Fort Worth, Lt. Gen. Barton K. Yount and his staff of more than 700 officers, enlisted personnel, and civilians directed every aspect of Army Air Force training. Over 25,000 aircraft were assigned to the Training Command at one point in 1944, more planes, speculated the *Star-Telegram,* than Adolph Hitler could find in all of his *Luftwaffe*. More than 80,000 pilots were graduated each year.

In addition to flight schools for pilots, navigators, and bombardiers, the Fort Worth facility also supervised the training of mechanics, armorers, machinists, metal workers, clerks, photographers, weather observers, radio operators, and parachute riggers. Additionally, the center directed flying training programs for foreign airmen from China, France, Great Britain, the Netherlands, and South and Central America. Military security prohibited the newspaper from divulging the exact number of personnel assigned to the gigantic command, but it was announced there were training installations in each of the forty-eight states, with the curious exception of Wyoming. It was also revealed that the training program had increased a hundredfold in the five-year period from 1939 to 1944.[29]

Fort Worth was understandably proud of the important role it played in World War II. With its massive Air Training Command Headquarters, its mile-long Consolidated Aircraft Plant, and the bustling Army airfield, the city clearly saw itself as a vital part of the overall war effort. Should any resident of the booming city find even temporary cause to believe otherwise, Amon Carter and his *Star-Telegram* conducted an inexhaustible public relations campaign to reinforce the importance of the city's massive contributions toward attaining victory. As one of Carter's biographers put it, "World War II was the exclusive copyrighted property of the *Star-Telegram*."[30] Daily, the publisher implied to his readers that the war was in reality an all-Texas affair, with "all others being nothing but spear-carriers in the drama." Reports of the enlistment, training, assignment, promotion, and battlefield accomplishment of every West Texan in the service received more than ample coverage in Mr. Carter's newspaper. The publisher generously offered his personal advice on how to win the war to Generals Eisenhower and Arnold, as well as to Admirals Nimitz and Halsey. Fort Worth was a major player in the deadly game of war, and the influential publisher of its leading newspaper was the very visible and very vocal coach of the city's wartime team.[31]

The entire community benefited from Amon Carter's relentless campaign to make airpower the cornerstone of the city's role in the war effort. In the ten-year period between 1940 and 1950, Fort Worth banks reported a 300 percent increase in earnings, while county payrolls jumped by more than 700 percent. According to one historian, "Fort Worth Army Airfield was the driving force behind that growth."[32]

On frequent bleak occasions, however, even the *Star-Telegram* was forced to recognize that the stakes of war were often higher than economic statistics could possibly indicate. As the flying training at Fort Worth Field continued at an ever-accelerating pace, an all-but-inevitable rash of fatal air accidents occurred.

In December 1942 a Liberator on a training mission from its Fort Worth base crashed into a cliff five miles north of Council

Bluffs, Iowa, killing all sixteen men on board. Five of the dead officers had been scheduled to graduate from transition school on the very next day.

Seven other men were killed on September 2, 1943, when two of the giant Fort Worth-based B-24s collided in midair near Birdville, Texas. Eyewitnesses reported that the early-morning crash occurred when one aircraft that was flying in close formation with other Liberators suddenly banked sharply and smashed into the plane flying alongside. "They spiraled down just like footballs," said A. J. Sanders. County Commissioner Jess Holder reported hearing a "crash like a cannon followed by a flash of light." C. N. Medley, a Birdville resident, saw the wing of one plane shear off the tail of the other, and J. E. Flory believed that it took at least five minutes for parts of the ruined aircraft to start hitting the ground, even though the collision occurred at an altitude of only 1,000 feet. The bulk of the wreckage from the two aircraft was found less than a mile apart. According to newspaper accounts, a crowd of several thousand onlookers formed shortly after the planes hit the ground. Military police forced the crowd away from the crash sites to protect it from any explosions that might occur.[33]

Just over a year later, another midair collision of B-24s killed eight more Fort Worth fliers. The two aircraft collided early on a Sunday morning about five miles southwest of the airfield. Each plane carried approximately two thousand gallons of gasoline, four hundred quarts of oil, and forty oxygen tanks. The deadly combination of these highly inflammable elements resulted in intense fires following the crash, making recovery of the crewmembers all but impossible.[34]

Despite these and numerous other fatal accidents, the Fort Worth Airfield was able to boast an impressive flying safety record due to the enormous number of training hours flown from the base. In an eighteen-month period of flying in all kinds of adverse weather and at night, the base recorded an "exceedingly low rate" of only .093 fatal crashes per 1,000 flying hours. According to reports from the airfield, this low fatality rate was largely due to a policy that directed that instructor pilots be asked if they personally would want to be a crew member on any plane their student was piloting. If the answer was even a conditional no, the student pilot was immediately washed out of the program.[35]

As the flight training in the B-24s continued at the Fort Worth field, production of the giant bombers at the Consolidated plant began to slow as the war entered its final year. In total, nearly 20,000 of the airplanes had been built, with 3,000 of them rolling off the production line at Fort Worth's plant. The Liberators had dropped an impressive 634,831 tons of bombs on Axis targets during 312,734 sorties. Their gunners had downed 4,189 enemy aircraft. Even though more Liberators had been deployed than any other four-engine bomber during the war, changing strategies dictated that longer-range aircraft were needed to bring hostilities to a final conclusion.[36]

Although Boeing's B-29 Superfortress was seen as the answer to the Air Force's late-war needs, it seemed prudent to have a backup aircraft available in case the B-29 failed to live up to its highly vaunted expectations. Consequently, the Consolidated plant, newly named Convair, was chosen to produce the new B-32 Dominator bomber. More than 1,200 of the aircraft were ordered built at Fort Worth, and delivery began in September 1944. By then, the course of the war indicated that the plane was already obsolete, and only 114 of the Fort Worth–made Dominators were completed. The short and unhappy career of the B-32 was marked by two curious events. Its nickname was changed from Dominator to Terminator because of what one sourcebook cryptically refers to as "political reasons," and then one of the newly renamed planes managed to shoot down the last Japanese aircraft to be lost in the war, unfortunately on the day following the surrender of Japan.[37]

At any rate, the changeover from Liberator to Terminator production at the Fort Worth plant resulted in a concomitant change of training aircraft at the adjacent Army airfield as the new B-32s came off the assembly line. According to the August 1, 1945, issue of *The Tarranteer*, the base newspaper, the transition from B-24 to B-32 training marked the first time during the war that a new tactical aircraft was assigned to the Air Training Command before it was actually engaged in operational use. The article pointed out that the rival B-29 aircraft went directly to the Continental Air Force Command before going into combat. The Air Training Command routine, the article concluded, was both more efficient and quicker, requiring only two months for crews to become combat-ready.[38]

The same issue of *The Tarranteer* also announced the first use of the B-32 in combat in the Pacific Theater of War. Two of the newly built aircraft were involved in a raid against a Japanese supply base on the island of Luzon in the Philippines. The planes flew unescorted and dropped their 1,000-pound bombs with great precision, according to a mission report issued by the Army Air Force. The report also noted that the aircraft had made their way across the Pacific to their new base in less than three days.[39]

Back in Texas, August 1, 1945, was a red-letter day for Fort Worth Army Airfield and its resident B-32s. The date marked the thirty-eighth anniversary of the Army Air Force and, as was the case at airfields all across America, the Fort Worth installation celebrated by staging an open house. Gates to the base opened at 10:00 A.M., and an estimated 10,000 visitors boarded army buses and trucks to be transported to the flight line. There they watched in awe as formations of the new bombers, escorted by P-38 fighter aircraft, flew past at low altitudes. Mrs. Emory Crane traveled from Lockridge, Iowa, to watch her son pilot one of the B-32s in the formation. Dazed and admittedly slightly deafened by the tremendous din created by the massed engines, Mrs. Crane managed to express wonderment about "how they keep a big plane like that up in the air."[40]

Visitors were permitted to closely inspect one of the big planes from a specially built ramp. In addition to long rows of B-32s, spectators also were able to get close to a B-17, a P-47, a B-25, and a battle-scarred B-24, dubbed "Little Audrey," that had gone from Fort Worth into a combat zone earlier in the war.

Children were given rides in Army jeeps while their parents watched firefighting and water-survival demonstrations. In the afternoon, additional flyovers by B-32s, complete with mock bombing runs, attracted another crowd estimated to be nearly 15,000 strong. The planes also flew at low altitudes over downtown Fort Worth for the benefit of those who had to work on the bright Wednesday afternoon. The activities on the base concluded at 6:00 P.M. with "an impressive retreat ceremony in front of post headquarters." The article did not disclose if the bell-and-cannon duo were used during the ceremony.[41]

Just a few days after the open house, the battles in the Pacific ended and World War II came to its conclusion. By September, airmen stationed at Fort Worth had been going through the often-tedious process of becoming civilians once again. In four weeks, some 1,300 had been discharged, and an article in the September 21,

1945, *Fort Worth Press* said the base was capable of processing up to 800 soldiers per week for separation from the service. Among those soon to leave the Army was a fifty-year-old veteran of World War I who had two sons currently in the military. Rather than return to his dairy farm in Wood County, Texas, however, the old veteran had applied for a GI loan to open in Fort Worth what was to become one of the country's first laundromats.[42]

The end of the war and the reduction in the size of the armed forces naturally raised concerns about the future of Fort Worth Army Airfield and its contribution to the economic well-being of the community. On October 14, 1945, it was announced that the airfield would be one of 150 installations to remain open, at least on an interim basis. More than 300 other Army posts were scheduled to close. In addition to remaining in operation, it was further disclosed that the Fort Worth facility would be receiving $2 million in federal funds for improvements to its runways and taxiways.[43]

Two months later, on December 8, 1945, the War Department announced that the 7th Bombardment Operational Training Wing was on its way to Fort Worth. Over 6,000 men were expected to arrive as part of a training program involving Boeing's B-29s, the very aircraft that had rendered Convair's B-32s obsolete almost as soon as they had been ordered into service. Intercorporate rivalries aside, the news that the base was to become a permanent peacetime installation was greeted with great enthusiasm throughout the business community.

Recent history has clearly shown that the adjective "permanent" should never be connected with the term "military installation." Used in tandem, the resulting phrase is just short of being an oxymoron. To be sure, Fort Worth's "permanent military installation" enjoyed a much longer life than most such facilities, but eventually the base simply outlived its usefulness.

From the end of World War II until its closing in 1991, however, the big field continued to be a vital cog in the nation's defense machine. In 1948 the facility received a new name when it was designated Carswell Air Force Base in honor of Maj. Horace S. Carswell. A Fort Worth native, Carswell had been a B-24 pilot during World War II and had posthumously received the Medal of Honor for his heroism in the Pacific Theater in 1944. As Carswell

AFB, the field long continued its close relationship with the aircraft plant located just across the runway. Later known as General Dynamics, the successor to Consolidated and Convair continued to build many of the aircraft used on the base, including the B-36, the B-58, and the FB-11A.

On December 7, 1948, one of the base's massive B-36s flew from Fort Worth to Honolulu and back, some 8,000 miles without refueling, to stage a mock attack on Pearl Harbor. As had been the case just seven years earlier, the aircraft had arrived over its target totally undetected. An embarrassed U.S. Navy successfully blocked nearly all post-raid publicity about the attack.[44]

In 1955 Carswell AFB received nationwide exposure when it served as the setting for the motion picture *Strategic Air Command*. The film's star, Jimmy Stewart, who was in real life an Air Force general, spent time on location at the base during the filming of the movie.

As the years passed, the giant air base grew in importance, both as a major Strategic Air Command installation and as a vital part of Fort Worth community life. In 1980, for example, it was estimated that the base had an aggregate economic impact of over $260 million per year. Some 5,400 military personnel were stationed on the field, with their combined families totaling 15,532. The base payroll equaled $61 million, and more than $1 million in federal aid went to the Fort Worth Independent School District on behalf of the 1,751 children from the base who attended the city's schools. As evidence of what was assumed to be Carswell's permanence, the government earmarked nearly $9 million for further base expansion and improvements in fiscal year 1980.[45]

Two years earlier, John Martin, an assistant Air Force secretary, had told high-ranking city officials that Fort Worth is an "Air Force city" and that Carswell AFB definitely would never be closed. Later, Harold Brown, the secretary of defense, confirmed to his audience that the base was going to remain open. Antonia Handler Chayes, another assistant Air Force secretary, reiterated later the same day that "Carswell was not even a candidate for closure."[46]

By the late 1980s, however, it became increasingly apparent that despite all the official promises to the contrary, Carswell was definitely a leading candidate for closure. After a period of lengthy meetings and occasional glimmers of hope, the axe finally fell on

April 12, 1991, when Defense Secretary Dick Cheney officially announced that the 3,400-acre base would indeed be closed by 1993. Local and national political leaders continued to press for a reversal of the decision, but to no avail. On June 1, 1992, the proud flag of the Strategic Air Command was lowered for the final time at Carswell, and the last B-52 roared off the base's 12,000-foot runway and climbed over Lake Worth on its way to a new home in Louisiana.[47]

With the departure of the huge bombers, an almost eerie silence fell across the western edge of Fort Worth, where for more than half a century, America's newest aircraft had almost continuously flown. Layoffs at the General Dynamics plant contributed to the gloom that settled over the city. Retail sales plummeted, house values decreased, and population numbers began to recede for the first time in decades.

Not completely idled by the deactivation, Carswell was designated a reserve base and home to an Air National Guard unit. As plans were being set in motion to utilize the vast amount of unused building space on the old airfield, the Tonkawa Indians sought to claim all the base as their own, acting upon a disputed 1866 land grant from the Texas Legislature. The Tonkawas contended that their ancestors had been promised the land for helping early-day Texans battle Comanches. Although the issue has not been resolved, tribal lawyers have privately expressed doubt that their client will likely gain title to the nearly vacant air base.[48]

While the Indians did not gain possession of what is left of Carswell, at least for the time being, the Navy did. This brought about yet another name change, one that required a considerable degree of mental capacity to recite without error. No longer just Carswell Air Force Base, the facility now bears the title "Naval Air Station Fort Worth Joint Reserve Base, Federal Medical Center, Carswell Field." Perhaps someday the phrase "a wholly owned subsidiary of the Tonkawa Nation" will be tacked onto the already ponderous title.[49]

Be that as it may, to old-time residents of Fort Worth, the base is and always will be simply Carswell, the lost heir to a long legacy of Air Force service and tradition. Now the shrill jet whine of reserve fighters manages to break the late-afternoon silence west of the city, but the sounds are pallid imitations of the almost holistic effect of years ago, when rumbling Consolidated B-24s, earthshaking Convair B-36s, and heart-stopping B-52s eased down on a northerly heading to land on Carswell's massive runways. Names can change, commands may shift, and missions will always be drastically altered, but nothing can ever erase the haunting memory of those huge and powerful airplanes suspended in stark silhouette against a brilliantly setting West Texas sun over Fort Worth, Texas.

Midland Mayor M. C. Ulmer welcomes Lt. Col. Isaiah Davies to his new command at Midland Army Airfield in 1942. Davies, who soon became a brigadier general, probably felt right at home with the welcoming horse. He had once been a private in the cavalry.

— Courtesy Midland County Historical Museum, Midland, Texas

Newly assigned trainees take the Bombardier's Oath at Midland. Note the two rifles held at the ready and the shrouded bombsight.

— Courtesy Permian Historical Society Archival Collection, The University of Texas of the Permian Basin, Odessa, Texas

Two bombardier trainees carry a bombsight to their aircraft.
— Courtesy Midland County Historical Museum, Midland, Texas

Early in the war, Midland Field's practice bombs had to be hand-filled with sand.
— Courtesy Midland County Historical Museum, Midland, Texas

Cadets use presumably unfilled bombs to augment their morning calisthenics.
— Courtesy Midland County Historical Museum, Midland, Texas

Bombardiers give thumbs-up to their school's "Hell From Heaven" insignia.
— Courtesy Midland County Historical Museum, Midland, Texas

Who wants to be a bombardier? The Future Bombardiers of America Club was started by General Davies to solidify civilian support of Midland Field.

— Courtesy Midland County Historical Museum, Midland, Texas

A bombardier trainee and friends. The cadet's theatrically blackened eye was perhaps enhanced a bit for photographic emphasis.

— Courtesy Midland County Historical Museum, Midland, Texas

Army personnel attend a picnic hosted by Midlanders, circa 1942.

— Courtesy Permian Historical Society Archival Collection,
The University of Texas of the Permian Basin, Odessa, Texas

Midland Field officers heap their paper plates high in what a USAAF photograph captions as a "5730 Combat Barbecue." Note the U.S. Navy man among the servers.

— Courtesy Midland County Historical Museum, Midland, Texas

Odessa's famous "Chuckwagon Gang" serves barbecue to South American air officers visiting Midland Airfield. The officer nearest the camera looks suspiciously like Argentina's Juan D. Peron.

— Courtesy Permian Historical Society Archival Collection, The University of Texas of the Permian Basin, Odessa, Texas

Local musicians entertain Midland's officers at a picnic at the J.E. "Bob" Hill residence, October 22, 1944.

— Courtesy Midland County Historical Museum, Midland, Texas

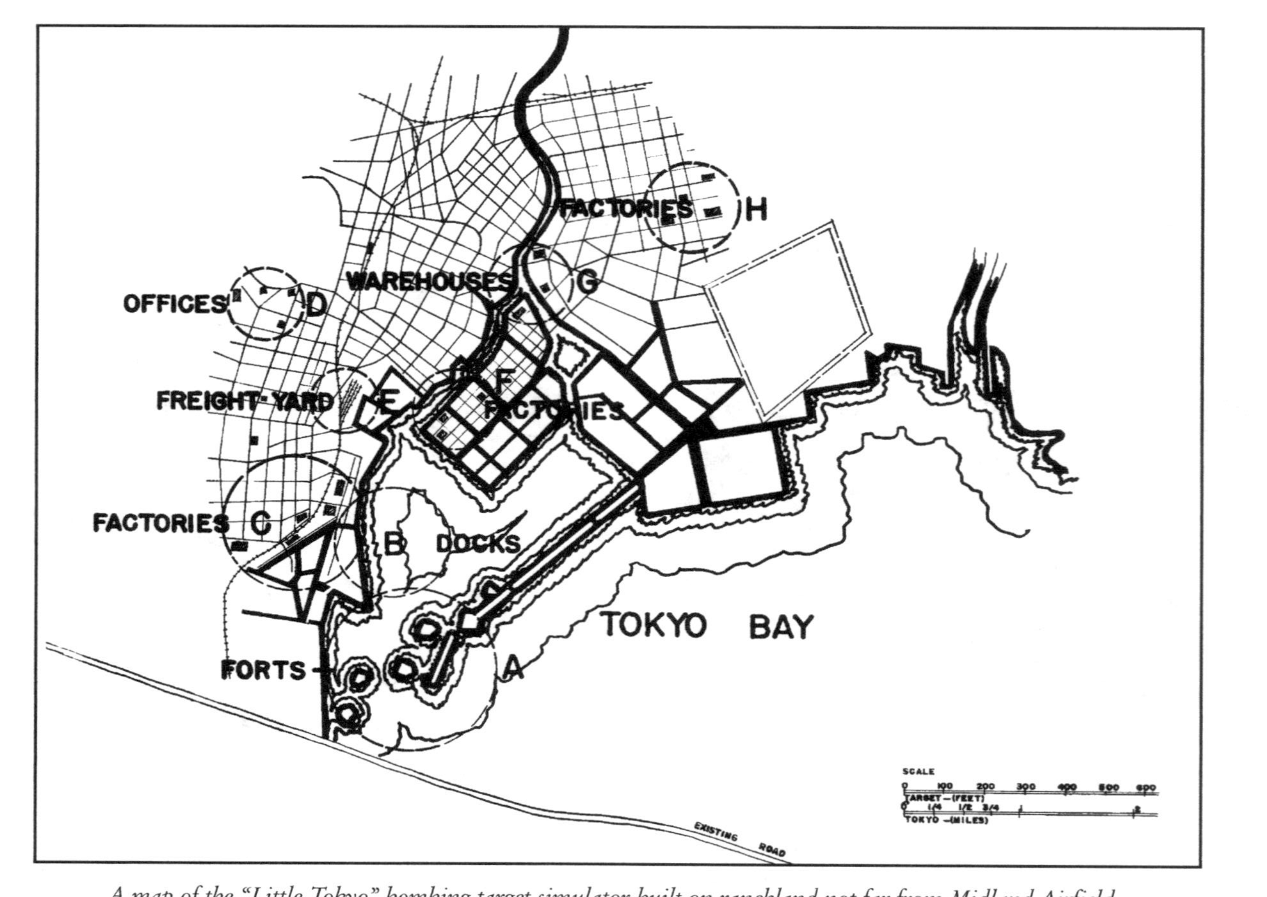

A map of the "Little Tokyo" bombing target simulator built on ranchland not far from Midland Airfield.

— Courtesy Midland County Historical Museum, Midland, Texas

Practice bombs fall as training aircraft approach "Little Tokyo," July 4, 1942.

— Courtesy Midland County Historical Museum, Midland, Texas

"Little Tokyo," complete with model ships in the bay, comes into view as the bombs continue to rain downward. Hollywood movie cameras were at Midland to capture this action.

— Courtesy Midland County Historical Museum, Midland, Texas

Maj. Bill Walmsley flies his plane over the smoldering remnants of "Little Tokyo."

— Courtesy Mrs. Mimi Walmsley, Fredericksburg, Texas

An apparently satisfied Gen. Isaiah Davies gets an up-close view of what was once "Little Tokyo." Cameramen from RKO-International Pictures filmed the July 4, 1942, bombing excercise to get footage for the movie Bombardier.

— Courtesy Permian Historical Society Archival Collection, The University of Texas of the Permian Basin, Odessa, Texas

Marfa Field's main gate in a wintry setting, circa 1943.

— Courtesy Museum of the Big Bend Archives, Sul Ross University, Alpine, Texas

What remains of the Marfa gate, 1999. Note the identifying hinge post.

— Author's photograph

A 1943 aerial shot of Marfa Airfield showing the huge scale of the base. The dark line at upper center is Highway 67/90 connecting Marfa on the left to Alpine on the right. The viewing site for the famous Marfa Mystery Lights eventually would be near the black vertical object just off the highway at the photograph's center.

— Courtesy Bryan Wildenthal Memorial Library Archives, Sul Ross University, Alpine, Texas

Marfa Field with its distinctive angular apron configuration, 1944.
— Courtesy C. M. "Fritz" Kahl, Marfa, Texas

Rooftop arrows point the way to Marfa Field.
— Courtesy C. M. "Fritz" Kahl, Marfa, Texas

Marfa's control tower, circa 1943.

— Courtesy Bryan Wildenthal Library Archives, Sul Ross University, Alpine, Texas

The base theater at Marfa, circa 1943, with the chapel in the background. Later the little church would be moved to Alpine.

— Courtesy Bryan Wildenthal Library Archives, Sul Ross University, Alpine, Texas

Marfa's base hospital, 1944.
— Courtesy Bryan Wildenthal Library Archives,
Sul Ross University, Alpine, Texas

The tarpaper mess hall with coal smoke blowing in the West Texas wind.
— Courtesy Bryan Wildenthal Library Archives, Sul Ross University, Alpine, Texas

Chinese student pilots get outfitted in the Marfa PX late in the war.

— Courtesy Bryan Wildenthal Library Archives, Sul Ross University, Alpine, Texas

Known as Alfred Arnold Coccozza when he was stationed at Marfa Airfield during WWII, Mario Lanza later became a popular Hollywood star.

— Courtesy Metro Goldwyn Meyer Studios

A sign points to the Marfa Mystery Lights viewing area, located just yards from what was once the airfield's main gate. The sign also helpfully advises that lights are best viewed when it is dark.
— Author's photograph

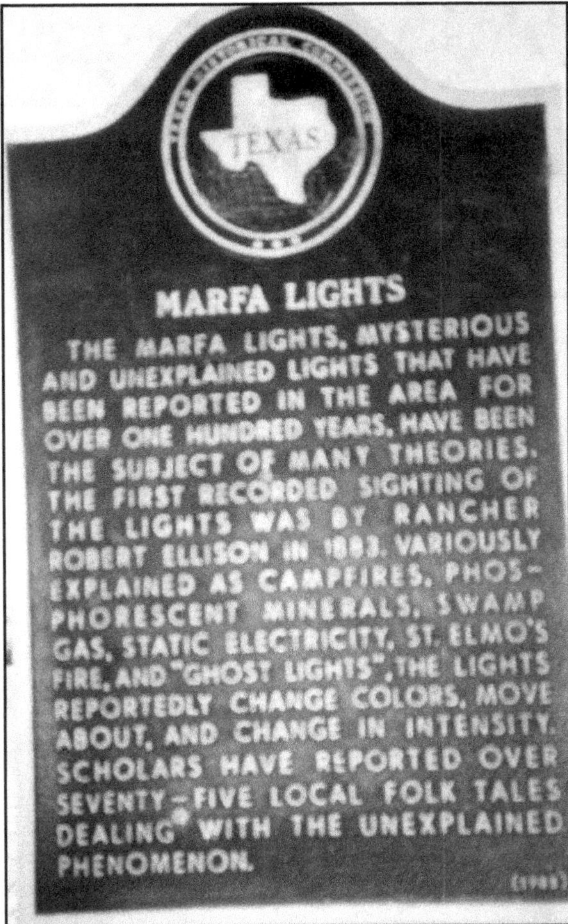

A Historical Commission sign tells the Marfa Lights story, but the impressive record of Marfa Army Airfield, which was located just yards from this sign, goes untold.
— Author's photograph

When the light is just right, the foundations of a few WWII buildings can be seen on the Marfa Airfield site.

— Author's photograph

This slab probably marks the location of the gatehouse shown in a previous photo.

— Author's photograph

The chapel was moved over Paisano Pass to a new location in Alpine.
— Author's photograph

This Alpine school gymnasium was once a WWII hangar on Marfa's airfield.
— Author's photograph

Was Pancho Villa the inadvertent father of modern American airpower? At least he proved that the United States Flying Service was in woeful shape and in desperate need of overhaul.

— Courtesy The University of Texas Institute of Texan Cultures at San Antonio

Brig. Gen. John J. Pershing, on the border, learned that his Army's air arm could not catch Villa and could only seldom get off the ground.

— Courtesy The University of Texas Institute of Texan Cultures at San Antonio

The first hangars at Biggs Field housed lighter-than-air surveillance craft.

— Courtesy Fort Bliss Historical Museum, El Paso, Texas

Brig. Gen. Billy Mitchell and Capt. Eddie Rickenbacker, two genuine airpower icons, meet at Biggs Field in 1927.
— Courtesy Fort Bliss Historical Museum, El Paso, Texas

A World War II training squadron uses a B-24 as an appropriate photo prop, 1944.

— Courtesy Fort Bliss Historical Museum, El Paso, Texas

At the end of the twentieth century, Biggs Field once again belonged to the U.S. Army.

— Author's photograph

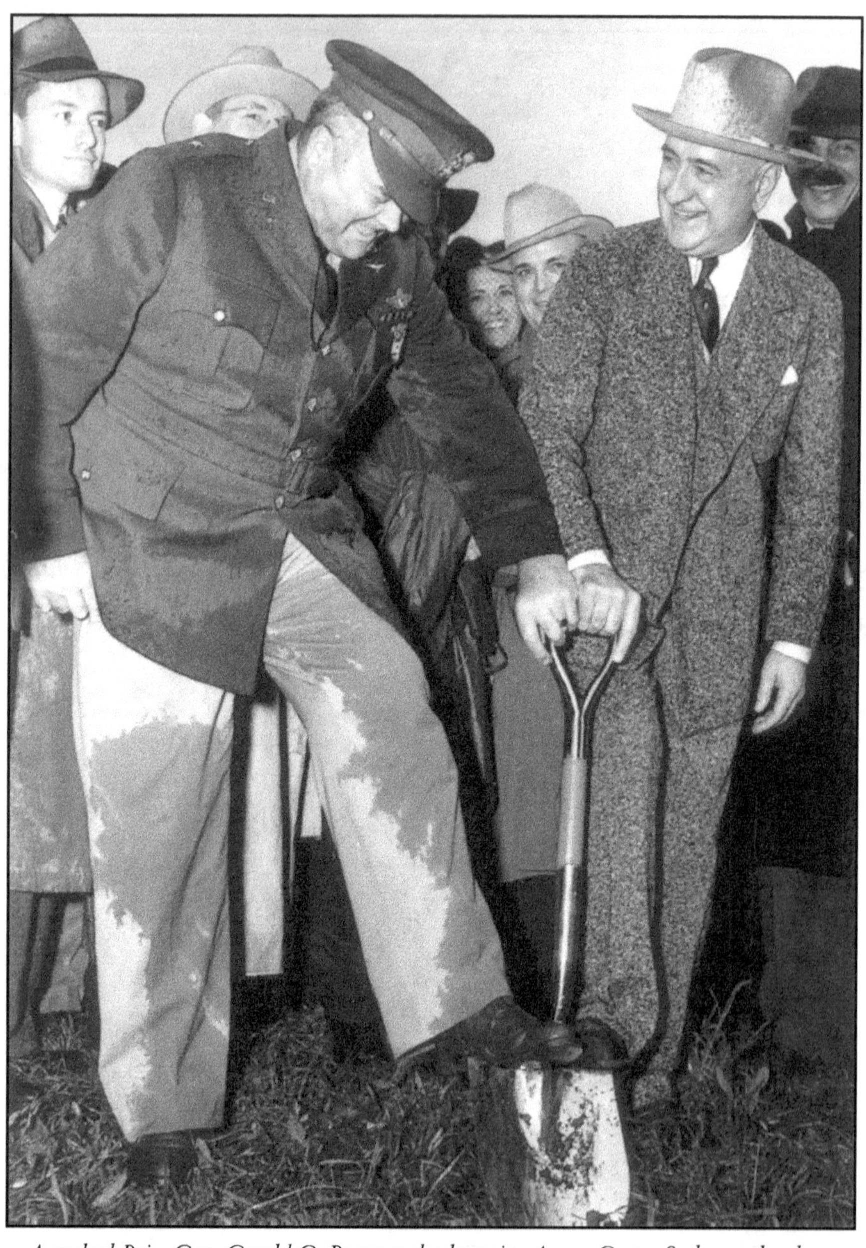

A soaked Brig. Gen. Gerald C. Brant and a beaming Amon Carter Sr. brave the elements to break ground for Consolidated Aircraft's new plant in Fort Worth, 1941.

— Courtesy The University of Texas at Arlington Libraries, Special Collections Division

Consolidated's mile-long assembly line mass-produced B-24 Liberators during the war. Many of them were assigned to Fort Worth Army Airfield, located just across the runway.

— Courtesy Tarrant County Historical Commission, Fort Worth, Texas

This old army howitzer was fired twice daily at Fort Worth Army Airfield during WWII, much to the dismay of nearby civilian neighbors.

— Courtesy The University of Texas at Arlington Libraries, Special Collections Division

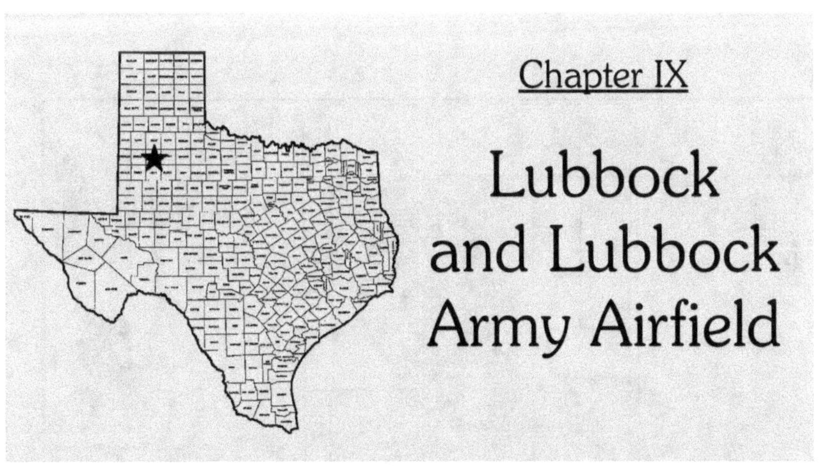

Chapter IX

Lubbock and Lubbock Army Airfield

I think this has always been a bootstrap city. It took root out here on this windblown prairie, got itself hooked up to the big railroads, and then somebody convinced the powers that be that it was just the right place to put a big university. How they did it all, I'll never understand, but boy howdy, look at it now!

Eugene R. Gilmore
Lubbock, Texas

Lubbock's transition from windblown prairie village to modern Texas city has not always been easy. Located some 120 miles south of Amarillo, the site for the town was initially chosen by real estate promoters who saw the need for a hub city to serve what they correctly envisioned would someday become a rich agricultural region. The settlement that began to take shape in 1891 took its name from Lubbock County, which had been created in 1876 but for fifteen years had remained too sparsely settled to require a county seat. With little in the way of any serious competition, the honor of becoming the county seat easily devolved upon the eponymous little settlement.[1]

Its future thus apparently assured, the town began to grow as farmers and other settlers arrived to take advantage of extremely low land prices and high agricultural expectations. A newspaper was

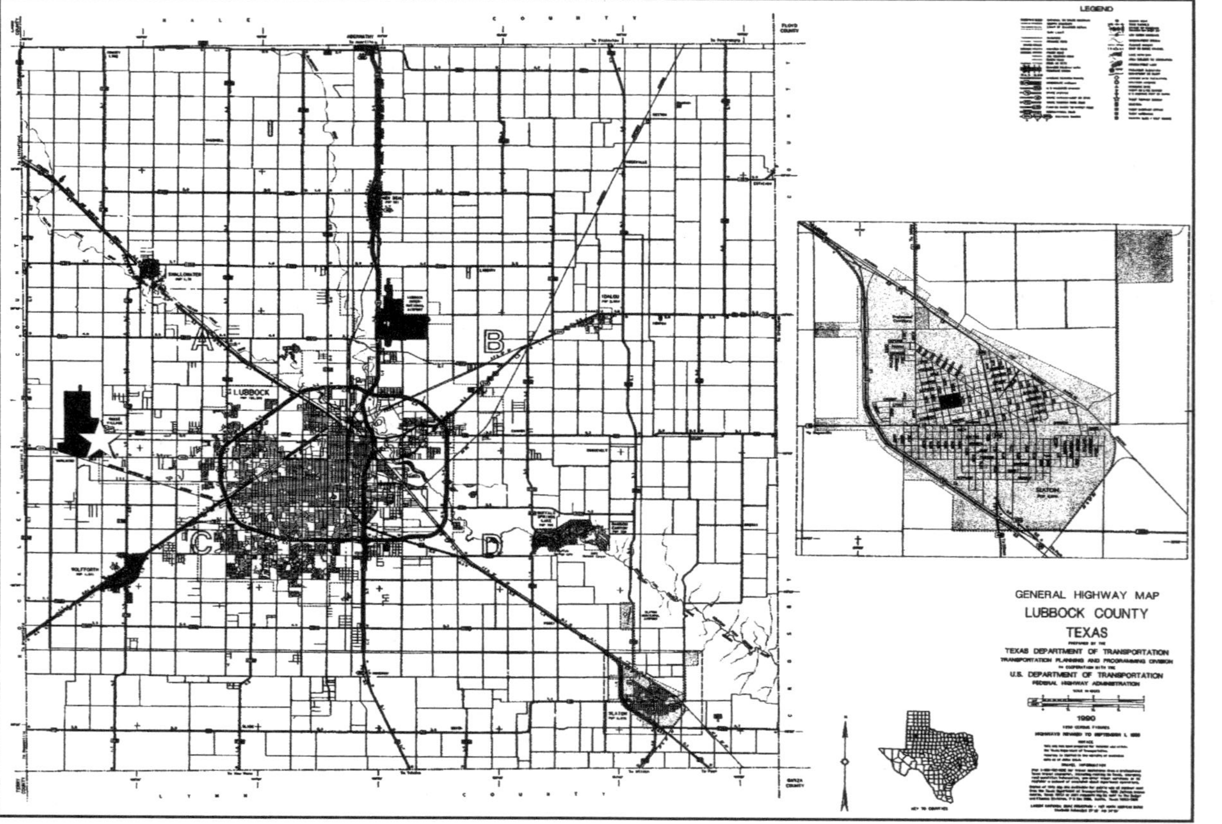

Lubbock County Map

This map of Lubbock County shows the location of Lubbock Army Airfield during the war years. An inset map of Texas shows the location of the county within the state

soon in operation, along with several stores and hotels. A courthouse was eventually built, complete with a jail, and as buildings were still somewhat scarce in the tiny community, the jailhouse doubled as a schoolhouse on those rare occasions when there were enough empty cells to provide space for the students.

Even though the small town had become the county seat, there was little else to distinguish it from other rough-hewn communities that had sprung from the dusty soil of the South Plains. For years, streets remained unpaved, and most buildings were made of wood and often were too poorly constructed to effectively resist the frequently vicious winds that roared across the prairies and into town.

As was usually the case in West Texas, it was the coming of a railroad that gave Lubbock its first key to permanence. The great east-west transcontinental railroads had bypassed the town both to the north and to the south, so it was a connecting line of the Atchison, Topeka and Santa Fe, running down from Plainview, that gave Lubbock its initial significant access to major agricultural marketplaces. Through the Santa Fe's rail system, area farmers were at last provided with an economical way to transport their products, and Lubbock soon became the marketing hub of the South Plains.

The city, with a population of nearly 2,000, incorporated in 1909, the same year the railroad came. Just over a decade later, the population had doubled.

In the early 1900s, the State of Texas began a search to find a site for a major college to serve the West Texas region. The result of that search proved pivotal to Lubbock's future. Competition to acquire the college became heated among Lubbock and the other six towns that submitted proposals to the Texas Legislature. In their zeal to be the successful candidate, the petitioning communities quite often amplified their virtues, glossed over their faults, and took egregious liberties in presenting their population and economic statistics.[2]

After years of rumors, lobbying, and sheer skullduggery, it was officially announced by the Texas Legislature in 1923 that Lubbock had been selected as the home for the school to be known as Texas Technological College. Perhaps no other single factor contributed as significantly to the city's growth and its future than its selection as the site of what would eventually become the large and influential Texas Tech University.[3]

The new school, industry, and manufacturing plants had combined with the strong agricultural and marketing sectors to make Lubbock the center of economic influence over a fifty-one-county region that included parts of eastern New Mexico. By 1930 Lubbock's population was reported to be just over 20,500, a growth of 19,000-plus in only twenty years.[4]

The onset of the Great Depression in the early 1930s, however, began to slow the rate of Lubbock's impressive growth. Reduced buying power impacted the agricultural market, and manufacturing activity diminished. Even though the city's population had expanded dramatically, unemployment and reduced household incomes were taking their toll on the economy.

Lubbock's Chamber of Commerce, however, was by no means content to stand idly by until conditions improved on their own. Perhaps remembering the success of the coordinated civic effort that had won the contest for Texas Tech a decade earlier, the city's leaders began a campaign in 1932 to convince the federal government to construct an Army airfield somewhere on the wide-open spaces that surrounded the city. It is interesting to note that this well-orchestrated campaign began several years before there were any significant indications that the United States might again be involved in an international war that would require an enhanced military aviation force. The eventual success of the chamber's airfield campaign provided Lubbock with an economic stability that would endure for nearly fifty years. Much more important at the time, it also provided the United States with thousands of sorely needed, well-trained pilots who would soon see combat action in several international military conflicts.

LUBBOCK ARMY AIRFIELD

Even from the beginning, the people of Lubbock were most supportive of the military and Lubbock Army Airfield.

Gordon Treadaway
Lubbock, Texas

Longtime Lubbock citizen Gordon Treadaway was a captain assigned to Lubbock Army Airfield on the day it was officially dedicated. The warm reception given the new base and the genuine hospitality extended to its personnel were reflections of the persistence with which the city had pursued the War Department to gain approval for the installation.

At the forefront of the decade-long campaign was the chamber of commerce manager, Mr. A. B. Davis. A review of his correspondence with his ally, Congressman George Mahon, and his prey, who was virtually anyone who might someday influence a decision to give Lubbock an airfield, shows the zeal with which he sought his prize. Davis was tireless. No detail of the ongoing lobbying effort escaped his notice as he relentlessly pursued Army Air Force officers, became their personal friend, and then used that friendship as best he could to the advantage of his city's quest for an airfield.

Davis besieged important officers with invitations to join him on hunting and fishing trips in the Lubbock vicinity, so that he could continue his sales pitch in person around the campfire. He made certain that key Army personnel received free annual fishing passes to Buffalo Lake State Park so that he would have more frequent access to them when they came to the South Plains to catch bass.[5]

Elaborate "fact-finding" sojourns were arranged in Lubbock, during which visiting officers received all the entertainment that the city could provide. Long before World War II commenced, A. B. Davis was on a casual first-name basis with virtually every high-ranking army officer who might have any influence on the final decision to give Lubbock an air base.

Sometimes, his tactics failed. When one officer declined Davis's repeated invitations to join him on a hunting trip "because he didn't have a gun," the chamber manager then suggested that they go fishing. When the officer again declined, writing, "I only rarely fish," Davis exploded, in private of course, saying, "Well, he's the damnedest officer I've ever met."[6]

In all of his lobbying efforts on behalf of an Army airfield, Davis avoided publicity. He preferred to be behind the scenes, and at his insistence, the local newspaper refrained from publishing any photographs of him or mentioning his name unless it was absolutely necessary to do so.

The *Fort Worth Star-Telegram* had no such agreement with Davis and once sent its reporter Frank Reeves on special assignment to get a photograph of "Mr. Lubbock" at work. Learning that the man would be attending a luncheon in Odessa, Reeves soon found Davis having lunch and quickly snapped the desired photograph. According to a report that appeared in the *Star-Telegram*, Reeves was immediately pelted by "salt shakers, spoons, knives, and heads of lettuce" thrown by the obviously highly incensed Davis. After the picture appeared in the Fort Worth paper a few days later, the Lubbock executive wrote Reeves a letter in which he claimed it was "the durn best picture I ever had made." Davis closed his letter by ordering a half-dozen of the prints be sent to him, even though he made it clear that he had no intention of paying for them.[7]

After at least eight years of effort and many hunting and fishing parties but no tangible results, the publicity-shy Mr. Davis began to show signs of discouragement. On May 31, 1940, he wrote, "I am very, very doubtful that there will be an air base established at Lubbock or anywhere in this vicinity." The reason for this uncharacteristically negative statement perhaps stemmed from one Army officer's comment that the service was opposed to "primary training centers in areas in excess of 2,000 feet [elevation]." If this were indeed true, Lubbock's 3,256-foot altitude above sea level automatically disqualified it from further consideration.[8]

Discouraged, perhaps, but by no means undaunted, A. B. Davis continued to press his case, regardless of the extra 1,256 feet in the city's elevation that might cause his efforts to fail. On May 26, 1940, he sent a telegram to R. D. Shinkle, his lobbyist in Washington. Sensing, correctly, as it developed, that Amarillo was also vigorously pushing for an Army airfield, Davis stated that the terrain around Lubbock was far better for pilot training than that in the "north," a thinly disguised reference to Amarillo, which lay in that direction from Lubbock. While he was at it, Davis also suggested that Shinkle remind the Army high command that the air over San Antonio was already "saturated," just in case there were plans afoot to award another air facility to the Alamo City. In closing his message to Shinkle, Davis admonished the man to do what he himself had been doing for years on behalf of a Lubbock air base, "work like hell."[9]

While Shinkle worked the scene in Washington as ordered, his boss continued to bombard Texas-based Army officers with letters enumerating the many benefits to be derived from building a major military installation in Lubbock. Brig. Gen. Gerald C. Brant, the commanding general of the Gulf Coast Air Training Center at San

Antonio's Randolph Field, was the officer singled out by Davis to receive the greatest amount of pro-Lubbock information, and the general responded to some of the invitations to visit the city. It is clear that Brant and Davis became lifelong friends during their airfield negotiations, for their later correspondence, conducted on a first-name basis, continued for many years. The two men apparently spent considerable leisure time together, as the relative successes or failures of their hunting and fishing trips were often recounted in the letters that they exchanged.[10]

Almost every officer on Brant's staff who might have a role in the decision-making process was frequently the recipient of broadsides from Davis. One officer finally found it necessary to take steps to stem the flood of correspondence rushing his way from Lubbock. In a curt and apparently effective one-sentence letter to Davis, Major T. W. Spurgin stated "pls [*sic*] omit my name from your mailing list." Spurgin had obviously heard more than enough about Lubbock, Texas, from its most ardent promoter.[11]

Despite such very rare examples of failure to communicate successfully, A. B. Davis's campaign on behalf of his city finally bore rich economic fruit. On April 15, 1941, a delegation headed by General Brant visited Lubbock to inspect various sites that had been offered to his command as a location for a flight-training base. The so-called "Lindsey Site," a 1,400-acre plot some ten miles west of town, seemed particularly attractive to the general and his staff, perhaps in part because the City of Lubbock offered it to the War Department at no cost. Promising to consider this generous offer fully, Brant and his men returned to San Antonio.[12]

A few days later, a team of Army engineers appeared at the site and began taking measurements and testing the soil. In view of such obvious interest, it had clearly been prudent of the city to make prior arrangements to acquire the site from its owner, Mrs. J. H. Lindsey, at a purchase price of nearly $50,000, or $35 per acre.[13]

When their analysis was complete, the engineers forwarded the results to Brant on May 5, 1941. The general quickly endorsed the engineers' report and sent it on to Army headquarters in Washington without further delay.

Aside from A. B. Davis and General Brant, apparently few others seem to have been aware of the impending success of Lubbock's decade-long campaign. On May 6, Davis wrote a letter to Col. Charles H. Dowman, who was a senior staff officer under Brant at Randolph Field. Apparently believing that the colonel was unaware of Brant's endorsement of the Lubbock site, the chamber manager reported "very, very confidentially" that the inspection by Brant had taken place and that the outlook for the base was favorable. A postscript to his letter to Dowman reflected Davis's optimism by endorsing the bid of local pilot Clint Breedlove for a contract to provide civilian training for primary flight students when the flying school actually opened.[14]

On June 21, 1941, the message that A. B. Davis had been waiting for at least ten years was received at the chamber of commerce offices. In a telegram, U. S. Representative George Mahon proudly stated, "I am authorized to announce that a flying school for Lubbock has been approved here [Washington, D.C.]."[15]

Accounts differ as to exactly how much the War Department had appropriated to construct the school on the 1,400 acres provided free of charge by the city. A Lubbock newspaper placed the initial estimate at $5.2 million, noting that around $600,000 had been trimmed from the allocated funds somewhere along the legislative pathway. Other sources reported that the new field would cost only $3.2 million. All accounts do agree that the construction contract clearly specified that the base was to be completed within 120 days of the agreement's August 21, 1941, execution date.[16]

In order to meet the tight construction schedule, up to 850 workers arrived on the site at least two weeks before the contracts were let. A barbed-wire fence was erected around the perimeter of the future flying field to prevent curious onlookers from interfering with work on the massive project. The Santa Fe Railroad hurriedly built a spur leading to the site to facilitate the handling of building supplies.[17]

The primary contracts for base construction went to the W. G. McMillan Company, the W. S. Moss Company, and the C. S. Lambe Company, all of Lubbock. Mr. W. G. McMillan, owner of one of the principal contracting firms, was also a member of the city commission and a veteran of "several extended trips to the nation's capital to promote the base," according to the *Lubbock Daily Journal* of June 13, 1941.[18]

More than 1,600 construction workers found steady employment, and local merchants rejoiced at the prospect of a large contingent of over 4,000 military personnel who were poised to arrive in their city. The *Lubbock Avalanche-Journal* ran an editorial confirming the approval for the base and the economic projections that popular approval signified. "Lubbock has worked hard for this project," declared the newspaper. "It is enough to say that it has not been a one-man job nor a one-man accomplishment."[19]

Despite the paper's assertion to the contrary, it really had been just one man who had doggedly persisted when prospects for getting the base seemed all but dead. He had formed genuine friendships, pulled legislative strings, arranged for Army officers to catch hundreds of fish, shoot whole herds of deer, and consume copious cases of liquor, and finally was able to procure a major air base for his beloved city. Yet, the newspaper singled out Representative Mahon, Senator Tom Connally, and General Brant for special praise in obtaining the field, while the herculean efforts of A. B. Davis went without praise. In keeping with his wishes, his name was not mentioned in the laudatory editorials. As we shall see later, however, his failure to gain public credit for getting the base in no way daunted Davis's enthusiasm nor curbed his effectiveness in future dealings with the U.S Army Air Force and its successor, the U. S. Air Force.

As the plaudits were being handed out and deep bows being taken, the next real task of building an airfield began in earnest. The magnitude of the project came into focus when it was revealed that, given the thickness and length of the runways, the quantity of paving materials to be used on the base would be sufficient to "replace approximately two-thirds of all of the pavement that has ever been laid in the city of Lubbock." Wells had been dug to a sufficient depth to provide 500,000 gallons of water daily to the flying school, with more than adequate storage capacity provided in the newly completed red-and-white-checkered water tower that would become a familiar landmark for years to come. The three runways under construction would each measure 6,500 feet by 150 feet, and the field's three hangars were each 184 by 100 feet.[20]

The contractors working on the project were faced with some radical temperature extremes as the work progressed. Official Army Air Force data reported that average temperatures for the Lubbock area ranged from -10° to 108° F. As air-conditioning was not even a consideration in any construction plans drawn in 1941, the men assigned to the base would have to learn to cope with the heat factor, but perhaps wood-burning stoves might help in the barracks when the temperature outside dropped well below freezing.

Other weather factors also affected the progress of construction on the base. Strong springtime winds often reached velocities in excess of 70 to 80 mph, usually triggering blinding dust storms that could last for several days. The wind-driven particles of dirt and sand that created the storms made any outdoor activity unpleasant, if not downright unhealthy.

Despite frequently intemperate weather conditions, work on the base continued. Following the Japanese attack on Pearl Harbor, the construction timetable was accelerated to a seven-day-a-week schedule. More workers were hurriedly imported to ensure completion of the base and the opening of the pilot-training facility. With war now a reality, the need for fully trained flight crews became increasingly urgent.

On January 4, 1942, the War Department announced that additional buildings would be added to the air base still under construction. It was further announced that 95 percent of the building construction originally let for contract had been completed, although the task of pouring concrete for all runways and taxiways was only 60 percent complete. Due to the extended workweek and authorized overtime, however, the Army predicted that the base would be finished by mid-February 1942.[21]

Contractor W. G. McMillan lent his voice in praise of the patriotic spirit that had prompted the construction workers to exceed all expectations. Pointing out that the entire period of the construction had endured some of the worst conditions in Lubbock's long history of notoriously bad weather, McMillan saluted "the morale of the workers that had virtually nullified the effects of ice, mud, and blowing dust." McMillan continued, "The men working on the project are keenly conscious that they have an opportunity to hit a lick for Uncle Sam, and believe me, they are hitting it."[22]

On February 25, 1942, the base was sufficiently completed to allow the arrival of Class 42-E, the first group of seventy-four cadets to be assigned to Lubbock. Although the school was built to produce multi-engine pilots, 42-E and the following two cadet classes received flight instruction in the single-engine T-6 "Texas" aircraft, due to a shortage of twin-engine training planes.[23]

The first class of cadets graduated from what circumstances had temporarily made a single-engine flight school on April 29, 1942. Before receiving a commission as a second lieutenant and the silver wings of a pilot, each cadet had spent seven weeks accumulating two hundred hours of flying time plus a commensurate amount of ground-school and Link simulator training.

Early in the war, the government's growing need for qualified pilots seemed greater than the flight schools' ability to produce them. In an effort to balance supply with demand, new pilot programs were put into effect at Lubbock Army Airfield. At first, all pilot officer candidates were required to have completed at least two years of college to be accepted into the flight-training program, but it soon became necessary to modify that rule. Candidates lacking the previously required amount of college studies were then admitted to what was termed the Sergeant Pilot Program. They received the same training as the officer candidate pilots, but upon earning their wings, they remained noncommissioned officers and earned noncommissioned officers' pay.[24]

Many of these sergeant pilots went on to become commissioned officers as the war progressed. Owen Clark, who was in the first class of graduating sergeant pilots, came out of the war as a lieutenant colonel. In reflecting on his military career, Clark explained that simply being permitted to fly had meant much more to him at the outset of his enlistment than anything else. "We wanted to fly," he recalled, "and we really didn't care that much about rank at that point in our careers. We just wanted to fly."[25]

As the flight-training program at Lubbock Airfield accelerated, the base was formally dedicated on June 21, 1942. Gordon Treadaway, who was present that day, estimated that more than 30,000 people attended the dedication ceremony. As the city of Lubbock had an estimated population of some 50,000 at the time, it is evident that citizens from all across the South Plains found their way to what less than a year before had been known only as "Mrs. Lindsey's land."[26]

The visitors admitted to the base for the first time saw over 215 newly constructed buildings, including three large hangars, scores of barracks and classrooms, a theater, a chapel, and nearly four miles of still-pristine concrete runways. Eventually some 4,000 military and civilian personnel lived and worked on the giant facility.[27]

As the war progressed, Lubbock Army Airfield grew even larger. An additional 62 acres were purchased from George W. Dupree in December 1942, and the Lindsey Estate sold the government 182.5 more acres in January 1943. The price for the additional Lindsey land amounted to $8,000, or just $9 per acre more than the price of the original parcel. At war's end, the base contained slightly more than 1,651 acres.[28]

Beginning with the fifth class of cadets, multi-engine aircraft finally became available for training purposes. From 1942 through 1945, AT-7s, AT-9s, AT-17s, and UC-78s were in use at various times on the base. Expanding the facilities to accommodate the different types of aircraft, however, proved costly. By the time the war was over, nearly $6 million had been spent on Lubbock Army Airfield, roughly 20 percent more than had originally been allocated for the project.[29]

The ongoing construction work on the base meant continued employment for area workers and attracted others to move to the region. Meanwhile, the huge government payroll further enhanced the Lubbock economy. As evidence of its attractiveness to outsiders, the city reportedly became the second-fastest-growing metropolitan area in the entire United States during the war years.[30]

As might be imagined, the ever-growing number of Lubbock residents, enjoying a buoyant economy and genuinely proud of their important air base, gave military personnel a warm welcome. The Baker Hotel, located at 1211 Thirteenth Street in the heart of the city, was the location of the Lubbock Service Organization (LSO), the official welcoming center for visiting airmen. As the entire area was legally dry and consequently all but devoid of the off-base entertainment usually sought by soldiers, the LSO swiftly became the main focus of military and civilian social interaction.[31] When the city had petitioned the national United Service Organization (USO) to open a facility downtown, the request had been rejected on the grounds that there would not be an adequate number of personnel on the base to warrant a USO facility. In a typical reaction to such adversity, the city's leaders simply formed their own service organization.[32]

Operating both day and night, the LSO offered all military personnel a variety of recreational activities, including games, reading rooms, and indoor sports. Of particular interest to most soldiers, however, were the regular dances, hosted by a group of young Lubbock ladies known as the Hub-ettes. According to those who belonged to the group, soldiers far outnumbered girls at the first dance, but as the word spread to coeds attending Texas Tech about the availability of hundreds of young and attractive men, the odds soon became more even.[33]

Even though the dances were heavily chaperoned and dating between the soldiers and the Hub-ettes strictly forbidden, the rules were frequently (but discreetly) violated. Izora Edwards, a wartime Hub-ette, met a young soldier named Harlan Fisk at the LSO and eventually became his wife. "Oh, I dated a lot of [soldiers]," Mrs. Fisk recalled, adding that both she and Fisk were dating someone else they had met at the LSO when they were first introduced.[34]

The LSO published a monthly newsletter that provided a schedule of all planned activities for servicemen, including movies, athletic events, variety shows, and, of course, the "heavily chaperoned" dances. Hub-ettes, it was noted, were to be admitted to the dances by invitation only. When the South Plains Army Airfield Glider School was opened north of town, personnel from the new facility also enjoyed their leisure time at the Baker Hotel's LSO.

Among the few who were not welcome at the LSO were the African-American soldiers assigned to either base. Black personnel had an entertainment center of their own, located at East Avenue "C" and Twenty-first Street. Although World War II–era rules of racial segregation were strict and, by today's standards, unacceptable, some of the former servicemen affected by them seem to harbor pleasant memories of their assignment to Lubbock's Army Airfield. Although most of the field's two hundred black soldiers were required to live off-base in substandard housing, had to eat in segregated areas, and were admitted to only a few theaters, Rudolph Delvan, who was a private in 1943, sums up his time at Lubbock by saying, "I wouldn't change the experience for nothing."[35]

In addition to black personnel, the base also hosted a contingent of WACs, the female aviators of the WASP, and for a time toward the end of the war, a large group of Axis prisoners of war.

More than two hundred German soldiers, mostly from Erwin Rommel's *Afrika Korps,* arrived in Lubbock in March 1945.[36]

The POWs were put to work throughout the city, laboring in various industries to alleviate serious employee shortages created by the war. The ex-soldiers could often be seen in trucks on city streets being transported to feed mills or cotton presses for a day of work. In August 1945, Italian POWs replaced the Germans and continued to involuntarily reinforce the local labor pool as Rommel's men had previously done.[37]

The growing number of POWs and the lessening demand for new pilots signaled that the war might soon be coming to an end. On October 23, 1945, a month following the ceremony marking the Japanese surrender, the base received notification that it was to be placed on inactive status. The final graduation of cadets took place two days later, and on December 31, 1945, the base was officially closed. Exactly 7,008 pilots had earned their wings at Lubbock during the war. Although city leaders launched an earnest campaign to keep the field active, it seemed likely that the region was no longer to be in the military aviation picture.[38]

Mayor Overton Ribble made a trip to Washington to plead for the continuation of base activity, and when agricultural experts released a gloomy forecast that the region's vital cotton crop was all but doomed for the year, the mayor's efforts on behalf of Lubbock Army Airfield were redoubled.

Other, perhaps more experienced, players of the air base game were also involved. Chamber manager A. B. Davis once again began lobbying behind the scenes for the retention of the Lubbock field. Throughout the war, Davis had maintained his personal relationships with various Air Force leaders, entertaining them when they came to town and making sure they still enjoyed plenty of hunting and fishing. As various senior officers retired, Davis wrote each of them glowing letters of praise and gratitude, vowing to remain a close friend to each. By all accounts, he kept his vows.

When it was painfully obvious to all but a zealous few that the base was definitely marked for closure, Davis wrote his old congressional ally George Mahon seeking top-level assistance to avoid what was likely inevitable. In a letter dated November 6, 1945, Mahon informed Davis that the War Department was facing a $30 billion reduction in budgetary funds and that the department was "having its troubles over that." Despite what the congressman deemed the "personal basis" upon which he had built his appeal to keep the airfield open, Mahon conceded that the outlook was bleak indeed. Consequently, he did not feel he should encourage Davis to go to Washington in an effort to once again promote Lubbock as a permanent site for a peacetime air base.[39]

On November 10, A. B. Davis replied. Judging from the tone of his letter, the old campaigner was tired and perhaps more than a little disappointed that his constant public relations effort now accounted for so little. "Of course, down through the years we have done a lot of good with the Army in getting ranking officers on a personal basis at parties for them," Davis wrote to Mahon in Washington, "and on hunting and fishing trips, but my thinking now is that it is too late to do any more of these things."[40]

For a fleeting moment, however, the old A. B. Davis resurfaced. "I have just been wondering," he stated, all but refuting his own argument, "if someone from here was up there and could give a few parties for the right officers . . ." In the next sentence, weariness set in again, and Davis conceded, "frankly, I doubt it would do any good." Underlined in the letter is a phrase that shows that Davis seemingly had accepted the inevitable defeat, "I don't want to go to Washington now." The old lion was finished.[41]

The war was over and the battle for Lubbock Army Airfield was lost. Yet, unlike the scenario in most other Texas cities that had suffered the postwar closure of their military bases but had been given title to the properties, the federal government retained ownership of Lubbock Field. Closed airfields at Pecos, Hondo, and elsewhere, for example, had reverted to public or private ownership only to fall into disrepair and dereliction. Lubbock's field was merely padlocked.

Less than four years later, on August 1, 1949, the field's suddenly unlocked gate swung open again. It is easy to speculate that the seeds of goodwill sown by A. B. Davis, George Mahon, and other energetic Lubbock boosters for decades had proved fertile enough to bring the old World War II base back into full operation. Although the Cold War was showing signs of becoming appreciably warmer when the base was reactivated in 1949, the United States was not involved in actual combat at the time.

The operational catalyst for reopening the old field, now

known as Lubbock Air Force Base, was directly linked to the Cold War, however. When the Strategic Air Command, America's prime weapon in its growing confrontation with the Soviet Union, assumed control of Barksdale Air Force Base in Louisiana on August 3, 1949, it became necessary to transfer the 3500th Pilot Training Wing to another location.[42]

With its long history of excellent relations with the Air Force, Lubbock became the choice for the new home of the abruptly displaced pilot-training wing. On October 26, 1949, after the transfer of the unit was complete, the field's name was again changed, to Reese Air Force Base, in honor of onetime area resident Augustus F. Reese Jr., who had been killed in combat over Sardinia during World War II.[43]

The newly named base rapidly regained its momentum as a major pilot-training installation. Its impact on the economy of Lubbock was both instantaneous and enormous. Shortly after it reopened, the base had more than 2,000 military and civilian personnel assigned to it, with an annual payroll estimated to be in excess of $11 million.[44]

In May 1950 the U.S. Air Force announced that Reese AFB had been designated a permanent installation, immune to the traditional budgetary cutbacks that historically imperiled nearly all military bases. The citizens of Lubbock were both elated and relieved to learn that Reese was apparently to be their neighbor forever.

On June 15–16, 1991, the base celebrated its fiftieth anniversary with an open-house event that attracted thousands of visitors from all across the South Plains. It is possible that the event also saluted the good news that Reese had not been included on the April 1991 base closure list that had just been published. In view of the earlier guarantee that their base was a permanent one, the people of Lubbock had been shocked when news had leaked out of Washington that Reese was being considered for closure.

At the time of the fiftieth anniversary, and the unofficial "we dodged the bullet" celebration, it was announced that the base's annual payroll had risen to nearly $60 million, with approximately 3,100 personnel actually employed on the field. Off-base services generated by Reese also figured significantly in the region's financial well-being. A Lubbock Chamber of Commerce report put all of the statistics into stunning perspective when it revealed that with all factors considered, Reese AFB fueled a full one-third of Lubbock's total economy.[45]

In view of this report, it was unthinkable to civilian and military officials alike that the 3,954-acre air base, with its 1,200,000-square foot building space, all valued at nearly $90 million, would ever lose its coveted permanent-installation status. While the prospect of closure may have been unthinkable to Lubbock's supporters, it was apparently foremost in the minds of the Defense Department experts who determine what base survives and what base dies, regardless of any promises made a half-century earlier.[46]

The possibility of closure hovered over Lubbock for almost six years, but in mid-1997, the long-feared announcement at last came from Washington. Mighty Reese AFB was indeed to be deactivated, its pilots and its planes moved away from the South Plains, this time probably forever. Although the blow to Lubbock was both swift and painful, the bootstrap city managed to absorb the loss in a remarkably short period of time. The base facilities were rapidly converted into Reese Technology Center, with a declared mission to become a world-class research-training and business center. All the while, an expanding Texas Tech University continued to spark the city's growth, as it had since 1923.

Today, Lubbock continues to grow and prosper, even as memories of its once-vital airfield have dimmed. Veterans' groups return to the city from time to time to reminisce about the old days and to tell and retell their stories of war. Many of the men who were once stationed at Lubbock Army Airfield married local girls and came back to live in the city. It says much for Lubbock that these veterans returned to the town for the rest of their lives. "I can't imagine being anywhere else," one former pilot declares, "but I've got to tell you, it just isn't the same with Reese shut down now. I sure miss the sounds of those airplanes taking off and landing day and night. No, sir, it's just not the same anymore."[47]

A. B. Davis did not live to see his beloved Lubbock Airfield die. In his obituary, which appeared in the *Avalanche-Journal* on November 7, 1967, the editors no longer felt obligated to remain silent about the man and his many accomplishments for the city he loved. At long last, he was given full public credit for causing the base to be established, and he was saluted as the man known "throughout the U.S. Air Force as 'Mr. Lubbock.'"[48]

However, a few years after his death, the Air Force created a place of honor at the base for a select group of twelve men who were given the distinction of being designated "Friends of Reese." According to the *History of Reese Air Force Base and 64th Flying Training Wing*, this was "the highest honor the base could bestow on a private citizen." Topping the list was George Mahon, the U.S. congressman who indeed had done much to bring the airfield to Lubbock in 1940. Absent from the list, however, still far from the glare of public acclaim, was the late A. B. Davis, the man who had truly orchestrated the entire process from start to finish.[49]

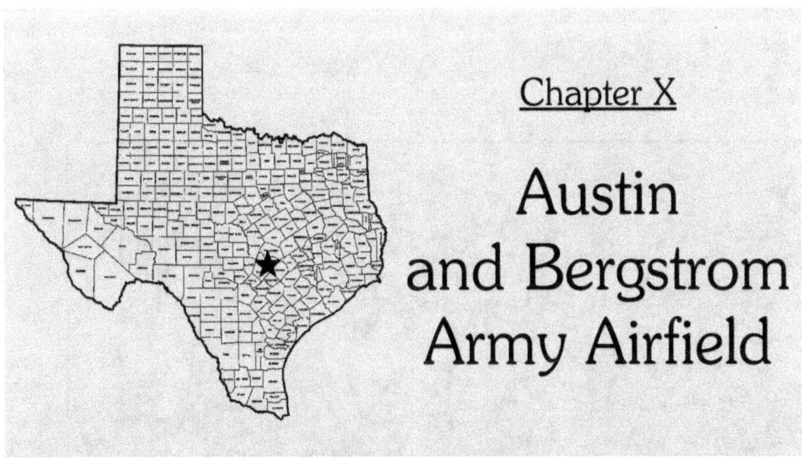

Chapter X

Austin and Bergstrom Army Airfield

I think we can all fully understand that Stephen F. Austin could easily have had his pick of any land located within his massive grant to claim as his own personal homestead. According to his papers, however, the empresario had his eye on "some rough mountain land, well-watered by springs, with wild scenery" situated on the banks of the upper Colorado River. There, Austin initially hoped to build a working farm, but his longer range plans called for "the establishment of an academy" which he hoped would serve to benefit "all those who might come to Texas."

W. Harris Schaeffer
East Texas Historical Association
March 4, 1953

Stephen F. Austin, empresario and founder of Anglo-American Texas, held managerial control of millions of acres of land in the years immediately prior to the Texas Revolution of 1836. When he found good reason to choose a sizable tract of land for his personal use, however, he selected only several thousand verdant acres on the Colorado River, eighty miles or so northeast of San Antonio, just outside his area of immediate control. Austin, fatigued from his constant travails with the Mexican government and his often frustrating duties as empresario, sought a refuge for his retirement years. His death in 1836 cut short those plans, but

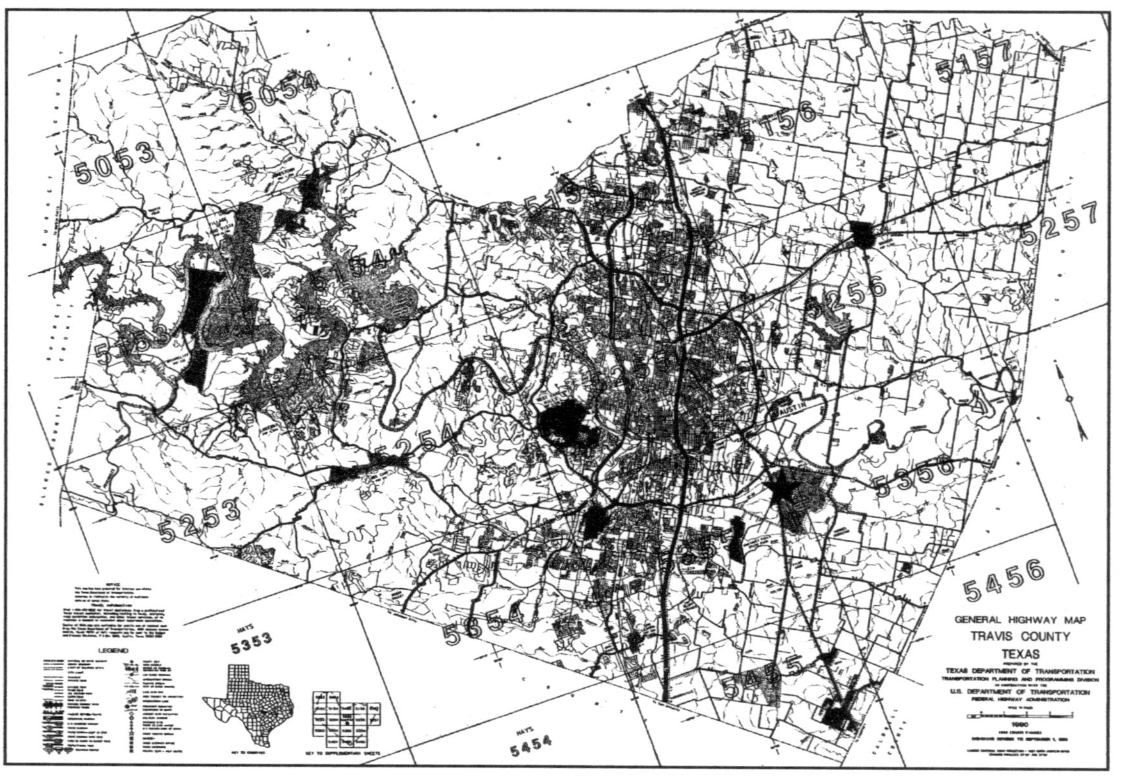

Travis County Map

This map of Travis County shows the location of Bergstrom Army Airfield during the war years. An inset map of Texas shows the location of the county within the state.

the tract of land he had desired above all others in Anglo-Texas now comprises a large portion of what is today Austin, Texas. The academy that he hoped to establish on his land did in fact come into being as the University of Texas many years after his death. In 1839, with Stephen F. Austin gone but the Republic of Texas very much alive, an appropriate site was needed to become the capital city of the new republic. Over the objections of many prominent Texans, including General Sam Houston, Mirabeau B. Lamar, the Republic's president, selected 640 acres out of Stephen F. Austin's original 7,735-acre tract to be the location of the capital of the Republic and promptly announced that the town to be built on the site would be named in honor of the land's original owner.[1]

Never one to waste time, President Lamar saw to it that the new capital would be ready to host the Texas legislative session of November 1839. Hastily constructed temporary buildings were erected to accommodate the legislators of the Texas Congress, and the tiny town seemed primed to flourish. By the time the gavel fell convening the first session of the Republic's legislature, residential lots were being auctioned, a church had been established, and a newspaper was being printed. Just under a thousand permanent inhabitants were in residence at the beginning of the next year, as were diplomats from England, France, and the United States.[2]

However, despite this deceptively auspicious beginning, Austin's days as the capital city of the Republic were short-lived. When General Houston succeeded Lamar as president in 1842, he immediately ordered all of the young government's records removed to what he considered a safer location at Houston, the city he had arranged to be named for himself. Military incursions by Mexico in March 1842 saw San Antonio again fall into foreign hands, and the new president, who had by no means ever been a supporter of Austin as a capital, found this reason enough for the rapid transfer of the government.

Houston's unilateral action was not at all well-received in Austin, and local citizens and militiamen attempted to forcibly prevent the movement of the records. This resistance triggered the so-called Archive War, which at once proved both acrimonious and futile. The seat of the Republic stayed only briefly in General Houston's namesake city before moving once again, in

1845, to Washington-on-the-Brazos, which was to be the final capital of the Republic just prior to its annexation by the United States.

While the government's records and its leaders were shuffling about from town to town, the once-promising city of Austin languished and all but disappeared. By 1845 the population of the formerly bustling village had dropped to fewer than two hundred hardy souls.[3]

With the annexation of Texas to the United States in 1845, however, the citizens of America's newest state voted to return its government to Austin for a trial period of at least twenty years. In an effort to ensure that this be the permanent location for the capital, key state and local leaders saw to it that new buildings were erected and provisions made for future expansion of the seat of government. By 1850 the town's population had again reached nearly a thousand inhabitants.[4]

By 1860 Austin had more than tripled in size, but as the threat of civil war loomed ominously in the eastern United States, concerns for the economic future of Texas caused the state's growth to slow. Even though area residents voted against secession from the Union by a margin of 704 to 450, Texas nonetheless became a Confederate state on February 1, 1861.[5]

Following the devastating war, Austin resumed its role as the capital of the reunited nation's largest state. By 1870, five years after the Civil War had ended, the town's population had reached 4,428. The first railroad to serve the Austin region arrived the following year, making the city a trade center and causing the population to double by 1876. When a second rail line then bypassed the town a short time later, however, growth slowed once again.

In 1883 the opening of the University of Texas at last ensured the continued growth of Austin and virtually guaranteed its future. When subsequent efforts to attract major industry failed, the city fathers drafted a farsighted plan in 1928 that called for Austin to forego additional efforts to attract industry and to concentrate instead on the political and educational strengths it already possessed. This wise decision, coupled with the subsequent efforts of Mayor Tom Miller and Congressman Lyndon B. Johnson in the late 1930s and early 1940s to bring significant federal flood control and concomitant federal water and electrical power projects to the region, placed Austin firmly in a position to become a progressive and stable major municipality.[6]

A further collective, if often rancorous, effort on the part of the mayor and his congressional colleague gave Austin another powerful asset from which it would benefit for decades to come. In 1940, as world conditions clearly indicated that America was likely to become involved in a war of major proportions, Miller and Johnson set about procuring some form of national defense activity for the Austin vicinity. Through their skillful and forceful leadership, that activity eventually took shape as Bergstrom Army Airfield.

BERGSTROM ARMY AIRFIELD

Just before I got my orders for Bergstrom, I heard from a couple of my buddies who'd been sent to Pecos and Big Spring, so when I saw Austin and that great big school full of beautiful gals, I knew the gods had smiled on me.

Ernie L. Blumenthal
Chicago, Illinois

The land upon which Lyndon Johnson and Tom Miller were to create Austin's wartime airfield had a colorful history that stretched back for well over a century. On March 8, 1832, Don Santiago Del Valle obtained a grant from his employer, the Mexican government, for the eleven leagues of raw land that would many years later become an airfield. The huge tract of some 35,424 acres cost Don Santiago a mere 1,100 pesos, even though it was well-irrigated by the Colorado River and obviously very fertile. To ensure that his claim to the land would not be easily disputed, the new owner gave his family name to the entire area.[7]

Even though his newly acquired land seemed to hold great potential for agriculture, Don Santiago was apparently more interested in dealing in real estate than in crops. By 1846 sections of the vast property had been sold to a group headed by Thomas Freeman McKinney, an early Texas entrepreneur and associate of Señor Del Valle. The McKinney group acquired much of Del Valle's holdings for less than 75 cents per acre before dividing it into smaller parcels that promptly sold for more than $5 per acre.[8]

The growth of Austin, just six miles to the northwest, quickly created a demand for the fertile land around the Del Valle community. By 1878 there was a post office, and within ten years, there were three churches, a general store, a school, and fifty inhabitants mostly living on large estates. With the coming of the Great Depression in the late 1930s, demand for Del Valle's agricultural products dwindled, and the little community's prospects for continued growth were considered dim at best. America's sudden entry into World War II in December 1941, however, served to quickly change the rural face of Del Valle for all time.

According to a somewhat naive history of Bergstrom Field written by an Army historian in 1943, the decision by the War Department to transform the idyllic Del Valle countryside, with its "peaceful landscape," into a military installation was an arbitrary and almost whimsical one. The historian noted that after surveying the Austin area from the air, government representatives had easily identified 3,000 of Del Valle's acres as the best possible site for a new Army airfield. The 1943 account goes on to relate that in November 1941, the Army then simply notified the Austin Chamber of Commerce of its interest in acquiring the highly desired acreage "if possible."[9]

Other, perhaps more credible, accounts, indicate that Austin's business and political leaders, namely Congressman Johnson and Mayor Miller, had in fact long been pressuring the Army to locate some kind of defense installation in or near the city as soon as possible in anticipation of America's likely entry into the war already engulfing Europe and Asia. In a letter to Johnson dated April 9, 1941, Mayor Miller told the congressman of Austin's "fervent desire" to get some kind of defense installation, preferably an air base. Recognizing both the short-term benefits of massive construction and military payrolls and the long-range prospects for a postwar civilian airport to succeed a wartime Army airfield that might be built, the mayor indicated that his city was even willing to buy the land for the air base and lease it to the government for the customary token fee of one dollar per year.[10]

The November 29, 1941, visit to Austin by the Army survey team so casually mentioned in the airfield's history in all likelihood came about directly as a result of Johnson's well-known powers of persuasion, which in this instance coincided with the War Department's urgent need to find sites for new military airfields before the already raging world war involved the United States.

The base historian's account of the selection of Del Valle as Austin's wartime facility indicates that Mayor Miller for some obscure reason apparently attempted to discourage the Army in its choice of the Del Valle site. No explanation is given as to why the mayor, who had worked for at least six months toward arousing the Army's interest in his community, would suddenly find reason to create obstacles to the chosen site. One possibility might be that the Austin City Council, having committed to buy the approximately 3,000 acres the War Department required, hoped to find a less expensive tract of land elsewhere in the immediate vicinity. One account makes the unlikely claim that the mayor was reluctant to take Del Valle's valuable farmland out of agricultural production, while another historian believes that Miller did not want to dispossess the area's inhabitants for some unrecorded humanitarian reason.[11]

Whatever the motive behind the city government's uncharacteristic hesitation to acquire land to obtain a guaranteed federal windfall, a concentrated effort was indeed expended to dissuade the Army in its vigorous pursuit of the Del Valle site. The Austin Chamber of Commerce provided food and lodging at the city's prestigious Driskill Hotel for the Army survey team for over a month while local officials took them on daily tours to inspect possible alternate air base sites.[12]

At the end of the month-long visit, the wining, dining, and inspecting proved futile when the Army team refused to budge from its original intent to build its airfield in Del Valle. As the base historian succinctly put it in his 1943 text, "the Army knew what it wanted."[13]

What the Army so singlemindedly wanted was 3,000 acres of flat land with good highway access and with all utilities either in place or readily available. The very first flyover by the Army's survey aircraft had apparently told the officers nearly all they needed to know about the desirability of the Del Valle site. It was quite obviously big enough and flat enough, and it was well-served by state and county roadways.

Curiously, this rather cursory flyover method of airport site selection had been employed by the federal government once before in the Austin area. In 1927 the Army had been asked by the city to find a likely site for the construction of its first municipal airport. The service had willingly obliged, sending one of its pilots north from San Antonio's Kelly Field with instructions to fly over the Austin vicinity to determine just where an airport might be situated. The pilot chosen for that important mission was Lt. Claire L. Chennault, who later rose to fame in the skies over China during World War II. Chennault selected a location that the city apparently accepted without question.[14]

Fourteen years later, the Japanese attack on Pearl Harbor not only thrust the United States into World War II, but also accelerated interest in building an Army airfield near Austin. On January 3, 1942, the Army formally asked Austin's city government if it would indeed be willing to acquire the acreage long before specified by the survey team as a suitable site for an airfield. With no trace of the curious earlier reluctance, the mayor and his city council quickly committed to proceed at long last with the acquisition of the Del Valle site.

Having told the War Department that it would buy the land outright, it obviously became immediately necessary for the city to raise the funds with which to make the purchase. Plans were promptly put in place to hold a bond election on March 4, 1942, to raise the $600,000 that would likely be needed.[15]

A newspaper article dated February 17, 1942, noted that the city had tried desperately to keep the proposed airfield project a secret from other Texas communities, located in the domain of some unnamed but nonetheless "rival congressman." The article went on to rather dryly note that since the city government had so openly been seeking price quotes on acreage in the Del Valle area for some weeks, the whole airfield project and the likely location had "scarcely been a secret."[16]

The citizens of Austin, exposed to a vigorous pro-airfield campaign in the local newspaper, easily passed the bond issue by a margin of fifty-to-one. Curiously, the turnout at the polling place was quite light in view of the obvious significance of having a large military installation come to the area. According to the *Austin Statesman* of March 4, only some 1,500 voters were projected to cast their ballots. In a city whose total population in 1942 was estimated to be well over 100,000, the meager showing at the polls must have proved disconcerting to the city fathers and particularly to the local newspapers that had wholeheartedly promoted passage of the bond issue.[17]

Embarrassed or not by the apparent lack of public interest in the airfield project, the city government swiftly sent a cashier's check in the amount of $466,600 to the government to be used to buy the 2,750-acre parcel finally acquired for War Department use. Along with the check, dated March 9, 1942, went a note asking that after the price for the parcel had been finally resolved, any money not expended be returned to the City of Austin. Moreover, the note further stated that if the amount covered by the check was insufficient to consummate the purchase, the City was willing to send an additional check to Washington to make up any shortfall.[18]

Even with the check in the mail and the promise of more checks if needed, negotiations between Austin and the federal government became very delicate. Austin wanted to hold the title to the land and lease it to the federal government, which in turn would be expected to arrange and pay for all improvements on the site. The War Department, on the other hand, insisted on holding clear title to the land until after the war. Further, Austin demanded that the whole entity, including all improvements, should revert to the City when the Army no longer needed it, while the War Department held a differing opinion. As the intensity of World War II increased overseas, both sides were under mounting pressure to resolve the differences so that construction could commence. In the end, the City of Austin agreed to grant title to the land to the federal government for the duration of the war, and both sides agreed to let the question of the timing of postwar reversion remain unresolved. Some fifty years later, the lack of resolution on the reversion matter would again become a thorny issue.

When the negotiations between Austin and the War Department became most crucial, city leaders again turned to the office of Congressman Lyndon B. Johnson for assistance. By early 1942, however, the congressman had joined the Navy and had been dispatched to the southwest Pacific on a fact-finding mission. In his absence, the day-to-day workings of his office had come under the direction of his highly capable wife, Lady Bird. Working closely with Mayor Tom Miller, Mrs. Johnson quietly brought the negotiations to a successful conclusion. An article in the March 14, 1942, edition of the *Austin Statesman* reported that she had just notified city officials that the new base had at last been "Okayed" by the War Department. In the same article, an apparently euphoric Tom Miller publicly thanked Lyndon Johnson for his work on obtaining the airfield, but the efforts of the congressman's wife were not mentioned.[19]

In an oral history interview conducted in 1980, Mrs. Johnson recalled that she had asked an assistant secretary of war to let her know ahead of anyone else once a decision about the airfield had been reached. "We wanted the announcement to come from the congressman's [LBJ's] office, so people would know that he was on the job, his deputy [herself] was on the job still working for them."[20]

Evidently, there were still lingering questions, even though the base was now approved. The mayor addressed the subject of postwar use of the soon-to-be-constructed airfield, although in somewhat guarded terms. In view of the new airfield which "will supposedly revert to the city for use as an airport" after the war, he announced that Austin's government had determined not to spend an estimated $100,000 to build a suitable terminal at the city's Robert Mueller Municipal Airport. According to Austin City Manager Guiton Morgan, until the war ended, "air travelers alighting at the municipal airport will have to continue to sneer at the meager accommodations."[21]

By late May 1942, any civilian air travelers who had been given to sneering at Austin's aviation activities quite likely had second thoughts. Approaching the city from the southeast, incoming airliners flew within sight of the massive construction project that would soon become an Army airfield. Some thirty large homes had been removed from the Del Valle site, along with "innumerable tenant houses." The schools and churches that had marked the progress of the little community for decades had been demolished to make way for hangars, runways, and barracks.

Some 1,600 men working for the Austin construction firm of Montgomery, Page, Hemphill and Page were rapidly clearing, leveling, and paving most of the vast acreage that only weeks before had been fields of cotton and groves of pecans. Additional workers were constantly being sought to keep up with the accelerated construction timetable. The chamber of commerce launched an employment campaign to recruit the men so urgently needed to keep the project on schedule.[22]

The first official history of the base states that an average of ten to fifteen buildings were being erected each day during the summer months and into the early autumn of 1942. In addition to hangars, ramps, and taxiways, six paved runways were soon completed, the longest measuring 7,000 feet in length.[23]

On September 19, less than four months after work had commenced, the field was officially activated as the Del Valle Army Air Base. Initially, the facility was intended for photographic and observer training, but changes in the Army Air Force's needs soon caused the mission to become an Air Support Command facility. Within weeks, the base's role was again changed, to become part of the Troop Carrier Command. According to the base history, pilots trained in single-engine aircraft came to Del Valle to learn to fly larger multi-engine transport airplanes such as the C-47. The pilots also received extensive instruction in low-altitude flying, navigation, code communication, and "flying techniques," whatever that term might have meant.[24]

Strong evidence of Del Valle's air-transport mission was presented to the citizens of Austin on September 29 when fifty C-47 aircraft of the 316th Troop Carrier Group flew in from Georgia in what was described at the time as the "largest mass flight of transport planes in the history of aviation." The formation flew proudly if noisily over the city of Austin before landing at Del Valle Airfield at three-second intervals. The commanding officer of the 316th, Lt. Col. Jerome B. McCauley, piloted the lead plane in the gigantic formation.[25]

On October 11, just two weeks after Colonel McCauley brought his flight of C-47s to Del Valle, the base chapel was officially opened. Dr. Homer P. Rainey, the president of the nearby University of Texas, gave the opening address, while the Reverend J. H. McCauley, the colonel's father, delivered the sermon. The chapel was of the classic military design seen on installations all across the nation, complete with an impressive spire and a sparkling coat of bright white paint.[26]

Other buildings on the hastily constructed airfield were without exception far less imposing than the chapel. The exterior walls of the barracks were covered with black tarpaper, and a few had only dirt floors. Some of the larger buildings, such as the base exchange and the officers' clubs, had somewhat more impressive interiors, but to most passersby who felt inclined to comment, the outward appearance of the entire base was definitely that of the "early-Depression era."[27]

Colonel McCauley and his 316th Troop Carrier Group did not have long to consider the unattractiveness of the new base. On November 4, 1942, the entire unit was ordered to fly to North Africa to participate in the Anglo-American offensive against the forces of Gen. Erwin Rommel. Again, the group flew toward its new assignment in a massed formation, arriving without incident. After months of surveying, negotiating, and constructing, Austin, Texas, had at last actually gotten into the war.[28]

On January 10, 1943, the nearly completed airfield staged an open house to thank Austinites for their support. While only 1,500 had bothered to vote in the bond-issue election called to raise funds to acquire the base, over 30,000 local citizens eagerly responded to the invitation to visit it. In addition to a tour of the facilities, the visitors were treated to a flyover of glider aircraft, a demonstration of chemical warfare, and a fairly realistic mock battle involving tractors simulating tanks and jeeps "playing the role of armored vehicles." According to the base history, the Del Valle event was the first of its kind to be held on any military installation since the war had started. "It established," the history recorded, "a closer connection between the City of Austin and the Base, a feeling of neighborliness and friendship."[29]

By most accounts, Austin did enjoy friendly relations with its new military neighbors during the World War II years. There were some early complaints by citizens about aircraft flying low over the city, and eventually an order from the base commander instructed pilots to avoid flying over the city whenever possible and to forego any overt buzzing of Austin buildings. When complaints of low-flying aircraft continued to reach his office, the commander, believing his pilots to be innocent of such misadventures, sent letters to other nearby bases asking that they avoid Austin's civil airspace.[30]

Perhaps as a result of a negative impression gained by some of its members during the January open house, Austin's garden clubs initiated a program to beautify the base as much as possible, despite the less-than-appealing tarpaper buildings that existed on it. Evergreens and fruit trees were planted, streets were bordered with shrubbery, the flagpole island received tall pink yucca, and "the bed south of Base Headquarters [was] planted thick with several hundred roses."[31]

Apparently, the Army's efforts to be friendly and neighborly with the civilian community bore fruit, at least if judged by the number of weddings held in the base chapel during the course of the war. In the city, the USO served as the key meeting place for the airmen and the local girls. Although dating of USO volunteers by the military men was officially prohibited, the rule was constantly overlooked. Austinites frequently opened their homes to the fliers, and various clubs staged dances and parties to entertain the men and to introduce them to the many young ladies who attended the university.

Numerous athletic events pitted the men from the airfield against teams from the University of Texas and Texas A&M. On one occasion, the Air Force team dared to challenge a baseball squad fielded by the Internal Revenue Service's Austin headquarters. As is all too often the case, the challenge to the IRS proved futile, with the agency winning the game handily.[32]

When not engaged in athletic contests, off-duty airmen enjoyed a variety of other activities at facilities located on the base. A large recreation hall boasted such state-of-the-art appliances as a radio and a music box, along with Ping-Pong tables, a library, and "almost of greatest importance during warm weather, a good sized Coke machine." A theater, featuring both training films and feature motion pictures, adjoined the recreation hall.[33]

Despite the prevailing descriptions of the Del Valle Airfield as a Depression-era eyesore even with its civilian-provided colorful landscaping, the post exchange was apparently one of the most attractive such facilities in the country in the early 1940s. The overall design motif was described as "Rancho Southwest," with all fixtures and decorations made of Texas cedar. The counters and showcases were faced with unfinished split logs of cedar, and the countertops were of the same material, "clear varnished to show the full beauty of the natural wood." Ceiling, office walls, and even doors were of cedar, and the lighting was from fluorescent tubes that gave "a pleasant illumination" to the enormous room that was, not surprisingly, "at all times heavy with the fragrance of cedar."[34]

On March 3, 1943, Del Valle Army Airfield had its name changed in an effort once again spearheaded by the office of Congressman Lyndon Johnson. Reacting to the pleas of a close associate who was the vice president of the Austin National Bank, Johnson launched an all-out campaign to change Del Valle's name to Bergstrom Army Airfield in honor of Capt. John August Earl Bergstrom, a former employee of the bank and reportedly the first Austinite to be killed in the war.

Captain Bergstrom, a reserve infantry officer, had been called to active duty in October 1941 and sent to Clark Army Airfield in the Philippines as an administrative officer. He was killed on the first day of hostilities when the Imperial Japanese Air Force bombed Clark Field on December 8, 1941.

Johnson, never easily dissuaded, was eventually able to override the Army's objections to naming a facility for a local hero, and Del Valle's new name officially became Bergstrom Army Airfield. On November 11, 1943, the name of the base was shortened to simply Bergstrom Field.[35]

Shortly after the Del Valle name was dropped, the first members of the Women's Army Corps (WAC) arrived at Bergstrom Field. In an effort to provide the new arrivals with some degree of privacy, base officials leveled a small parade ground for their use and created an enclosure of trelliswork for their outdoor recreational activities. Five buildings were designated for the WACs, placed "far away from everything else," as the base history reported. In addition to the three barracks, the WAC compound included an administration building and a day room complete with a beauty parlor. It was also noted that while the buildings were neat and clean, the entire WAC area was "without a tree to shade them."[36]

Although she tried to avoid publicity, one comely WAC private attracted attention by virtue of her family connections. She was Pauline Ogden, the wife of a brigadier general and the cousin of Lt. Gen. Jacob Devers, commander of all U.S. Army forces in the European theater of operations.[37]

The Officers' Club, strategically located well away from the treeless WAC compound, boasted a setting of evergreen shrubbery as well as a broad verandah. The interior gave the impression of a luxurious country club, with red leather seating throughout, a massive stone fireplace, and a bar constructed of glass bricks. The dining room reportedly served an average of 6,000 meals each month to officers, their families, and their visitors.[38]

Perhaps just in case the opulence of the Officers' Club lulled at least some of its personnel into a false sense of security, it was determined to stage what was termed a "baptism of fire" mock attack on the base on June 8, 1943. Beginning at 8:00 in the morning on the day of the impending attack, all base personnel were required to go about their duties wearing their gas masks in anticipation of the mock air raid that all knew was soon coming their way. The actual zero hour, the moment of truth for the so-called baptism of fire, was a closely guarded secret, but a series of thirty-second blasts of the alert siren commencing at 1:30 P.M. left no doubt that the attack was imminent. The gates to the base were instantly closed, and no one was allowed to enter or leave the field.

Apparently in an effort to create an aura of realism, smudgepot smoke bombs were ignited, promptly blanketing the whole base area with thick, dirty clouds of foul-smelling smoke. Just what possible enemy action might have included the use of smudgepots was not explained. Aircraft were rapidly deployed to Austin's Robert Mueller Airport, "there to hide until needed," according to the base history. Surely an inbound enemy air force would not notice many C-47s sitting on the ramps at the municipal airport. Other base aircraft were taxied through the smoke to various remote sections of the field to avoid becoming part of a massed target.

Other base aircraft were assigned the role of attack planes and, after taking off, turned back to the runway they had just left to drop flour-sack bombs. Yellow gravel was also thrown from the hatches of the mock attack planes to simulate machine gun bullets, and men on the ground fired blank ammunition in the general direction of the diving aircraft. Bombs that had been secretly planted in various unpopulated areas of the field were set off by ground detonators, while trucks were hurriedly driven to the active runway to form a barricade to deter any "enemy" pilot who might be foolish enough to attempt to land amid the dense smoke and pelting gravel.

The chaos continued for a full hour before the all-clear siren sounded. Although base officials claimed that the exercise was an unqualified success, one enlisted man found the whole affair more than slightly ridiculous. "It was just plain silly," said Jerry Lawrence. "I guess people did what they were supposed to do, but most of them were laughing so hard they could hardly do anything." As the base history noted, "Around three o'clock, the gates were opened again, the cars began to drive in and out, [and] the smoke clouds blew away."[39]

As amusing as the mock attack might have been to some, few if any Bergstrom personnel found much to laugh about in the base's regular training routine as the war continued. By early 1944, it had become widely known that the Troop Carrier Command would be taking part in the forthcoming invasion of Hitler's Germany. Planes carrying paratroopers, and those towing combat personnel-laden gliders, were seen as key components of the planned cross-Channel invasion, and the men and aircraft of Bergstrom Field were vital parts of those components. As foreseen, planes from the airfield were in the thick of the action when the long-awaited invasion took place on June 6, 1944.

Following the surrender of Nazi Germany shortly thereafter, and the formal capitulation of Japan in September of 1945, the world again became, at least temporarily, peaceful. The beginning of massive reductions in America's military forces caused many to wonder and worry about the future of Bergstrom Field. It had been a good neighbor to Austin and a significant contributor to a strong economy.

Once again, Lyndon B. Johnson weighed in on behalf of the airfield he had done so much to obtain for the Texas capital. He vigorously pressured the Army Air Force's top generals in an effort to exclude Bergstrom from the growing list of air bases marked for closure. Although much reserve activity was in time materially reduced, the big base remained open, seemingly shielded by Johnson's powerful protective arms. In fact, by 1949, rather than being closed, the field began receiving federal funds for new building programs.[40]

By protecting Bergstrom, Johnson and his colleagues were intent on maintaining and expanding the field's invaluable contribution to the community's economic well-being. By 1947 it was estimated that Bergstrom Field generated $5 million in spending in the Austin area. Its monthly payroll at the time equaled a stunning 92 percent of the total University of Texas payroll, while some $60 million was spent by the base on supplies each year. Clearly, Austin needed Bergstrom.

For many more years, the U.S. Air Force needed Bergstrom as well. From 1945 through September 1993, various Air Force commands continued to make the base a vital part of America's defense force. The Troop Carrier Command gave way to the Strategic Air Command in late 1948, and elements from Bergstrom Air Force Base participated in the Korean War in the early 1950s. By 1957 the base was reassigned to the Tactical Air Command, but just over a year later, the field was again controlled by the Strategic Air Command.

As president of the United States in the mid-1960s, former congressman Lyndon Johnson often flew in and out of Bergstrom on his frequent visits to his Texas White House. During one winter trip from Washington, the president commented on how much he was looking forward to seeing the green grass of Texas rather than the brown grass he had observed on the dormant lawns of the nation's capital. To his loudly proclaimed dismay, he found that an unusually severe winter had caused the normally verdant grass at Bergstrom to assume a distinctly Washington-like shade of brown. When the base commander learned of Johnson's displeasure over the unexpected color of Bergstrom's lawns, he ordered that henceforth, any brown grass along the president's usual route as he drove from or to the field was to be dyed a natural-looking green color. No record exists to indicate if Mr. Johnson ever speculated why only certain parts of Bergstrom AFB could somehow manage to maintain brightly green grass despite the severest of Texas winters.[41]

In 1966 it was announced that the field with perennially green grass, at least that part along what had been designated Presidential Boulevard, was to become the new headquarters of the Twelfth Air Force, dispelling any nagging rumors that the base was among those even remotely being considered for closure. As evidence of the airfield's apparently secure future, a huge doughnut-shaped headquarters building was constructed. With one floor below grade level and two above and a circular atrium at its core, the building contained over 120,000 square feet of office space. In time, it also contained massive colonies of Mexican free-tailed bats that somehow seemed to delight in the building's unusual circular design. Valiant efforts by base engineers and local exterminators proved futile as the bats somehow continued to gain almost unlimited access to the interior of the building.[42]

As the bats and the Twelfth Air Force high command learned how to coexist in their shared round building, Austin was experiencing a population growth and expansion that virtually surrounded the city's Robert Mueller Municipal Airport. Consequently, a consulting firm was retained to study the problem and to recommend a solution to the growing municipal airport problem. Among the alternative plans suggested was a joint-use scheme at Bergstrom that would have commercial and military aircraft sharing the base's runways to alleviate the congestion and safety problems at the existing city-operated air facility. The Air Force quickly rejected this concept.

As the congestion and noise problems at Robert Mueller Airport worsened, the man who was perhaps Bergstrom's greatest champion made his final flights from the runways he had made possible. On January 24, 1973, the body of Lyndon Baines Johnson was placed on board Air Force One for a final trip to Washington, where approximately 40,000 mourners would pay their respects. The next day, the presidential aircraft brought the body of the thirty-sixth president back to Texas for burial at his beloved LBJ Ranch. The funeral procession made its way out of Bergstrom Air Force Base, moving slowly along a wide boulevard trimmed with grass significantly tinted a beautiful green, despite cold temperatures of a harsh late January day.[43]

It is easy to speculate that even had such an advocate as Lyndon Johnson still been in the White House, the closing of Bergstrom could not have been avoided as the twentieth century wound down. A surging Austin needed a new, bigger municipal airport and the Air Force required fewer bases. By 1990 the base was listed as a candidate for closure, and by 1993, despite last-minute negotiations and political maneuvers, nearly all of the Air Force had left it forever. Only skeleton elements remained, along with several reserve components. The City of Austin, faced with the loss of an estimated $317 million in military payroll and 10,000 jobs, was on the one hand justifiably concerned. Yet, under orders to either close down its municipal airport or comply with a State of Texas directive to soundproof thirty-nine churches and eight public buildings in the airport's immediate vicinity, Austin clearly needed the runways and less-crowded acreage that a closed Bergstrom could provide. The decision to occupy the Air Force's once mighty installation was one easily reached by the city fathers. The Bergstrom-Austin Community Council, a unique thirty-year-old, non-political civic organization, played a significant role in facilitating the decision.[44]

There was one nettlesome problem, however. No one, nation or city, seemed to know who actually owned the giant base. Record searches showed very clearly that no contract nor written agreement had ever existed between the City of Austin and the United States of America. Even though the city had assumed in 1942 that the land and all improvements would revert to it if Bergstrom ever closed, that assumption was based largely on wishful thinking.[45] All the same, on January 9, 1992, the *Austin American-Statesman* carried a lead story announcing that a Justice Department ruling had determined that Bergstrom, land, runways, and buildings, presumably including a sizeable population of bats, were now the property of Austin, Texas, free of any charge.[46]

In the face of such a windfall, the city moved with amazing speed for such a large community. In May 1993, Austin voters approved by 63 percent a $400 million revenue bond to create a new airport at the Bergstrom location. Just four months later, the base officially closed, and the property legally reverted to Austin's ownership. On November 19, 1994, with all legal issues resolved, ground was broken for the city's new airport. With an all-too-rare civic tribute to military heritage, it was decided that the modern facility would carry the proud title of Austin-Bergstrom International Airport.[47]

On May 23, 1999, the impressive, state-of-the-art air center opened for passenger service. No longer would air travelers arriving in Austin have any reason to sneer at the city's terminal building. Dedicated to Barbara Jordan, Texas's legendary stateswoman, the terminal is sleek, functional, and contemporary. The airport's main runway, originally built to accommodate the huge B-52s of the Strategic Air Command, appropriately bears the name of Bergstrom's principal advocate, Lyndon B. Johnson.

The transition from active Air Force base to modern commercial air center had been relatively seamless, given the initial confusion over ownership of the property. A few relics of the military era remain, but only the immense Air Force–built main runway and the doughnut-shaped headquarters were readily identifiable. Plans called for the former roosting spot for bats to be refurbished as an airport hotel. In a sense, the melding of the past with the present creates a viable foundation for Austin's even brighter future, a future that will owe much to the still-palpable legacy of historic Bergstrom Field.

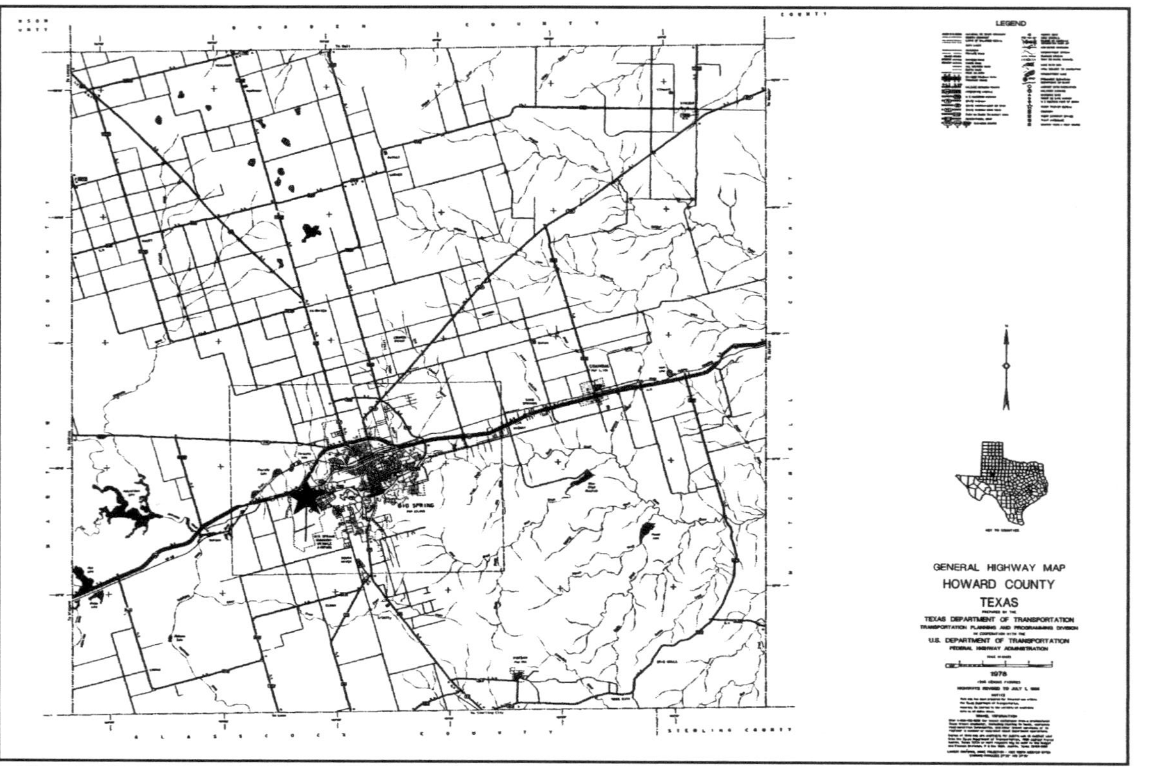

Howard County Map

This map of Howard County shows the location of Big Spring Army Airfield during the war years. An inset map of Texas shows the location of the county within the state.

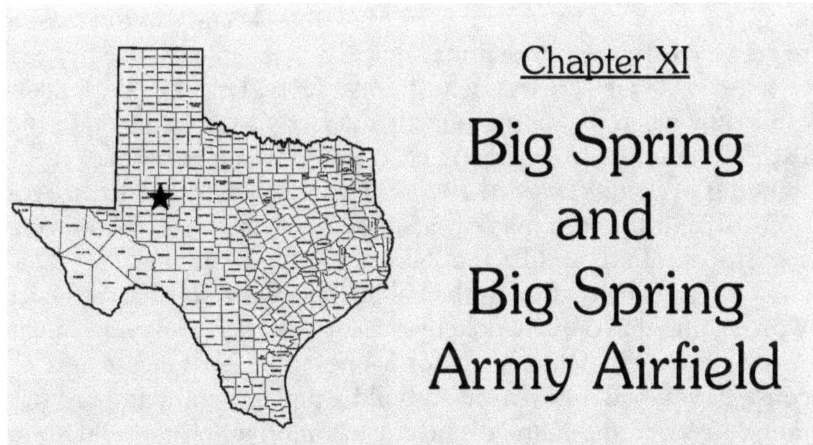

Chapter XI

Big Spring and Big Spring Army Airfield

*I never seen [*sic*] as many of them critters [bison] in one place as I usually did around that big spring out there on Marcy's Trail. They'd seem to just hunker down around it for weeks and we'd put down near as many as we wanted to every day.*

J. R. Bonifield
Buffalo Hunter
1880

On a cool October day in 1849, the intrepid Capt. Randolph B. Marcy became the first U.S. Army officer to make official note of the natural big spring from which a town would eventually take both its name and its water. Under government orders to seek and mark a clear route between Fort Smith, Arkansas, and Santa Fe, New Mexico, Marcy, guided by his Native American guide Manuel, had followed well-used Indian trails to the spring on his return from the western terminus of his newly created overland trail.[1]

Although gold-hunting or adventure-seeking pioneers had followed Marcy's route for more than thirty years, permanent settlement of the area around the spring, one of Texas's rare natural reservoirs, was slow to develop. When the massive herds of bison that had long dominated the area were finally annihilated by hunters such as J. R. Bonifield, only bone gatherers, a handful of hardy travelers, and a few enterprising saloon keepers found reason to stay close to the giant spring.

As was true across much of West Texas, lasting development came only when the railroads made their way westward toward the Pacific Ocean. In 1879, greatly encouraged by the state's generous standing offer to reward the railway companies with sixteen sections of land for each mile of mainline track that it laid, surveying crews of the Texas and Pacific Railway explored the area.

As the construction of the rail line moved westward from Fort Worth along the route marked by the surveyors, the tiny settlement around the spring flourished for a brief time. Advance teams of construction workers arrived to build a pipeline and pumping station to service the railroad's steam locomotives that would soon arrive, and more tented saloons to service the construction workers promptly appeared. As the rails came closer, the little community moved some two miles to the north to be nearer the proposed site of the Texas and Pacific's railway depot. When the train station finally opened, it was given the appropriate name of Big Spring, Texas.

On May 26, 1881, regular rail service finally rolled into Big Spring from the East. The rough frontier settlement that had so eagerly awaited the coming of the railroad began to both grow and improve. By the end of 1881, the Texas and Pacific had opened maintenance shops at its new division point, and company personnel and their families began to move into what just months before had been for the most part a brawling, cowboy-dominated, raw-whiskey town. Rail traffic flowed through Big Spring from both the Atlantic and Pacific coasts as America's long-cherished dream of a transcontinental railway system at last became a reality.

Within a year of the arrival of the railroad, the village had voted to organize, having just become the seat of government of newly created Howard County. By 1884 the town had a post office, a newspaper, four general stores, and a population of just over 1,000. Apparently not completely weaned from its tumultuous past, the county seat also generously supported six saloons.

Even with its enviable location on the mainline of the Texas and Pacific, however, the moderately reformed village of Big Spring grew slowly. By 1900 the population had increased by only fifty-five people. Within a few years, however, expanding agricultural activities began to take full advantage of the rail service. The area soon experienced an accelerated growth, and by 1920, over 4,000 citizens lived in the town.[2]

The breaking-up of the region's huge cattle ranches into smaller homesteads did much to encourage growth and development, but Big Spring and the entire region soon virtually exploded with the discovery of vast quantities of oil and gas beneath the West Texas prairie land. When the Owens and Sloan No. 1 Chalk well blew into life on the Chalk Ranch in April 1926, the oil boom was on, and the Big Spring region became a major petroleum center.[3]

Within four short years, the town's population more than tripled, while that of the county increased fourfold. New businesses flocked to the area as big oil companies rushed into the community. More than a dozen automobile dealerships appeared in Big Spring seemingly overnight, and three multi-story hotels were rapidly built, to accommodate throngs of new arrivals. New, larger churches were built and a series of modern schools was constructed to replace the modest facilities that were suddenly found wholly inadequate. Even the railroad, which had been the very foundation of the now-burgeoning community, deemed it necessary to expand and improve its facilities to provide adequate service to the oil-driven boom times.[4]

Too soon, however, the seemingly inevitable bust came to Big Spring. With the arrival of the Great Depression across the nation, the demand for petroleum products dwindled as the funds to pay for those products became all but nonexistent. An overextended local government found itself with a rapidly shrinking tax base and too many building projects under construction. For the first time in decades, the town's population decreased as regional petroleum activity vastly diminished. However, as was the case at Midland, Pecos, Greenville, and in towns and cities all across the Lone Star State, an international event of stunning magnitude brought an end to the Depression, although often at a great and tragic cost. In 1941 America went to war, and the wartime Army, with millions of dollars to spend, came to Texas.

BIG SPRING ARMY AIRFIELD

*Who ever [*sic*] decided on the construction of the buildings at Big Spring AAFB must have been an extreme pessimist and believed that we* *would loose [*sic*] the war in a hurry or an extreme optimist and believed we would get it over with, right off.*

Bill Steagald
Big Spring, Texas

Prior to World War II and the construction of Big Spring Army Airfield, the city's economic existence had been based almost exclusively on the railroad, agriculture, and, most significantly in the recent past, the petroleum business. During the war years, however, and for nearly three decades thereafter, aviation arguably became the most important and reliable pillar of the area's fiscal well-being.

The first aircraft to visit Big Spring had landed on pastureland north of the city in 1911, just thirty years after the railroad had constructed its rather primitive depot alongside its newly laid track. By the end of World War I, local interest in the increasingly popular pastime of flying caused former Army pilots to make the town something of a regular stop for their barnstorming aerial circuses.

One such military aviator, on a surveying mission to identify potential sites for future Army landing fields, selected a location just west of Big Spring for possible development. The town's leaders apparently concurred with the airman's unofficial recommendation, and in 1928 purchased the 275-acre site as the future location for Big Spring Municipal Airport.

A hangar, terminal building, and runways were soon under construction, and by March 1, 1929, the first commercial flight had landed at the new facility. Transcontinental airmail service began landing at the airport early in 1932, with Capt. Eddie Rickenbacker of World War I fame on hand for the event. Within a few years, Big Spring's strategic location between Fort Worth and El Paso ensured that its airport became a regular stopover point for several major airlines. The economic collapse that had so disastrously affected the region's petroleum and agriculture markets also brought nationwide civilian air travel nearly to a standstill, and as a result, activity at the new airport all but ceased.[5]

In early 1941, perhaps remembering that the now all-but-dormant airport had been built on a site originally chosen by an Army aviator, Big Spring's Chamber of Commerce officials launched a well-orchestrated political campaign to convince the War Department that the thirteen-year-old facility would be an ideal site for an Army flight-training base. Following the Japanese attack on Pearl Harbor, the city's efforts came to a swift fruition.

The wartime-generated demand for flight-crew personnel had caused the Army to acquire or build training facilities all across Texas, with its largest school for bombardiers located just forty miles west of Big Spring at Midland. When it soon became apparent that what was being hailed as the "World's Largest Bombardier School" could not graduate its cadets fast enough to compensate for both the deadly attrition of combat and the ever-increasing need for flight-crew members, other schools were speedily opened in relative proximity to the big mother base at Midland.[6]

Because of its location, its existing facilities, and the persuasive selling techniques of its civic leaders, Big Spring's airport was among those chosen to become a bombardier-training school. As the *Big Spring Herald* proudly proclaimed in a lead story on April 22, 1942, the refitting of the airport would require some $5 million, to say nothing of a massive amount of cooperation between civilian and military authorities. It was estimated that the construction phase of the Army field would generate an increase of at least 40 percent in the area's population and that the school district would likely experience at least a 30 percent growth in enrollment. New water lines were to be built by the city to carry the projected million gallons that would be required by the completed base, and miles of roads and highways were slated for construction, expansion, and upgrading. While the cost to the city was certain to be sizable, the paper assumed, the prospect of a $5 million annual military payroll somehow seemed to make any startup expense more than worthwhile.[7]

Just days after the announcement of the plan to open the bombardier school, construction on the field was in full sway. When the facility was officially declared operational just four months later, a small city had been created on what had only recently been a municipal airport smaller than three hundred acres. Three 6,200-foot runways had been constructed, and two huge hangars had been erected, along with barracks, classrooms, a gymnasium, a chapel, an auditorium, and miles of streets and sidewalks. The entire installation now sprawled across nearly 1,300 acres.[8]

On August 22, 1942, the first cadre of military personnel arrived at the new Big Spring Bombardier School, having traveled the forty miles from Midland in Army trucks. The reaction of one enlisted man perhaps best expresses the initial impression the soldiers had of their new home. "Hey, Lieutenant," he cried in dismay, "you gonna tell me this is an Army base?" Only one-story tarpaper shacks were visible to the new arrivals, and caliche dust covered everything. The hastily built facility would continue to grow as the war went on, but the quality of the buildings seemed to most soldiers to be practically substandard, with the exception of the hospital and the hangars.[9]

As noted in the official history of the 812th Bombardier Training Squadron, which was made up mostly by the initial cadre at the new base, "there was clear evidence that the carpenters had not done much more than build." The barracks were filled with rubbish, the latrines lacked many important things, including mirrors, shelves, and, as the squadron historian noted with heavy irony, "even water." The men of the cadre unit soon acquired enough brooms and shovels to make their accommodations at least livable. Other personnel found hammers, nails, and lumber to start building partitions and shelving that had apparently been overlooked in the original government building specifications.[10]

A temporary post exchange was organized by the men and located in the library building, which was already completed and open for use but was devoid of any books. According to the unit history, the availability of cigarettes, candy, and particularly cold drinks, "greatly helped the morale of the newly arrived men."[11]

Not content to wait until the Army Air Force provided for their recreational needs, the men of the 812th continued to build and enhance their barracks and immediate area when not training the bombardier candidates. The airmen built a day room for their leisure hours, complete with writing desks, Ping-Pong tables, and magazine racks. Lamps, chairs, and a radio were purchased with money from the squadron fund. Eventually, two pool tables were acquired for the dayroom, much to the delight of many of the off-duty personnel. In a further effort to make their existence more pleasant, the men bought grass seed to sow across the sunbaked caliche that seldom if ever experienced much in the way of rainfall. Amazingly, the undertaking was at least in part successful, as the unit history records that the seed "did not blow away, sprouted and grew, thereby enhancing the appearance of the area."[12]

Shortly after the apparently less-than-enchanted but highly resourceful cadre had arrived, the first class of 130 bombardier candidates began their training on the base, even though it was still under construction. The course of instruction lasted twenty-four weeks and included ground school, an introduction to the secret Norden bombsight, and actual in-flight practice bombing experience. The flying training was conducted in the Beechcraft AT-11 on an around-the-clock basis, with the 100-pound practice bombs dropped on area target ranges both day and night.[13]

The prime target used by all bombardier schools was a wooden shack, located at the center of a series of concentric circles marked with lime. The shack was lighted for night practice, with the power coming from generators located about a half-mile from the structure. If and when a cadet managed to score a direct hit, crews from the base were dispatched the next day to repair both the shack and its electrical system. The AT-11s from which the practice bombs were dropped had a 35mm camera on board. Photos of the bombing pattern were delivered to the base photography lab upon completion of the mission. The film was developed overnight and the prints used by instructors to evaluate their pupils.[14]

As had been the case at the big Midland Bombardier School, the practice bombs occasionally missed their intended targets, causing damage to livestock and sometimes allegedly starting fires. One sergeant, whose duty it was to patrol the bombing ranges, wrote long after the war that some area ranchers would use naturally caused fires as an excuse to falsely blame errant bombs as the source of combustion in hopes of gaining a sizable recompensation from the Army for damages. Some ranchers would find a previously dropped practice bomb elsewhere, transport the mangled object to the site of a range fire that had been caused by lightning or carelessness, and then indignantly telephone the bombardier school to demand a settlement. The Army's range inspectors would visit the burned field, look at the remains of the bomb, and then advise the reward-seeking rancher that since the bomb itself was not burned and as it had not created even the slightest crater, clearly "something else must have started the fire." Presumably, a rancher seldom tried this particular ruse again.[15]

Aside from a few unscrupulous opportunists seeking money for alleged damage done by poorly aimed bombs, the citizens of Howard County and Big Spring warmly welcomed the young men and women who were assigned to the base located just west of town. At any one time during the field's wartime operational peak, there were more than three thousand military personnel stationed on it. Some lived off the base with their families in town, where the population had soared to nearly seventeen thousand, up from only twelve thousand in a very short time.

Despite an acute housing shortage and a city infrastructure that fairly groaned under the influx of people and their vehicles, the relationship between the military and the civilians was open and friendly. Although the Texans clearly enjoyed the flow of federal dollars created by the base, they also were proud of the airfield and its mission. The patriotic fervor that enveloped America during the war years was keenly felt and regularly demonstrated all across the Lone Star State.

Soldiers from the airfield made the less-than-three-mile trip into town quite often, particularly on weekends. As it was against Army regulations for military personnel to wear civilian clothes off base, they were easily recognized in their olive drab or khaki uniforms as they flocked to Big Spring's four movie houses and drugstore soda fountains. A few saloons such as the Blue Bonnet were placed off-limits by airfield authorities, but the men from the base generally were welcomed in all places of business.[16]

A USO facility was opened in downtown Big Spring, providing a well-chaperoned rendezvous spot for local girls and lonely soldiers. According to both oral histories and newspaper articles of the war years, many marriages eventually grew from the dances and social hours held at the USO building. Some soldiers and their dates found the lush green lawn of the courthouse to be a comfortable spot for a tête à tête. Military Police routinely cleared the lawn each night at 11:00 P.M.[17]

Most parents of young Big Spring girls were understandably wary of the intentions of the soldiers. One veteran remembered seeing a beautiful girl, dressed in her finest gown, sitting alone at a USO dance. As he watched, several airmen approached the girl and asked her to dance, only to be pleasantly but firmly turned down. At last, the observer decided to test his ability to persuade the girl to join him for a waltz. "Oh, no thank you," she answered with a smile, "my Daddy said I could come here tonight, but only if I promised him I wouldn't dance or talk with anyone." [18]

Not all parents were quite as restrictive. If a soldier met an interesting girl at the USO or the drug store, he might well find himself invited to her family home. After meeting her parents and having supper with them, the duo might go to the movies, making sure to be at her home no later than 11:00 P.M. If the next day happened to be Sunday, the soldier would likely attend church with the girl and her family and then enjoy dinner with them before returning to the airfield. A thoughtful airman might carry some of his food ration stamps along with him to the family dinners to leave behind, a technique that was often particularly effective in gaining the endorsement of the girl's mother.[19]

When without passes to go into town, service personnel found much in the way of recreation and entertainment on the base. There was a theater, a gymnasium, service clubs, and a library, as well as numerous athletic fields for use by the soldiers.

Traveling shows frequently performed at the field. In 1943 Bob Hope came to Big Spring to entertain the troops, as he did at so many other military installations during the war. He was accompanied by his popular cast, which included songstress Frances Langford, sidekick Jerry Colonna, and the usual bevy of beautiful Hollywood starlets.[20]

Occasionally, base officials would invite local high school boys to come out for an orientation visit. As the invitation was extended to senior boys only, the purpose behind the airfield tour was rather transparent. A photograph of a group of the young men on the base appears in the Big Spring High School Annual of 1945 with the biting caption, "Draft Bait." [21]

As in every wartime military town, a seamy underside flourished despite the combined earnest efforts of base and civilian authorities. The provost marshal and his military policemen in Big Spring, for example, were particularly diligent in stamping out, or at least controlling, prostitution on the city streets. Army men were advised to tell their wives to be certain to bring their marriage licenses with them when they came from out of town for a visit, as the MPs were under strict orders to call for the arrest of any female found with a male in a public accommodation who could not conclusively prove that said male was her legal spouse. Just why the carrying of a marriage license was deemed to be a wifely responsibility was never fully explained. Despite such unusual precautions, however, Big Spring was considered "a fine military town" by the majority of the soldiers stationed on the airfield.[22]

Bill Steagald, who came to the newly built field with the group trucked over from Midland, loved Big Spring but had some serious problems with the region's weather peculiarities. When it rained, he recalled, the caliche on the base would instantly be transformed into a clinging white mud. When one of the infamous West Texas "Blue Northers" struck, he was awed by the phenomenon of hurtling tumbleweeds thrust at unbelievable speeds by north winds of immeasurable velocity. The tumbleweeds would hit the north side of his barracks with a resounding crash and begin to accumulate in rapidly mounting piles. Once the pile had reached the roofline of the barracks, the next wave of tumbleweeds, having no place to stack, would blow over the roof to start a new pile on the north wall of the barracks next door. By the time the storm had blown itself out, the northern exposures of all the barracks were completely obscured by mountains of giant tumbleweeds.[23]

In its three and a half years of existence, the field amassed a high level of training intensity and proficiency. One contemporary bulletin issued by air base headquarters stated that 1,000 hours of in-air training were logged each month, with more than 4.5 million pounds of bombs being dropped on practice targets. "In just over one year," the bulletin declared, "a distance of 18,000,000 miles had been flown, with but one fatality." By the time the bombardier training school was closed, the final tally showed that 400,000 hours had been flown for a combined distance of 60 million miles. Unfortunately, four fatal accidents had occurred. In total, more than 6,000 bombardiers received their wings from the Big Spring facility during the course of World War II.[24]

A memorable feature of each graduation ceremony was the earnest singing of the official anthem of the Big Spring Bombardier cadet song. Written by a cadet, the words reflect the proud spirit of the airfield:

> The Big Spring Bombardiers
> have put their sights in gear,

and now they're waiting for the day
when they can all so proudly say,
we're all going over there.

We'll bring peace everywhere,
we'll fight until that day
we're flying home to stay.
But 'til that great day comes
we'll keep on dropping bombs
to keep our coastline clear.
For the honor of
the Big Spring Bombardier.[25]

As the war drew to a close and graduation ceremonies occurred less frequently, it became apparent that the Big Spring base and its bombardier-training mission would no longer be of use to the government. Despite an effort by chamber of commerce officials and the region's elected officials, the base was finally closed in early 1946, some five months after the war had ended.

Although the closing had a definite economic impact on Big Spring and all of Howard County, opinions differ as to just how severe that impact was. Joe Pickle, who was editor of the *Big Spring Herald* when the base closed, recalls that the "economic repercussions were not too pronounced." According to Mr. Pickle, the pause in economic growth was only momentary, and renewed activity in oil exploration and production soon erased any financial difficulties for the region.[26] A. J. Prager, who operated Prager's Men and Boys Wear when the base shuttered, recalls things differently. "There's no way you can take that much money out of Big Spring's economy," he said, "and not have it hurt each and every one of us, particularly the businessman."[27] Population figures for the time indicate that the region was not immediately severely affected by the closing of the base, with Big Spring reaching an all-time-high census count of over 30,000 by 1960, reflecting a robust growth from its previous high of 17,000 reached just after the base closed.[28]

The military facility itself reverted to municipal ownership, and Big Spring Airport once again occupied the site. The expanded runways and large hangars built by the Army were soon put to good use by commercial and general aviation interests.

Unlike many World War II air installations, however, the old bombardier school site was destined to again hear the sound of military aircraft. On October 1, 1951, Big Spring Air Force Base was reactivated and designated a pilot training base. On May 18, 1952, the field was renamed Webb Air Force Base in honor of Lt. James L. Webb, a Big Spring pilot who had lost his life in a plane crash in 1949.[29]

As most of the World War II–era buildings had been destroyed or moved off the site, the Defense Department spent over $3 million to provide the old base with all that it would need for its new jet pilot training mission. The first class of trainees arrived in April 1952 and graduated sixty days later. Eventually, the course of instruction would include all phases of pilot training and last for nearly a year. In the Air Force base's twenty-six-year history, some 14,000 student pilots received their silver wings at Big Spring.[30]

Even though the United States was involved in intensive air wars in Asia during Webb's existence from the early 1970s on, rumors of its impending closure were in almost constant circulation. The *Big Spring Herald* confirmed in its issue of March 10, 1976, that the base was marked for closure. Even though the city had deeded the airport property to the federal government in an effort to keep base-generated dollars flowing into the local economy, it became evident that Webb would soon be closed.[31]

In a last-ditch effort to stave off the inevitable, citizens were urged by J. D. Nelson of the Big Spring Chamber of Commerce to write directly to President Gerald Ford. Pointing out that Webb AFB, with its $128 million worth of facilities, generated a payroll of $33 million and thousands of jobs, Mr. Nelson asked that at least 1,000 letters protesting the proposed closing be hand-carried to the chamber's offices "no later than noon, Friday."[32]

Despite the correspondence to President Ford and the vow of Texas Senator John Tower to fight the closing "to the last bloody ditch," Webb Air Force Base ceased all operations on September 2, 1977. The property reverted to the city of Big Spring for use as an industrial park and, once again, a municipal airport. In time, a major federal prison was constructed on the property, and in a fitting Texas gesture, producing oil wells on the runways were eventually completed where AT-11s and T-38s had once roared.

Even with such diversified activity on the once-vital base, Big Spring still struggles with memories of its closing. "It's been real hard for the community to get over it," states current airport director Nelda Reagan, "the closing of this base just devastated the community."[33]

Not all of the memories of Big Spring's long-gone era of military aviation revolve around economics. Toward the end of the twentieth century, a group of local citizens set about to preserve something of the combined heritage of Big Spring's Bombardier School and Webb Air Force Base. Forming an organization called "Hangar 25 Air Museum," the resourceful group has caused a once-derelict hangar on the field to be completely restored to its original condition, complete with shining glass-paneled doors and a rare wooden interior ceiling. In answer to the organization's call, memorabilia from the old air base days is returning to be housed in the venerable, refurbished hangar.

Support for the project, both financial and material, has come not only from those who once served here, but also from the still-proud and patriotic citizens of the region who remember what the once-mighty base meant to them and to their nation a long half-century ago. Precious little physically remains to reflect the memory of the three decades of military aviation that flourished on this sun-baked stretch of West Texas caliche, precious little except a reborn and hauntingly beautiful old airplane hangar, a fitting symbol of a glorious time gone forever but clearly not forgotten by the people of Big Spring, Texas.

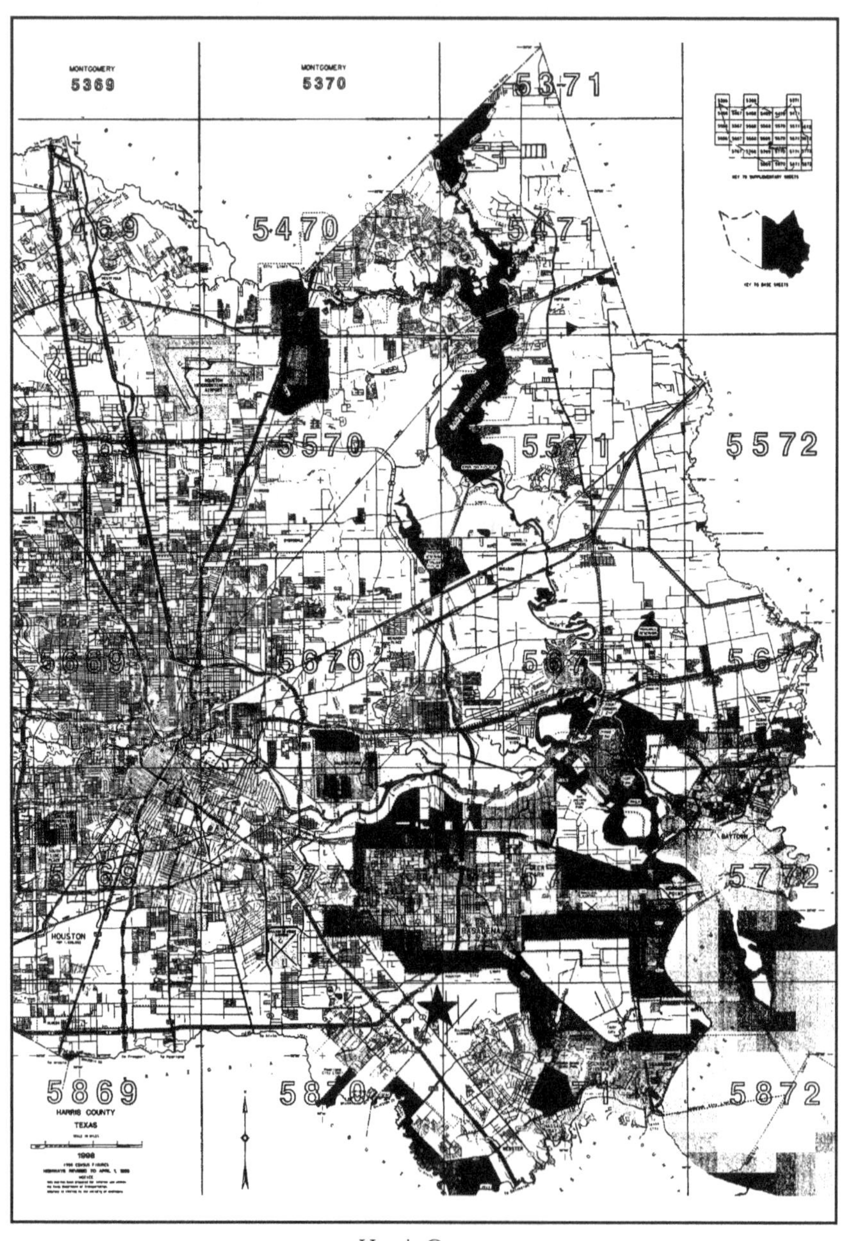

Harris County
This map of Harris County shows the location of Ellington Field during the war years

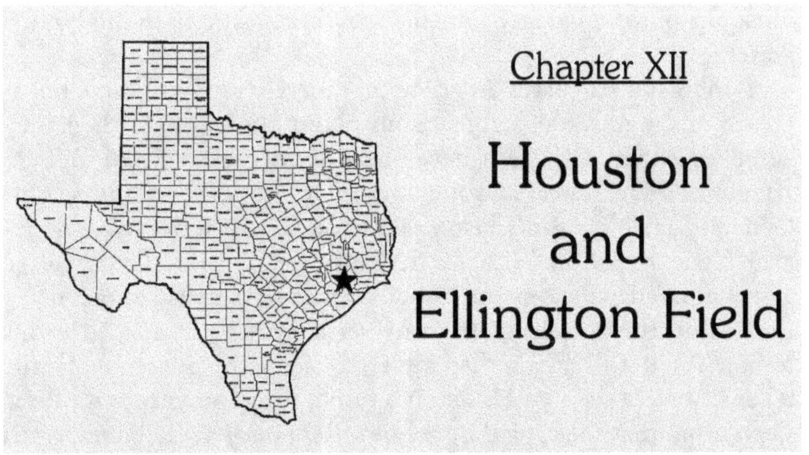

Chapter XII

Houston and Ellington Field

I read in the old Houston Post *many years ago that some scientist had come up with a wild scheme to enclose this whole city inside an air conditioned glass dome. I remember thinking that this was really a pretty good idea, but I also wondered if the exhaust fumes from the cars wouldn't just kill us all.*

L. K. Henderson
Houston, Texas

Although scientist Buckminster Fuller's plan to enclose all of downtown Houston within one of his trademark geodesic domes never developed, air conditioning on a somewhat lesser scale did help make it possible for the city to become one of the largest in the nation. Despite the fact that the community's founders, John and Augustus Allen, had claimed in an 1836 advertisement that their fledgling little town enjoyed "healthy, cooling seabreezes," early residents found the climate stifling and humid instead.[1]

The brothers Allen, being land speculators after all, also predicted that Houston would become "the great interior commercial emporium of Texas," and, in time, their prophecy proved to be inordinately accurate. It would take years for the city to grow into the prominence its founders had envisioned, but a combination of foresight, ambition, and technology worked to transform a lawless, mosquito-infested village into the fourth-largest city in the United States.[2]

John and Augustus Allen did not merely rely on simple boosterism and highly debatable claims about the climate when they launched their real estate development on the banks of Buffalo Bayou in 1836. Located some twenty miles west of the site of General Sam Houston's just won victory over the forces of Mexican General Antonio López de Santa Anna, the Allens' village gained immediate acceptance when they easily persuaded the victorious Houston to permit the tiny settlement to be named in his honor. As if this marketing masterstroke were not enough, the Allens, abetted by Sam Houston himself, next convinced the Texas Legislature that the capital of the new Republic should be relocated in the proudly named little town. In May 1837, just over a year after the Battle of San Jacinto had been so impressively won nearby, Houston indeed became the young Republic's capital city.

Even with such dazzling beginnings, the village on the bayou grew slowly and not without difficulty. For some reason, it initially seemed to attract a particularly lawless citizenry, apparently far more intent on hell-raising than city-building. According to *The New Handbook of Texas*, despite the efforts of the Masons and local churchmen, the town long remained "infamous for drunkenness, dueling, brawling, prostitution and profanity."[3]

In addition to the many problems created by the town's throng of hooligans, the residents were also plagued by disease epidemics in the early years. Nine major outbreaks of yellow fever struck in a twenty-eight-year period that started in 1839. More than 12 percent of the population was killed in the first epidemic alone.[4]

Despite disease and disorder, Houston managed to grow. By 1850 the population had reached nearly 2,500, and by 1900 the total was 44,633. By 1940, however, the year before World War II, nearly 400,000 citizens lived in what only a century before had been a one-log-cabin settlement with twelve hardy inhabitants.[5]

One of the keys to Houston's great growth in the mid-twentieth century was in fact World War II itself, and that key was forged in the city's tireless effort to create for itself a navigable deep-water link to the Gulf of Mexico some forty miles to the south. In 1914 the opening of the Houston Ship Channel, dredged into being from the shallow and often treacherous Buffalo Bayou, proved to be the single most important element in the city's emergence as the great commercial center so boldly predicted by the Allens in 1836. The industrialization and refining activity that soon flourished along the channel would become vital to the United States during two world wars.

ELLINGTON FIELD

It was kind of funny, I guess, come to think of it. My father was stationed at Ellington about twenty-five years before I was. I can still remember him telling me about how he saw the first airplane land at the field just after Thanksgiving Day, 1917.

Felix B. Neale Jr.
Houston, Texas

Houston was one of a handful of Texas cities to host military installations in both world wars. There were, in fact, two Army bases in the area during the first big war, with Camp Logan being located in what is now the city's Memorial Park and Ellington Field situated eighteen miles southeast of town, where it would reemerge in 1941 as a World War II flight-training facility.

Ellington had come into being as the result of a tireless civic effort orchestrated by the Houston Chamber of Commerce. In early 1917, just as the United States became fully involved in World War I, officials of the chamber had lobbied the federal government with claims of the consistently excellent flying conditions to be found in the Houston area, specifically between the city and Galveston nearly fifty miles to the south. In reality, the assertions of the chamber were almost as groundless as those made by the Allen brothers nearly eighty years earlier. Experience would soon prove that heavy ground fogs, frequent thunderstorms, and even occasional hurricanes often interrupted flight operations in the area. A quarter of a century later, author George Sessions Perry was still lamenting the government's decision to locate the air base in such an unfriendly environment. The field was supposed "to be a bombardment school," Perry wrote in 1942, "but Houston has a jackass-killing climate." Accepting the obvious fact that the giant field could not readily relocate from its site, Perry could only complain, "there it now sits, be-fogged, be-rained, be-mired, wasting precious hours of precious personnel and precious bi-motored training planes."[6] In its zeal, the chamber correctly made much of the flatness of the terrain and the existence of adequate roadways and railroads, but blithely omitted any reference to negative weather factors that might present problems for fledgling aviators.

At any rate, the lobbying campaign proved successful in mid-1917 when the U.S. government purchased nearly 1,300 acres of land from Dr. R. W. Knox and the Wright Land Company for the purpose of constructing a flying training base. Located less than twenty miles southeast of downtown Houston, the gigantic tract of land was "only thirty-three feet above sea level and as flat as a table," and, according to one governmental report, "covered with thick prairie grass."[7]

Actual construction on the airfield began on September 14, 1917, with the American Construction Company as the general contractor. Mules were used to pull earth-moving equipment while crews of laborers mowed, chopped, and eventually cleared the land to provide space for hangars, barracks, and runways on what had just recently been a swampy, wild tangle of thorny coastal brush and rope-like prairie grasses.

When heat, high humidity, mosquitoes, and backbreaking labor proved to be intolerable just a few weeks after the construction phase started, the workers went on strike. To keep the project on schedule, soldiers from Houston's Camp Logan were swiftly brought across town to serve as laborers. Deprived of their wages, the striking civilian workers promptly determined that conditions perhaps might not have been as bad as they originally had seemed, and they soon returned to their tedious tasks. Despite the strike, the base was nearly completed in less than sixty days. Hastily constructed wooden buildings served as hangars, headquarters, and officers' housing, while enlisted men were assigned to tents.[8]

As the construction work was nearing completion, the Army notified the city that the new facility was to be named Ellington Field in honor of Lt. Eric Lamar Ellington, who had been killed in a California air accident in November 1913. The lieutenant, an Illinoisan by birth, had graduated from the U.S. Naval Academy only to become a cavalry officer before earning his wings as an aviator. Aside from briefly serving at San Antonio's Fort Sam

Houston, Ellington had no connection with Texas, making the naming of the new field in his honor a rare tribute at the time.

By all standards, Lieutenant Ellington's namesake field was a large one. It consisted of twenty-four hangars, twelve barracks, four warehouses, two school buildings, and an array of mechanical shops. It had a hospital, an officers' club, two stores, and four movie theaters. The main runway was over 8,000 feet long and nearly 800 feet wide.[9]

The first aircraft flew from the newly completed runway on November 27, 1917, just seventy-three days after the first mule had been persuaded to begin the clearing phase of construction. The planes, all Curtiss JN-4s, were elements of the 120th Aero Squadron, which had transferred to Houston from Kelly Field at San Antonio.[10]

To dramatize the activation of the new airfield, base commander Lt. Col. John F. Curry led a formation of ten planes in a flight over downtown Houston. The city that had so eagerly awaited the opening of the field was by all accounts driven wild by the spectacle of so many aircraft over downtown. Whistles, sirens, and automobile horns were almost as loud as the combined drone of the JN-4s' powerful 150-horsepower engines.

Colonel Curry sought to maximize the event for the good of the war effort, instructing his pilots to throw out handfuls of Red Cross pamphlets as they flew over the city and made their way down toward Galveston Island. Unfortunately, a capricious Gulf breeze deprived the initial mission of its noble intent by blowing nearly all of the pamphlets away from the throng of spectators and well out into the Gulf of Mexico.[11]

When the ceremonial flight was completed, in less than an hour's time, the newly arrived squadron began the serious business of advanced flying training. Much of the actual instruction was conducted by civilian pilots, simply because the Army could not spare many of its experienced flyers from combat service in the skies over France. Despite a dismal record of flight safety, the field managed to produce a large number of well-qualified pilots who were sent to operational units in Europe as soon as they graduated.[12]

The early 1900s were difficult years of trial and error for an Army Air Force that was still very much in its infancy. Ellington Field, one of the better-equipped training facilities, was frequently used as a training laboratory during that fledgling period. Consequently, the field was properly given credit for many innovations in the development of flying training. For example, the base was the first to establish night and long-distance flights as part of the curriculum, the first to have its own newspaper, and perhaps of particular interest to the cadets and officers, the first to introduce what were termed "Girl Canteen Workers" to the military. In another war that was soon to follow, this innovation led to the creation of the highly appreciated United Service Organization (USO).[13]

Capt. Drury M. Phillips of the U.S. Army served at Ellington Field for over a year and in Texas for almost twenty years. He later remembered his service in the Lone Star State during the 1920s and 1930s as the most pleasurable in his long military career. Phillips recalled boxing carnivals, excursions to the beach, and dances, but most of all he cherished the memories of the hearty welcome that he and his fellow airmen received while serving at Ellington. "Houston opened its heart and homes to the men of the Air Service," he wrote, "and made them a part of herself, gave them cheer and encouragement . . ."[14] Although World War I, the "war to end all wars" was rapidly drawing to a close in November 1918, Houstonians would soon again demonstrate their legendary capacity to warmly welcome America's fliers into their midst.

A NEW ELLINGTON FIELD LITERALLY RISES FROM THE ASHES

I was only eight years old when the Big War ended in 1918, but I sure can remember how people around Houston celebrated on that Armistice Day. I know, too, that some folks began to worry that Camp Logan and Ellington Field would soon be closing up shop. Some others were afraid they wouldn't.

Mrs. Everett Simmons
Pasadena, Texas

On the initial Armistice Day, November 11, 1918, so well remembered by ninety-year-old Elva Simmons, Ellington Field was at the peak of its importance. With over 20,000 soldiers assigned to it, the field had established an enviable record in training pilots for combat service. With the war over, however, the Army saw little reason to keep the field active, even though no announcement of any plan to close the base was forthcoming from the War Department. In early 1920, however, it was formally announced by the government that Ellington was indeed to be deactivated.[15]

Less than a year after its closing, the old World War I base was reopened as a reserve air squadron field, and in 1923, operations at Ellington were transferred to the Texas National Guard. The base and the Guard thus began a close, if intermittent, relationship that would endure into the twenty-first century.

The National Guard's first occupancy of Ellington ended in 1925, and the Army began the destruction of all the buildings on the base. A major fire in 1926 contributed to the demolition, and by 1930 the sole remnant of the once-mighty World War I airfield was a solitary concrete water tank located on the south edge of the property. The government retained ownership of the now-vacant land, however, and leased it to area ranchers for grazing purposes.[16]

For the next ten years, only cattle were to be found in the wild marsh grasses that grew where airplanes had once taken off and landed. In early 1940, however, suddenly urgent national defense plans called for the construction of major air facilities throughout the United States. Because of fears of possible enemy action in the Gulf of Mexico, Texas, and Houston in particular, was the immediate beneficiary of those broad national plans.

Because of the vital refineries and other industries that had earlier been established along the Houston Ship Channel and throughout the region, the Army thought it prudent to locate one of its newly authorized air bases somewhere in the immediate area. As the federal government still owned the land upon which the old Ellington Field had been situated during World War I, it was clear that a new Ellington was both practical and vital to national defense.

The cattle were promptly herded off the 1,300-acre site, and construction of the second Ellington Field commenced. By June 1940, all utilities were in place and the enormous task of laying concrete on the native marshy soil had begun. Work on the apron alone involved nearly 3.5 million cubic feet of concrete, creating what the *Houston Chronicle* claimed was the largest one-piece slab of concrete in the world. It measured 7,500 feet in length and 740 feet in width and was eight inches thick.[17]

The original construction budget of $3 million was soon surpassed when more buildings and longer runways were added to the basic plan and over 600,000 man-hours were required to complete the base. Final cost of the resurrected Ellington Field was nearly $7 million. For that large sum, the Army received 301 buildings, six runways, and the huge record-breaking concrete apron. Until the actual runways were completed, pilots used the outsized apron for taking off and landing.[18]

By April 11, 1941, the field was deemed complete enough to receive its first troops, and within weeks, nearly 5,000 men were living on the base. It was projected that 7,280 pilots would complete their course of instruction each year, graduating at the rate of 1,456 every ten weeks. According to the *Houston Chronicle* of October 26, 1941, Ellington was poised to produce one-third of the nation's pilots under the Roosevelt administration's national defense program.[19]

As the pilot trainees flocked onto the nearly completed field, extra attention was being paid to their overall welfare. Houston's newspapers devoted much space to descriptions of Ellington's thirteen-building medical facility, universally credited as the finest in all of South Texas. Three chapels cared for the soldiers' spiritual needs, and service clubs, theaters, and sports facilities provided social and recreational activities. A post exchange required five branch outlets to cater to the shopping needs of the personnel. Daily sales at the combined exchanges were reported to be in excess of $5,000, a remarkably high sales volume for the time. Houston-area ladies' clubs donated time, money, and material toward the beautification of the field through elaborate landscaping projects.[20]

The first commander of the new Ellington Field was Lt. Col. W. H. Reid, an officer who had served on the old field in 1918. In 1920 Reid had again been assigned to the installation as an instructor pilot with the Texas National Guard. Reid had been the base commander in 1927 when fire destroyed all that was left of the World War I vintage wooden buildings.[21]

Having been stationed at Ellington previously, Colonel Reid was interested in keeping the heritage of the old field alive in some way. As a consequence, he was struck by the idea of having an artist paint a portrait of Lt. Eric Ellington to be prominently displayed as a symbol of the linkage between the World War I base and its successor, which had the same proud name. Presumably after due consideration, the colonel selected Mrs. E. Richardson Cherry, a widely known local artist, to create the oil portrait from a rare early photograph of the late Lieutenant Ellington. If Colonel Reid's choice of Mrs. Cherry as the artist was in any way influenced by the fact that she was his mother-in-law went unmentioned in the May 28, 1941, *Houston Press* story about the painting.[22]

Apparently, no one found reason to speculate how closely the painting resembled its subject until many years later. When Lieutenant Ellington's sister visited the base in 1958, she was shown the painting of her brother that was still hanging in the headquarters building. After a few moments of close study, she rather brusquely declared that it was "not a very good likeness."[23]

Perhaps better at running an air base than choosing artists, Colonel Reid and his staff established a demanding regimen for their student pilots. The ten-week course consisted of seventy hours of ground school and long days and nights of in-flight instruction. Navigators and bombardiers were also being trained on the airfield, but without receiving any actual flying experience. Following an intensive course of study in military fundamentals and related academic subjects, the navigators and bombardiers were then sent to specialized flight schools, where they earned their wings. From there, the men joined their pilots at combat crew training schools prior to going overseas to a theater of war.[24]

Because so many other training bases opened shortly after America's entry into World War II, the flow of pilots through Ellington's advanced school at first proved to be less than had been originally projected. Still, one of every ten Army pilots went through the school in the first two years of the war. As advanced trainees, the men first flew the AT-6 before moving on to the more challenging multi-engine aircraft such as the AT-10 or the AT-11.[25]

Later in the war, when the pilot- and bombardier-training programs were transferred to other airfields, Ellington became the location of the Air Force's Advanced Navigator Training School. From 1941 to the end of the war, more than 4,000 navigators graduated from the facility.

Tom Allen, a graduate of the navigation school, describes his experiences at Ellington with a combination of fondness and residual bewilderment. As a newly commissioned second lieutenant, Allen was assigned temporary billet in the visiting officers' quarters located directly across from the Officers' Club upon his arrival on the base. The room he was given was surprisingly spacious and equipped with two large oscillating floor fans that at least held their own against Houston's notorious mid-July heat and humidity. After quickly settling in, the new lieutenant walked across the road to the Officers' Club to sample a few cold Texas beers. Upon returning to his quarters some time later, Allen was surprised to find all of his belongings in a pile in the hallway and the door to the room securely locked. The clerk on duty informed the young officer that a senior full colonel had just flown in and, as was the custom, had been given the best room in the building, be it occupied or not. A disgruntled and overheated Allen, made suddenly wiser about the privileges of rank in the U.S. Army, soon found himself sharing a small and decidedly unairconditioned room with a fellow junior officer.

The next morning, Allen recalls, he was advised that the starting date for his class had been delayed by three days. As a result, he was given a leave and told to find other temporary quarters off base. Allen was also given a military police–produced booklet that described in fairly graphic detail all of the many establishments in the Houston-Galveston area that had been placed off-limits by order of the base commander. Under no circumstances, the lieutenant was sternly instructed, was he to visit any of the businesses that had been declared forbidden territory. The words of dire warning were particularly applicable to the port city of Galveston, which had somehow earned a reputation among military personnel as a center of sin rivaled only by Shanghai.

With the thoughtfully provided government-published Baedeker in hand, Allen swiftly set out for Galveston's Postoffice District in a conscientious effort to determine for himself if the findings of the military police were indeed accurate. Much to his delight, he found the saloons and other such nefarious establishments to be every bit as sinful as the Army had said they were. Allen was also pleased to discover that the military police on duty seemed totally uninterested in enforcing the off-duty sanctions so meticulously catalogued by the base commander's office.[26]

While some other Ellington graduates indicate that Lieutenant

Allen's response to the Army's warnings was in no way unique, many are more inclined to reminisce about the warm welcome they received when their schedules permitted them to visit Houston. There the families from the most affluent sections of town competed with the more modest neighborhoods in a show of genuine Texas hospitality.

Of particular interest to many student officers and cadets were the exceptionally friendly and, according to reports perhaps tempered by the passage of time, universally beautiful young women of the city's Rice Institute. One veteran, Ted Sherman, recalled steadily dating a graduate student who was working toward a higher degree in mathematics. She proved willing to help him prepare for his tests in trigonometry and calculus, two subjects in which he was apparently woefully deficient, and subjects that he never once used in his long career as an Air Force navigator.

Several decades later, Sherman could not quite remember if he had dated the girl for her mathematical expertise or for other reasons. He does recall, however, that after months of congenial tutoring, he sat down for his final math exam on the base. Of the twenty problems included in the test, Sherman found to his dismay that he was fully prepared to answer only one, despite the Rice girl's best teaching efforts. Desperate to pass the test so that he might earn his wings and go to war, Sherman resorted to the infamous college trick known as c-a-b-b-a. In this learned educational technique, it was suggested that making multiple-choice answers using the letters c-a-b-b-a in sequence would yield the student at least a passing grade. Although no logical nor remotely plausible rationale was ever offered as to how such a scheme might work, a nearly frantic Sherman found himself with no other option. To his complete surprise and that of his instructor, who had correctly surmised that the math test would overwhelm his less-than-apt pupil, Sherman scored an astounding 85 percent, graduated from the navigator school, and became a career Air Force officer. To illustrate that not all old veterans' stories are fairy tales with happy endings, he is quick to add that upon leaving Houston, he never saw the girl from Rice again.[27]

Bill Blanchard has memories of another side of Houston's social life in the late 1940s. A native of New York state, Blanchard had never heard country and western music until he was assigned to

Ellington Field as a student officer in the navigation school. Fascinated by the persuasive throb of the steel guitar and the often preposterous if heartbreaking lyrics associated with the Texas music, he could be found on most non-duty weekend nights in downtown Houston under a big tent that was taken down each Sunday before noon. From Friday at dusk until early on a Sabbath morning, both the music and the cold Lone Star and Pearl beer would flow in virtual rivers under the huge but tattered canopy. Occasionally, a Saturday night's revelry led Blanchard from the tented honky-tonk to other venues featuring the music he was learning to love.

On one memorable occasion, the very young lieutenant pursued his dedicated quest for pure Texas sound and authentic Texas beer through a succession of less than savory dance halls and saloons. An early Sunday morning sun found him awakening from a troubled sleep in the sand dunes on the Gulf beach near Freeport. As his eyes adjusted to the bright light and his brain groped for an explanation as to just why he had been sleeping on the beach, fully clothed in his best Saturday-night cowboy attire, Blanchard became aware of a large sign that stood not a foot from where he had slept. Unable to read the wording from his prone position, he struggled to his feet and read, "Danger—These Dunes Are Infested With Deadly Rattlesnakes—DO NOT ENTER." The startled New Yorker hurriedly departed, vowing to restrict his enjoyment of Texas nightlife to the relatively safe environs under the big tent in downtown Houston.[28]

Despite the colorful off-base adventures of its cadets and officers, Ellington Field played a significant role in the war effort. In addition to producing advanced pilots, bombardiers, and navigators for the Army Air Force, the airfield also trained a large number of aviators from several foreign countries through 1945.

While still in training, personnel from the many lands all enjoyed what by most accounts was one of the more generous distributions of rations in the entire Army. According to a May 25, 1944, article in the *Houston Press,* a typical weekday menu offered at any one of the five mess halls on the field was more than ample. Breakfast included cooked farina, fried potatoes, and the ever-popular creamed beef on toast, while dinner, as the Army dubbed the noontime meal, consisted of Swiss steak, mashed potatoes, beans with ham, spinach with fried bacon, lettuce and tomato salad, dessert, and punch. Supper, the final repast of the day, included roast pork, sliced cheese, bologna, salami, green onions, potato salad, and Italian plums, all washed down with gallons of coffee or milk.

To produce such relatively lavish feasts each day, the mess halls required 163 gallons of milk, 975 pounds of beef, 1,300 pounds of potatoes, 780 pounds of bread, 260 pounds of sugar, 390 pounds of lunch meat, and 39 gallons of Italian plums. It was estimated by the newspaper's reporter that the consumption of food would quadruple within a year after the article appeared, based on the Army's plans to increase the size of the training schools on the field.[29]

When the war finally came to a close in 1945, nearly 5,000 well-fed officers and men were assigned to Ellington Field. The City of Houston had lobbied the government to keep the base open following the war, but despite the efforts of Congressman Albert Thomas and other civic leaders, the closing of the facility was set for March 15, 1946. The last classes of foreign navigator trainees, including officers from France and China, were allowed to complete their training at Ellington, but U.S. Army Air Force navigator trainees were considered to be surplus and were reassigned to non-flying duties on other air bases.

Immediately upon its deactivation, the federally owned Ellington Field again became home to a unit of the Texas Air National Guard. The 111th Air Guard Squadron, which had been involved in much combat action during the war, moved onto the base, which had expanded in size during the war to include over two thousand acres. Soon, reservists from throughout the area were reporting to the field on weekends to retain and improve their flying skills. The base remained a busy Air Guard and reserve installation until July 28, 1948, when it was announced that once again, Ellington would become an active Air Force base as a result of Cold War tensions, which had escalated to ominous levels.[30]

The *Houston Chronicle* of July 27, 1948, reported that the challenge of again bringing the thrice-activated air base to operational readiness standards was once again going to be expensive. Many of the field's 600 buildings had fallen into disrepair, and despite the flying activities of the Air Guard, the runways were in need of resurfacing.[31]

Even though the field had again become an active USAF base, the Texas Air Guard was permitted to continue to fly from it. Efforts by the Air Force to relocate the Guard's 111th Fighter Squadron to nearby Houston Municipal Airport were stymied by widespread public concerns about the potentially dangerous overcrowding of the air space over the civilian facility.

The prime mission of the newest incarnation of a federally controlled Ellington Field was that of a radar navigator school. From 1949 through 1958, the 3605th Navigator Training Wing produced thousands of highly qualified fliers, equally well versed in the newly developing electronic technologies and the old and reliable, if often tedious, techniques of celestial, pressure pattern, and grid navigation. Ellington's graduates saw active service in all of the unheralded, often secretive, and generally unappreciated aspects of America's Cold War.

Two years before the navigation school closed in 1958, the Texas Air Guard returned from gallant duty in Korea to its old home at Ellington AFB. Eventually known as the 147th Fighter Group, the unit maintained what was termed a "constant state of readiness." Because of its proven proficiency and high quality of performance, the 147th continues to be regarded as one of America's top Air Guard outfits. Among those who served with distinction in the unit as a pilot was a future governor of Texas and the forty-third president of the United States, George W. Bush.

In 1960 the USAF again deactivated the base, only to reactivate it three years later. Finally, in 1976 the Air Force turned the base over to the 147th and withdrew from Ellington, this time possibly forever.

The Air Guard still flies on a regular basis from the often traded but still active old field, and the National Air and Space Administration (NASA) uses part of the facility and the runway for its astronaut program. The City of Houston, owner of most of the base since 1984, operates a small air terminal on the field as a third municipal airport.

Those who return to Ellington Field seeking a familiar sight to refresh dimming memories are sure to be disappointed. The only official memento of the field's rich historical past is a state-supplied marker that is strategically located inside the securely gated Air National Guard enclosure, safe from the prying eyes of anyone who might be interested in learning something of the eighty-year-long legacy of aviation that Ellington represents.

Some thirty years ago, there was still some physical evidence that a great base had once existed on this "table-flat land." One Air Force veteran, a graduate of Ellington's post–World War II navigator school, recalls driving alone to the old field at twilight on a misty day in October 1977 and finding only an eerie, ghostly enclave. Ramshackle barracks sagged under the weight of time. The once-festive Officers' Club swimming pool was filled with debris, and two life-preserver rings still hung from a tilting lifeguard tower.

The door to the clubhouse itself was ajar, and the former navigator entered the building just as he had so many times before some twenty years earlier. To his surprise, chairs and tables were still in place throughout the dining room and ashtrays remained on the bar. The bottles of liquor that had once been displayed on glass shelves back of the bar had mysteriously disappeared, but two cracked highball glasses clearly marked "Ellington Air Force Base" had somehow managed to survive.

The whole club was damp and clammy as only derelict coastal buildings can be, and the smell of decay was pervasive, but the one-time flier found it curiously difficult to leave. "If only," he remembers saying to himself, "if only it could be just like it was . . . maybe for just a minute." [32] But of course it could never again be as it once had been. Ellington Air Force Base, built and rebuilt, only to be abandoned time and time again, was now gone forever. After Hurricane Alicia flattened the few dilapidated buildings that still remained in 1983, nothing remained of the old wartime field but a rusting flagpole and the softening memories of those who had once served here. Old Ellington indeed was no more.

A. B. Davis, aka *"Mr. Lubbock," vigorously pursued his dream of an Army airfield for his city for nearly a decade prior to World War II.*

— Courtesy *Fort Worth Star-Telegram* Photograph Collection, Special Collections Division,

Maj. Gen. Gerald C. Brant was the commander of the Army Air Forces Gulf Region and the key figure in base location decision making.
— Courtesy Midland County Historical Museum, Midland, Texas

A page from a World War II guidebook to Lubbock Army Airfield, 1942.

— Courtesy Texas Tech University Special Collections Library/
Southwest Collection, Lubbock, Texas

A wartime view of the headquarters building at Lubbock Field, 1942.
— Courtesy Texas Tech University Special Collections Library/
Southwest Collection, Lubbock, Texas

An impressive array of training aircraft under a towering Texas sky.

— Courtesy Texas Tech University Special Collections Library/
Southwest Collection, Lubbock, Texas

Opening day at Lubbock Field, 1942.

— Courtesy Texas Tech University Special Collections Library/
Southwest Collection, Lubbock, Texas

The Lubbock Officers' Club in 1942.
— Courtesy Texas Tech University Special Collections Library/
Southwest Collection, Lubbock, Texas

A young officer thumbs through the latest issue of Esquire *magazine in the field's bachelor officers' quarters.*
— Courtesy Texas Tech University Special Collections Library/
Southwest Collection, Lubbock, Texas

A young Lubbock-based pilot contemplates his transition from a tiny trainer to a multi-engine aircraft.

— Courtesy Texas Tech University Special Collections Library/ Southwest Collection, Lubbock, Texas

The Lubbock Air Force Band strikes a formal pose in front of the administation building, 1944.

— Courtesy Texas Tech University Special Collections Library/
Southwest Collection, Lubbock, Texas

A rare photograph of Bergstrom's main gate as it appeared in 1943.

— Courtesy Bergstrom/Austin Community Council, Austin, Texas

Bergstrom's tower and one of its hangars, 1943.

— Courtesy Bergstrom/Austin Community Council, Austin, Texas

A Bergstrom-based Goony Bird. Note that the assigned pilot is a non-commissioned officer.

— Courtesy Bergstrom/Austin Community Council, Austin, Texas

A C-47 wings its way over Austin in the early 1940s.
Note the famous tower on the University of Texas campus at upper left.

— Courtesy Bergstrom/Austin Community Council,
Austin, Texas

President Lyndon B. Johnson, one of Bergstrom Field's greatest champions, returns to the base for the last time, January 1973.

— Courtesy Bergstrom/Austin Community Council,
Austin, Texas

Supporters of Bergstrom AFB rally to protest its closing, but to no avail.

— Courtesy Bergstrom/Austin Community Council, Austin, Texas

The bat-infested "Doughnut," headquarters building of the 12th Air Force in Bergstrom AFB's final years. It survived the base closing to become an airport hotel.

— Courtesy Bergstrom/Austin Community Council, Austin, Texas

The Lyndon B. Johnson Runway at the new Austin-Bergstrom International Airport.

— Courtesy Bergstrom/Austin Community Council, Austin, Texas

The Barbara Jordan Terminal Building at Austin-Bergstrom International Airport.

— Courtesy Bergstrom/Austin Community Council, Austin, Texas

The main gate at Big Spring Army Airfield, circa 1943.

— Courtesy Hangar 25 Museum, Big Spring, Texas

Cadets of Class 44-10 arrive in Big Spring for bombardier training.
— Courtesy Howard County Museum, Big Spring, Texas

According to their signs, the Army cooks are apparently out of soup, but doubly full of trust.

— Courtesy Howard County Museum, Big Spring, Texas

Bob Hope and Frances Langford entertain Big Spring cadets, 1944.
— Courtesy Howard County Museum, Big Spring, Texas

Two apparently unsuspecting "targets for tonight" are entertained at a Big Spring Service Club.

— Courtesy Howard County Museum, Big Spring, Texas

A dual engagement announcement party at the Service Club is symbolic of the many marriages that took place between local girls and Big Spring personnel.

— Courtesy Howard County Museum, Big Spring, Texas

The big day arrives for Big Spring Class 44-10. Note the foreign officer at the right of the photograph.
— Courtesy Howard County Museum, Big Spring, Texas

Boys of Big Spring High School's Class of 1944 are given a tour of the airfield. The caption beneath this yearbook photograph reads, "Draft Bait."

— Courtesy Howard County Museum, Big Spring, Texas

An excellent view of Big Spring's Hangar 25 before restoration began.
— Courtesy Gloria McDonald, Big Spring, Texas

The sun sets behind Hangar 25 just before the restoration.
— Courtesy Gloria McDonald, Big Spring, Texas

The completely restored Hangar 25 at Big Spring, now a unique air museum.

— Courtesy Hangar 25 Museum, Big Spring, Texas

An official USAAF photograph of Ellington Field, taken at noon on January 10, 1942. The wide white strip visible at upper center was at the time the largest single slab of concrete in the world.

— Courtesy Texas Military Forces Museum, Austin, Texas

Ellington cadets walk to their artistically arranged trainers.

— Courtesy Texas Military Forces Museum, Austin, Texas

The same dramatic ground formation of aircraft lends itself to a double "V for Victory" on Ellington's runway.

— Courtesy Texas Military Forces Museum, Austin, Texas

The Ellington Field Band sounds off during a 1944 review.

— Courtesy Texas Military Forces Museum, Austin, Texas

As the band plays on, Ellington's officers and cadets pass in review.
— Courtesy Texas Military Forces Museum, Austin, Texas

Men of the 79th Aviation Squadron march smartly between chapel and cannon.

— Courtesy Texas Military Forces Museum, Austin, Texas

Air Guard Pilot, future Texas governor and president of the United States, George W. Bush prepares for takeoff from Ellington in 1970.

— Courtesy Texas Military Forces Museum, Austin, Texas

A numerically arranged flight of training planes heads toward the Gulf of Mexico from Ellington Field.

— Courtesy Texas Military Forces Museum, Austin, Texas

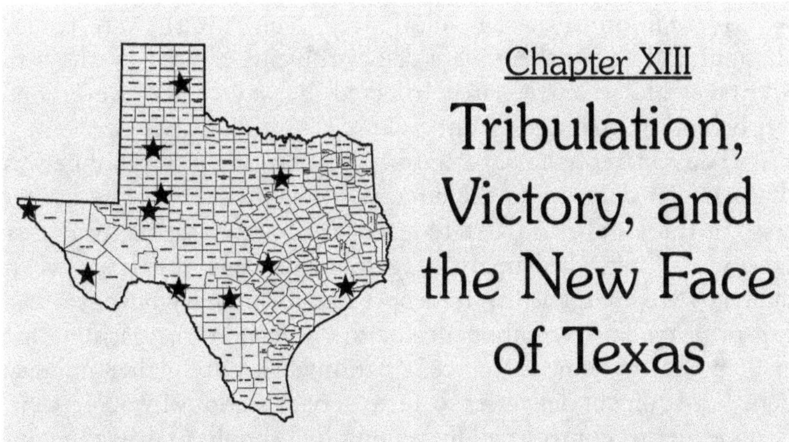

Chapter XIII

Tribulation, Victory, and the New Face of Texas

The very next day after the war started, my husband Tim was first in line to join the Navy. I was worried sick about him the whole four years he was in uniform, but when he came back safe and sound and kept telling us how rough he'd had it, I finally said, "Well, it wasn't any picnic around here either!"

Mrs. J. A. Timmons
Midland, Texas

Life on the Texas home front was anything but idyllic during the war years. The overriding concern among civilians, of course, was for the well-being of the state's 750,000 men and women in uniform. Overall, one of every ten Texans was in the service during the war, while roughly half of all men aged fifteen to forty-four were in uniform at some time between 1942 and 1945.[1] This drastic disruption in what had been a fairly static population pattern was made even more dramatic with the arrival of the thousands of military men assigned to the many Army and Navy installations located throughout the state. As pointed out in the preceding chapters, this relatively benign invasion of the Lone Star State resulted in a constant testing of long-held social standards and beliefs and frequently caused the weakening and eventual dissolution of traditional values that had never before been challenged.

In addition to these revolutionary changes in the way Texans thought and acted, there were daily problems created by the war. Shortages of certain resources affected the way of life of everyone left behind on the home front.

The apparent shortage and eventual rationing of gasoline was of particular concern to the citizens of what then was the largest state in the Union and a state legendary for its vast highway distances. At first, the supply of gasoline became restricted when tankers were compelled to transport fuel for military purposes as a top priority. This requirement cut the availability of gasoline for civilian use by some 20 percent nationwide, but further military demands soon cut deliveries to Texas service stations by 50 percent. In an effort to control rapidly waning fuel supplies fairly, the government instituted an unpopular rationing program. Although gasoline rationing was initially limited to the eastern part of the nation, perhaps out of recognition of the relatively shorter distances easterners were obliged to drive, it was eventually expanded to the entire nation.

Texans were perhaps understandably frustrated when most of the gasoline produced in such great quantities in their home state was virtually denied them under the expanded rationing program. In time, the government belatedly announced that the true purpose behind the rationing of gasoline had been in fact to conserve tire rubber, which was truly in dangerously short supply. Whatever the reason behind the rationing scheme, all Texans without a defense-related job were allowed only three gallons of gasoline per week.

If the fuel-restricted motorist chose to burn his weekly ration on the highways of Texas, he was compelled to observe a 35 mph speed limit to save both gasoline and tires. To make matters even more difficult, all prewar automobile assembly lines were converted to full war production on February 1, 1942, and the half-million automobiles left in stock were warehoused by the government to be sold only to worthy applicants for the war's duration. By 1944 all but 30,000 of the vehicles had been sold to individuals with high-priority defense positions, certain rural physicians, or law enforcement agencies. For most Texans, the government-ordered cessation of automobile production meant that whatever year, make, and model vehicle he was driving on the last day of January 1942 would have to endure to the end of the war.[2]

Many materials and items were either in short supply and rationed or totally unavailable until the conflict came to a close. Among these were sugar, meat, butter, cigarettes, matches, electric appliances, girdles, paper, and alcohol. In certain social circles, the shortage of alcohol, at least in its potable form, was among the more vexing of all of the war's inconveniences. As had been the case during the years of Prohibition, however, quantities of ardent spirits illegally shipped into Texas from Mexico served to materially reduce the liquor shortages in the state.

Ration books for staples were issued to every household in Texas and across the nation. The purchases of meat, sugar, and shoes, as well as gasoline, were limited to a buyer's ability to produce a mandatory ration coupon or stamp in addition to the necessary cash when buying the items. "Meatless Tuesdays" were introduced as a way to help conserve family meat-ration coupons, and in a state where hearty diners traditionally expected at least one meat entree each and every day, home economists concocted vegetarian recipes to fill the Tuesday void. Many Texans living in small rural towns simply arranged to purchase their beef or pork on the hoof, having it raised and fattened on a friend's farm until family appetites demanded the appropriate action be taken and the meat larder filled.

Quite often, people failed to understand why some items were subject to the troublesome and inconvenient rationing program while others were not. The official reason given for the rationing of an item not easily associated with military demands was simply that nearly all manufacturers had converted their facilities to produce items that were vital to the war effort.

Inconvenienced though they might have been, civilians wholeheartedly pitched into the war effort in other ways. They bought war bonds, collected scrap iron and rubber, gave blood, raised victory gardens, and even restricted themselves to taking only two baths per week in order to conserve soap. It was rumored at the time that some Texans considered taking two baths a week to be excessive and continued a lifelong practice of only indulging in a weekly bath, usually on Saturday night.[3]

In Texas, civilians worked at USO clubs located in the larger cities and at towns near airfields. Others served as volunteers at blood banks or at hospitals, while others provided transportation for relatives visiting servicemen stationed at nearby bases. Some volunteered to serve as air raid wardens in the Civilian Defense Corps, and still others served their time on the home front knitting or making bandages for military personnel.

The war also caused shortages that in turn created changes in how civilians dressed. A War Production Board (WPB) directive ordered a full 15-percent reduction in the yardage used to make garments. Consequently, men gave up wearing vests, women's skirts were shortened, and, eventually, ladies' nylon hosiery was taken completely out of production in order to produce sufficient quantities of parachutes for the Army Air Force. Certain garments were declared exempt from the WPB's orders. Included in this special group were infants' apparel, bridal gowns, maternity dresses, religious vestments, and even burial gowns. Perhaps somewhat inconsistent with this rather simplified cradle-to-the-grave rationale was a severe reduction in the production of metal coffins.[4]

While many of the restrictions brought about by the war may seem less than draconian in retrospect, it should be remembered that in Texas, as well as elsewhere, an economy kept long stagnant by the Great Depression had suddenly been made robust by money flowing from war-generated construction and production jobs. Most families had ample funds for the first time in many years, yet the shortages created by the same war that had made them relatively affluent made the most desirable items unavailable to them at any price. There was a heavy irony in this conundrum that was lightened only by a genuine patriotism and a sincere dedication to the winning of the war as soon as possible.

Another significant factor in the changes brought about in Texas by the war was a redefinition of women's role in society. Traditionally homemakers before Pearl Harbor, Texas women suddenly found themselves thrust into wartime jobs outside the home. Even though some 12,000 of the state's women had enlisted in the military service, there were still many females left behind who were eager to take over jobs formerly held by males in war production plants throughout the state. In Fort Worth's gigantic Consolidated Aircraft factory, for example, over 30 percent of the employees were women. They worked on assembly lines, wielded blowtorches, and drove trucks, each activity a far cry from their usual prewar occupations of cleaning house and tending flowers.[5]

The emergence of "Rosie the Riveter" signaled the beginning of an accelerated surge toward the independence of American women. For the first time in their lives, most of them were no longer reliant on the often indifferent and occasionally erratic generosity of men to provide them with both home and income. Learning new skills and gaining a previously unimaginable degree of self-reliance, the women of Texas swiftly achieved a level of empowerment during the war that would have otherwise taken decades to reach.

Sadly, many women and men alike lost something in the war that could never be replaced. More than 22,000 of the Texans who went to fight in Europe and in the Pacific were destined not to return alive. Virtually every community, large and small, had more than its share of Gold Star flags sadly but proudly unfurled in the windows of its homes. Each flag symbolized the death in service of a Texas man or woman, and in some windows, multiple Gold Stars mounted on a single flag told in muted ways of the heavy burden of crushing loss sustained in one household. To the few who can still remember in which windows those Gold Stars once hung before they were taken down, sun-faded and worn, it sometimes seems they left behind an indelible imprint on the glass, an eternal reminder of the terrible cost of war.

THE WAR ENDS, YET MEMORIES REMAIN

I can't really say which had changed more during the war, me or Texas.

Alton Kleinschmidt
San Antonio, Texas

By spring 1945, there was no doubt of an Allied victory in the war, and on May 8, with the capitulation of Nazi Germany, the fighting in Europe came to an official end. The event triggered enthusiastic celebrations throughout the nation, even though the War in the Pacific continued, with large losses of American lives reported every day.

The dropping of the atomic bomb on Hiroshima, Japan, on August 6, 1945, set in motion a series of events that culminated in the surrender of that nation a few days later. With the end of the Pacific War, the resulting celebrations were jubilant and without restraint.

World War II was over at long last, the boys would be coming home, and life would be getting back to normal, or so most people thought.

To be sure, the hundreds of thousands of men and women who had served their country did indeed begin to stream back into Texas, but both they and their home state had dramatically changed. The former soldiers and sailors had seen and done things they would have likely neither seen nor done had there been no war. Like most Texans before them, they would have probably stayed close to their homes their entire lives, but because of the war they had viewed the world and its people on a grand scale, and they were forever changed by the experience. They had acquired new attitudes and perspectives, and it was simply not possible for them to fully accept their hometowns and the people in them as they had been before the war.

On the other hand, the people in those hometowns had also changed. For many, the war had brought stunning personal loss and to all it had brought varying degrees of disruption, hardship, and deprivation. In the broader sense, however, jobs had been plentiful and the pay scale better than just good, and as a result, the Great Depression was only a bleak memory. Not everyone had grown wealthy because of the war, by any stretch of the imagination, but poverty had diminished, and the overall standard of living had risen across the state.

In the cities and towns that had hosted Army airfields, the new prosperity had directly contributed to the acceptance, or at least tolerance, of the disruptions created by the arrival of thousands of uniformed strangers. Despite the efforts of well-meaning commanders, Army personnel had broken laws from time to time, and most certainly had impudently challenged the old social order. Perhaps more important than all that, however, the Army also brought quantities of cash to communities that had previously been on the brink of economic disaster.

With money to spend and at least some time available to spend it, the soldiers had challenged longstanding traditions. Few individuals, and certainly no massive group, had ever challenged the social order to this degree before, particularly in the smaller communities where many of the airfields were located. Military personnel coming to Texas from other parts of the nation brought with them different and challenging views on racial and gender equality, a less-compliant respect for law and order, and a total rebellion against local archaic rules governing the sale of alcoholic beverages. The often-stringent local ground rules governing morality and legality were constantly probed and tested, and frequently broken by this gigantic force of high-spirited and freethinking individuals who had come to the state involuntarily. As they were only temporary Texans, the soldiers were in general not particularly inclined to warmly embrace locally conceived, hackneyed codes of conduct that they often perceived as bucolic and overly prohibitive, if not downright stupidly primitive. As long as no one got too badly hurt in this social revolution, the townspeople for the most part took the resulting challenges to their long-established order in stride, thankful to be doing their bit to win the war, and particularly thankful for the money the war had brought to their doorsteps.

In addition to the changes that had occurred to the returning veterans and their hometowns during the war, there was another element that further changed the face of Texas. Many of the servicemen who had been assigned to duty in the state during the war had grown fond of the place. After V-J Day in 1945, a surprisingly large number of these veterans from other states decided to return to Texas with their families. The cities of San Antonio and Harlingen gained a large share of the ex-GIs who decided to become permanent Texans. Bexar and Cameron counties, which contain San Antonio and Harlingen respectively, both experienced a population increase in excess of 50 percent from 1940 to 1950. Overall, the state showed an increase of 20 percent for the same period, with the western part posting a less-robust growth than the overall average.[6]

This large and influential group of new Texans continued the process of change that had begun with the arrival of the first detachment of soldiers in late 1941. These were the new pioneers who had liked what they saw during their service days and returned with their families to make their homes. Individuals in this group were a sort of social hybrid as far as Texan culture was concerned. They had undergone the sobering but liberating experience of direct exposure to a world at war, as had the veterans from Texas, plus they brought with them even greater permanent challenges to the prewar Texas way of life. After all, they and their families this time came to the state to stay, not just pass through on their way to a war. As full-time Texans, they demanded a voice in the way things were done.

These multiple forces of change brought about by World War II served to hasten the end of many lingering elements of the nineteenth-century mentality that had long pervaded parts of Texas prior to the conflict. It can, of course, be conclusively argued that eventually all of the state would have caught up with the twentieth century, war or no war. Such irresistible forces as immigration, mass communication, technology, better education, and vastly improved transportation would have surely combined, in time, to propel the state into the modern era, but it cannot be denied that the war greatly accelerated the transformation of Texas from a somewhat bucolic southern state into a more progressive, competitive, and highly influential social, economic, and political entity.

While tangible socioeconomic changes brought about by World War II were clearly in place by the end of the conflict in 1945, physical evidence of the massive military presence that had been in Texas for more than four years instantly began to disappear. Giant airfields, where thousands of men had learned to fight, were obliterated virtually overnight. Soon, only weatherbeaten water towers and a smattering of derelict hangars remained standing at what had once been bustling military cities, often bigger and far more active than the civilian communities located nearby.

Generations of people who live in those communities today have little if any knowledge that a major military installation ever existed near their town. Sadly, too many do not seem to care. Only a handful of the old fields have any sort of historical marker to inform those who do care about what occurred on the site nearly six decades ago. The veterans who served in World War II are dying at the rate of more than a thousand each day, and it seems only fitting that each former World War II military installation in Texas should have an easily accessible state historical marker to honor all who served there, before they, too, fade into history.

There are few curious and perhaps sentimental adventurers who care enough about the legacy of these once vital old airfields to seek some material evidence that they once existed. However, it is not always easy to find much that has survived nearly sixty years of vandalism, decay, and the force of often-harsh Texas weather. At Pampa, for example, an old hangar can be found on what is now private property, but instead of housing World War II B-24s, the once brightly painted building now shelters doomed Holstein and Angus feedlot cattle as they dumbly await their fate.

On the western edge of Hondo, gusting winds tear relentlessly at the little that remains of a wartime storage building, while hundreds of miles farther west, the ghostly mystery lights of Marfa dance eerily over what was once a giant air base. Only one wall and a few foundations remain, sagebrush and time having claimed everything else.

In other parts of the state, a keen-eyed observer can spot several old military water towers, with their distinctive checkerboard design only barely discernible after long years of exposure to the burning Texas sun. Many long concrete runways still exist, often in the most unlikely places. A twilight walk along those vast expanses of weed-choked surface can stir up images of the days when eager young pilots gunned the engines of their AT-6s here. Tie-down rings can still be found imbedded in abandoned airfield ramps, and rarely, some tiny artifact of a long-gone era can be discovered. A weathered coin, perhaps, or a shard of the typically thick ceramics used in military cups and plates, will bear silent witness to the historical truth that people once lived and worked on what is now an all-but-forgotten piece of earth.

For some who take the time and trouble to seek these old sites, there is an aura about them that is almost palpable. Something truly great happened there once, and a wisp of the spirit thus generated remains, even though only a few memories of all that happened have endured. It is as if all of the energy created by men and women intent on learning the skills of war was too intense to simply dissolve into the mists of time. Thousands of human beings once lived there, worked there, and died there, and an essence of them lingers still.

Although nearly all physical evidence of the great World War II experience has disappeared, memories of it do remain. There are still a precious few veterans and their survivors who can remember when the countless stars in the vast skies over Texas were joined by bright white stars so proudly emblazoned on the wings and fuselages of thousands of planes of the U.S. Army Air Force. In those cherished memories, doubtless enhanced and burnished by the inexorable passage of time, all of the wartime stars over Texas will be, forever, big and bright.

Appendices

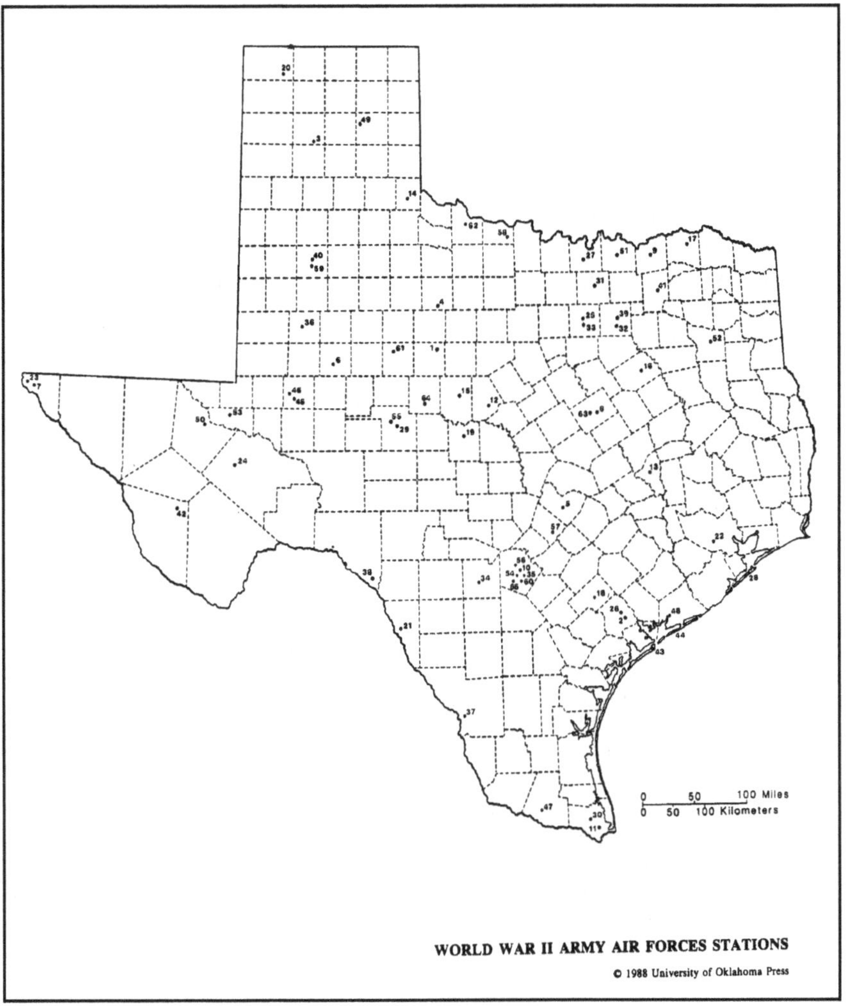

Map of Texas with airfields marked.

Copyright © 1988. Historical Atlas of Texas
The University of Oklahoma Press. Used by permission.

World War II Army Air Forces Stations

The wide expanse of relatively level terrain, coupled with a large number of clear-weather days, enabled Texas to become a major location for the establishment of Army Air Forces stations. The federal government started new flying fields and contracted for the use of existing municipal facilities to meet the need for trained pilots, navigators, bombardiers, and maintenance personnel during World War II. These installations had an influence on local services and lifestyles and brought changes to communities much more quickly than would have occurred under traditional conditions.

When the conflict ended, the federal government made some of the fields a permanent part of the national-defense system and transferred other properties to local governments. These acquisitions of improved air-power facilities by municipalities and counties led to a marked increase in aviation for agriculture, business, commerical traffic, industry, and personal flying pleasure.

The following list provides the names and locations of Army Air Force stations in Texas during World War II:

Army Air Forces Station	Location
1. Abilene Army Air Field	Abilene
2. Aloe Army Air Field	Victoria
3. Amarillo Army Air Field	Amarillo
4. Arledge Field	Stamford
5. Bergstrom Field	Austin
6. Big Spring Army Air Field	Big Spring
7. Biggs Field	El Paso
8. Blackland Army Air Field	Waco
9. Bonham Municipal Airport	Bonham
10. Brooks Field	San Antonio
11. Brownsville Municipal Airport	Brownsville
12. Brownwood Army Air Field	Brownsville
13. Bryan Army Air Field	Bryan
14. Childress Army Air Field	Childress
15. Coleman Flying School	Coleman
16. Corsicana Field	Corsicana
17. Cox Field	Paris
18. Cuero Municipal Airport	Cuero
19. Curtis Field	Brady
*20. Dalhart Army Air Field	San Antonio
21. Eagle Pass Army Air Field	Eagle Pass
22. Ellington Field	Houston
23. El Paso Municipal Airport	El Paso
24. Fort Stockton Field	Fort Stockton

*Author's Note: In the reference work cited here, Dalhart Army Airfield is shown to have been located in San Antonio. It was actually near Dalhart in the Panhandle.

25. Fort Worth Army Air Field .... Fort Worth
26. Foster Field........................ Victoria
27. Gainesville Army Air Field .... Gainesville
28. Galveston Army Air Field .... Galveston
29. Goodfellow Field .... San Angelo
30. Harlingen Army Air Field .... Harlingen
31. Hartlee Field....................... Denton
32. Hensley Field .... Dallas
33. Hicks Field......................... Fort Worth
34. Hondo Army Air Field .... Hondo
35. Kelly Field .... San Antonio
36. Lamesa Municipal Airport .... Lamesa
37. Laredo Army Air Field.............. Laredo
38. Laughlin Field...................... Del Rio
39. Love Field.......................... Dallas
40. Lubbock Army Air Field .... Lubbock
41. Majors Field .... Greenville
42. Marfa Army Air Field .... Marfa
43. Matagorda Island Bombing and
    Gunnery Range .... Victoria
*44. Matagorda Peninsula Bombing Range . . Childress
45. Midland Army Air Field............. Midland
46. Midland Municipal Airport .... Midland
47. Moore Field .... Mission
48. Palacios Army Air Field............ Palacios
49. Pampa Army Air Field.............. Pampa
50. Pecos Army Air Field............... Pecos
51. Perrin Field........................ Sherman
52. Pounds Field....................... Tyler
53. Pyote Army Air Field .... Pyote
54. Randolph Field.................... San Antonio
55. San Angelo Army Air Field .... San Angelo
56. San Antonio Municipal Airport....... San Antonio
57. San Marcos Army Air Field .... San Marcos
58. Sheppard Field .... Wichita Falls
59. South Plains Army Air Field .... Lubbock
60. Stinson Field....................... San Antonio
61. Sweetwater Municipal Airport........ Sweetwater
62. Victory Field....................... Vernon
63. Waco Army Air Field............... Waco
64. Bruce Field .... Ballinger
65. San Antonio Aviation Cadet Center
    (Lackland Army Air Field, 1946)...... San Antonio

—Courtesy *Historical Atlas of Texas*

*Matagorda Peninsula Bombing Range was not located anywhere near Childress, Texas, as listed in this reference source.

Pampa Army Airfield

U.S. Army Air Force Information Sheets
July 1944 (Formerly Restricted)

LOCATION:
from city: 12.5 mi. E; (airline); 12.8 mi. (road)
POSITION: lat. 35°32'00". Long. 100°44'00".
ALTITUDE: 3,130'.
CITY POPULATION: 12,895.

DESCRIPTION:
TYPE: Army (Advanced Twin-Engine Pilot School).
SIZE: 2,560 acres.
SHAPE: Square.

RUNWAYS: N/S 6,500' x 150', E/W 6,500' x 150', NW/SE 6,540' x 150', bituminous.
DRAINAGE: Natural and artificial.
SURFACE THROUGHOUT YEAR: Good.
OBSTRUCTIONS: None within 40/1 glide angle.
MARKINGS: Boundary markers; wind tee.
CAMOUFLAGE: None.
LIGHTING: Beacon (rotating); obst.; contact; runway (mobile); flood.

FACILITIES:
HANGARS: (1) 202' x 163', door 120' x 29'; (5) 122' x 80', door 121' x 25'; wood.
SHOPS: Major repairs.

GASOLINE:
At Airport: 73 and 91 octane, 465,000 gal.; tank capacity, 575,500 gal.; 8 servicing trucks, total capacity, 16,000 gal.
In Vicinity: 80 octane, 1,035 gal. at Pampa.

OIL:
At Airport: SAE 1120, 192,000 qt., in underground storage.
In Vicinity: None reported.

COMMUNICATIONS:
Telephone; telegraph; teletype; AACS station, call WXUD.

PERSONNEL ACCOMODATIONS:
At Airport: 75 officers; 500 enlisted men.
In Vicinity: At Pampa.

RADIO FACILITIES:
RANGE: 293 kcs.; ident. sig., DPW; mag. bearing, station to field, 124°, 3.0 mi.

INSTRUMENT APPROACH AND LETDOWN PROCEDURE:
Min. safe initial approach alt., 5,000'. Final approach, NW leg. Procedure turn alt., 4,500'. Alt. over range, final approach, 4,100'.
Min. safe letdown alt. over field, 3,600'. Missed approach, climb to 5,000' on SE leg.
CONTROL TOWER: 396 and 3760 kcs; continuous.

WEATHER:
PREVAILING WIND: S, except Feb., N.
PRECIPITATION: Av. mo, 0.50" (Jan.) to 3.24" (June); av. yr., 23.30".
TEMPERATURE: Av. min. and max., 44.4° to 72°; extremes, 15° to 114°.
FOG: Nov. to Mar.
FACILITIES: Class B weather station.

TRANSPORTATION:
RAILROADS: Fort Worth & Denver City; Panhandle & Sante Fe; at Pampa.
ROADS: State No. 152, adjacent N, paved.
FACILITIES: Bus service.

OPERATED BY: Army Air Forces.
OWNED BY: U.S. Govt.
AUXILIARY FIELDS: No. 1 (Reeves Field), 14.8 mi. WSW; No. 2 (Thompson Field), 16.2 mi. WNW; No. 3 (Hoover Field), 9.8 mi. NW; No. 4 (Laketon Field), 8.3 mi. ENE.

Hondo Army Airfield

U.S. Army Air Force Information Sheets
July 1944 (Formerly Restricted)

LOCATION:
from city: 2.2 mi. WNW (airline); 2.7 mi. (road)
POSITION: lat. 29°20'40". Long. 99°10'30".
ALTITUDE: 918'.
CITY POPULATION: 3,000.

DESCRIPTION:
TYPE: Army (Navigation School).
SIZE: 3,661 acres.
SHAPE: Irregular.

RUNWAYS: N/S 6,100' x 150', E/W 6, 100' x 150', NW/SE 6,100' x 150', concrete (under const.).
DRAINAGE: Natural and artificial.
SURFACE THROUGHOUT YEAR: Use runways only.
OBSTRUCTIONS: None within 40/1 glide angle.
MARKINGS: Wind cone; tetrahedron.
CAMOUFLAGE: None.
LIGHTING: Beacon (rotating); obst.; landing strip; runway (mobile); flood.

FACILITIES:
HANGARS: (3) 149' x 104', door 120' x 25'; (1) 200' x 161', door 120' x 28'; wood.
SHOPS: Major repairs.

GASOLINE:
At Airport: 91 and 100 octane, 102,348 gal.; tank capacity, 225,000 gal.; 8 servicing trucks, total capacity, 16,000 gal.
In Vicinity: None reported.

OIL:
At Airport: SAE 1120, 125,491 qt., in underground storage.
In Vicinity: SAE 20 to 50, at Hondo.

COMMUNICATIONS:
Telephone; telegraph; teletype.

PERSONNEL ACCOMODATIONS:
At Airport: 20 officers; 75 enlisted men.
In Vicinity: At Hondo.

RADIO FACILITIES:
RANGE: 230 kcs.; ident. sig., DHN; mag. bearing, station to field, 125°, 5.5 mi.

INSTRUMENT APPROACH AND LETDOWN PROCEDURE:
Min. safe initial approach alt., 5,500'. Final approach, W side of NW leg. Procedure turn alt., 3,500'. Alt. over range, final approach, 2,500'. Min. safe letdown alt. over field, 1,400'. Missed approach, climb to 3,000' on SE leg.
CONTROL TOWER: 317 kcs; continuous.

WEATHER:
PREVAILING WIND: SE, except Dec., Jan., N.
PRECIPITATION: Av. mo, 1.14" (Jan.) to 4.06" (May); av. yr., 27.39".
TEMPERATURE: Av. min. and max., 57.6° to 81.50°; extremes, 10° to 109°.
FOG: Dec. to June.
FACILITIES: Class A weather station.

TRANSPORTATION:
RAILROADS: Southern Pacific at Hondo. Sidings: On field.
ROADS: U.S. No. 90, 1.1 mi. SE, paved; county roads, adjacent N and adjacent E, improved.
FACILITIES: Govt. transportation; bus and taxi service.

OPERATED BY: Army Air Forces.
OWNED BY: U.S. Govt.
AUXILIARY FIELDS: Castroville Field, 19.9 mi. E; Kelly Field No. 5, 18.3 mi. ENE.

Laughlin Army Airfield

U.S. Army Air Force Information Sheets
July 1944 (Formerly Restricted)

LOCATION:
FROM CITY: 7.0 mi. E (airline); 8.0 mi. (road)
POSITION: lat. 29°21'48". Long. 100°47'15".
ALTITUDE: 1,073'.
CITY POPULATION: 13,343.

DESCRIPTION:
TYPE: Army (Specialized Twin-Engine Pilot School).
SIZE: 3,862 acres.
SHAPE: Irregular.

RUNWAYS: N/S 6,500' x 150', E/W 6,500' x 150', NW/SE 6,500' x 150', NW/SE 6,500' x 150', bituminous.
DRAINAGE: Natural and artificial.
SURFACE THROUGHOUT YEAR: Good.
OBSTRUCTIONS: None within 10/1 glide angle.
MARKINGS: wind cone; tetrahedron.
CAMOUFLAGE: None.
LIGHTING: Beacon (rotating); obst.; runway (mobile); flood.

FACILITIES:
HANGARS: (1) 202' x 162', door 162' x 29.5'; (1) 122' x 80', door 122' x 25'; wood.
SHOPS: Army.

GASOLINE:
At Airport: 65 to 100 octane, 252,500 gal.; tank capacity, 464,000 gal.; 10 servicing trucks, total capacity, 56,000 gal.
In Vicinity: At Del Rio.

OIL:
At Airport: SAE 1120, 26,000 qt.
In Vicinity: At Del Rio.

COMMUNICATIONS:
Telephone; telegraph; teletype.

PERSONNEL ACCOMODATIONS:
At Airport: 75 officers; 300 enlisted men.
In Vicinity: At Del Rio.

RADIO FACILITIES:
RANGE: 303 kcs.; ident. sig., DRD; mag. bearing, station to field, 259°, 4.9 mi.

INSTRUMENT APPROACH AND LETDOWN PROCEDURE: none.

CONTROL TOWER: 278 and 126.18 mcs; continuous.

WEATHER:
PREVAILING WIND: SE.
PRECIPITATION: Av. mo, 0.40" (Jan.) to 2.57" (Oct.); av. yr., 18.63".
TEMPERATURE: Av. min. and max., 58.5° to 79.9°; extremes, 12° to 111°.
FOG: Nov. to Mar.
FACILITIES: Class B weather station.

TRANSPORTATION:
RAILROADS: Southern Pacific at Del Rio. Sidings: On field.
ROADS: U.S. No. 90, adjacent NW, paved.
FACILITIES: Bus and taxi service.

OPERATED BY: Army Air Forces.
OWNED BY: U.S. Govt.

Midland Army Airfield

U.S. Army Air Force Information Sheets July 1944 (Formerly Restricted)

LOCATION:
FROM CITY: 8.0 mi. WSW (airline); 10.5 mi. (road)
POSITION: lat. 31°56'30". Long. 102°11'45".
ALTITUDE: 2,856'.
CITY POPULATION: 9,352.
DESCRIPTION:
TYPE: Army (Bombardier-School).
SIZE: 1,670 acres.
SHAPE: Irregular.
RUNWAYS: (2) N/S 6,500' x 150', NE/SW 6,500' x 150', NW/SE 6,540' x 150', asphalt.
DRAINAGE: Natural and artificial.
SURFACE THROUGHOUT YEAR: Good.
OBSTRUCTIONS: None within 40/1 glide angle.
MARKINGS: Boundary markers; wind tee, tetrahedron.
CAMOUFLAGE: None.
LIGHTING: Beacon (rotating); obst.; boundary; range; approach; flood.
FACILITIES:
HANGARS: (4) 180' x 120', door 80' x 20', steel.
SHOPS: Major repairs.
GASOLINE:
At Airport: 87 to 100 octane, tank capacity, 670,000 gal.; 20 servicing trucks.
In Vicinity: At Midland.
OIL:
At Airport: SAE 100 to 120, 15,000 qt., in tank.
In Vicinity: At Midland.
COMMUNICATIONS:
Telephone; telegraph; teletype; AACS station, call WZH.
PERSONNEL ACCOMODATIONS:
At Airport: 35 officers; 35 enlisted men.
In Vicinity: At Midland.
RADIO FACILITIES:
RANGE: 209 kcs.; ident. sig., DMD; mag. bearing, station to field, 48°, 3.5 mi.
INSTRUMENT APPROACH AND LETDOWN PROCEDURE:
Min. safe initial approach alt., 4,500'. Final approach, SW leg.
Procedure turn alt., 4,500'. Alt. over range, final approach, 3,800'. Min. safe letdown alt. over field, 3,400'. Missed approach, climb to 4,500' on NE leg.
CONTROL TOWER: 396 kcs; continuous.
WEATHER:
PREVAILING WIND: S, except Dec., Feb., SW; July, Aug., Sept., Oct., SE..
PRECIPITATION: Av. mo, 0.46" (Jan.) to 2.17" (May); av. yr., 15.91".
TEMPERATURE: Av. min. and max., 47.6° to 78.5°; extremes, -1° to 116°.
FOG: Dec., Jan., Feb.
FACILITIES: First-order weather station.
TRANSPORTATION:
RAILROADS: Texas and Pacific; at Midland. Sidings: On field.
ROADS: U.S. No. 80, adjacent S, State No. 158, 4.2 mi. NNE; paved.
FACILITIES: Bus service.
OPERATED BY: Army Air Forces.
OWNED BY: City of Midland.

Marfa Army Airfield

U.S. Army Air Force Information Sheets
July 1944 (Formerly Restricted)

LOCATION:
FROM CITY: 9.5 mi. ESE (airline and road)
POSITION: lat. 30°15'30". Long. 103°52'21".
ALTITUDE: 4,854'.
CITY POPULATION: 3,805.
DESCRIPTION:
TYPE: Army (Advanced Twin-Engine Pilot School).
SIZE: 2,717 acres.
SHAPE: Square.
RUNWAYS: N/S 7,525' x 150', NE/SW 7,500' x 150', NE/SW 6,000' x 150', E/W 7,500' x 150', (2) NW/SE 7,500' x 150', asphalt.
DRAINAGE: Natural.
SURFACE THROUGHOUT YEAR: Use runways only.
OBSTRUCTIONS: None within 40/1 glide angle.
MARKINGS: Wind cone; wind tee tetrahedron.
CAMOUFLAGE: None.
LIGHTING: Beacon (rotating); obst.; landing strip; approach; runway (mobile); flood.
FACILITIES:
HANGARS: (1) 202' x 160', door 120' x 27'; (1) 159' x 12', (1) 159' x 130', door 55' x 12'; (1) 153' x 87', door 120' x 27'; (1) 122' x 96', door 120' x 27'; wood.
SHOPS: Major repairs.
GASOLINE:
At Airport: 73 to 91 octane, 230,000 gal.; tank capacity, 383,500 gal.; 9 servicing trucks, total capacity, 36,000 gal.
In Vicinity: None reported.
OIL:
At Airport: SAE 1120, 62,000 qt., in bulk.
In Vicinity: None reported.
COMMUNICATIONS:
Telephone; telegraph; teletype; AACS station, call DMT.
PERSONNEL ACCOMODATIONS:
At Airport: 50 officers; 50 enlisted men.
In Vicinity: At Marfa.
RADIO FACILITIES:
RANGE: 293 kcs.; ident. sig., DMT; mag. bearing, station to field, 118°, 3.6 mi.
INSTRUMENT APPROACH AND LETDOWN PROCEDURE: None.
CONTROL TOWER: 3770 kcs; continuous.
WEATHER:
PREVAILING WIND: No data.
PRECIPITATION: Av. mo, 0.15" (Jan.) to 2.38“" (June); av. yr., 12.11".
TEMPERATURE: No data.
FOG: Not prevalent.
FACILITIES: Class A weather station.
TRANSPORTATION:
RAILROADS: Southern Pacific at Marfa. Sidings: Capacity, 260 cars, on field.
ROADS: U.S. Nos. 67 and 90, adjacent N, paved.
FACILITIES: Bus service.
OPERATED BY: Army Air Forces.
OWNED BY: U.S. Govt.
AUXILIARY FIELDS: No. 1 (South Field), 8.0 mi. SSE; No. 3 (Ryan Field), 27.3 mi. WNW; No. 4 (CAA Field), 11.3 mi. NW; No. 5 (Aragon Field), 18.7 mi. WNW; No. 7 (Marfa Municipal Airport), 8.5 mi. WNW.

Biggs Airfield

U.S. Army Air Force Information Sheets
July 1944 (Formerly Restricted)

LOCATION:
FROM CITY: 8.0 mi. NE (airline); 11.0 mi. (road)
POSITION: lat. 31°50'30". Long. 106°23'15".
ALTITUDE: 3,922'.
CITY POPULATION: 96,810.
DESCRIPTION:
TYPE: Army.
SIZE: 2,560 acres.
SHAPE: Square.
RUNWAYS: N/S 7,000' x 150', NE/SW 9,300' x 150', E/W 7,000' x 150', asphalt.
DRAINAGE: Natural and artificial.
SURFACE THROUGHOUT YEAR: Good.
OBSTRUCTIONS: None within 40/1 glide angle.
MARKINGS: Boundary markers; wind tee.
CAMOUFLAGE: None.
LIGHTING: Beacon (rotating); obst.; boundary; runway (mobile); flood.
FACILITIES:
HANGARS: (4) 122' x 80', door 122' x 25'; wood.
SHOPS: Major repairs.
GASOLINE:
At Airport: 73 octane, 91 octane, and 100 aromatic 635,000 gal.; 8 servicing trucks, total capacity, 48,000 gal.
In Vicinity: 91 and 100 octane, 200,000 gal., 3.0 mi.
OIL:
At Airport: SAE 60, 25,000 qt., in underground storage.
In Vicinity: SAE 60 to 120, 100,000 qt., 3.0 mi.
COMMUNICATIONS:
Telephone; telegraph; teletype; AACS station, call WZB.
PERSONNEL ACCOMODATIONS:
At Airport: 125 officers; 200 enlisted men.
In Vicinity: At El Paso.
RADIO FACILITIES:
RANGE: None.
INSTRUMENT APPROACH AND LETDOWN PROCEDURE:
None.
CONTROL TOWER: 396 kcs. and 126.18 mcs; continuous.
WEATHER:
PREVAILING WIND: E, except Nov., Dec., Jan., Feb., NW; Mar., Apr., May, W.
PRECIPITATION: Av. mo, 0.23" (Apr.) to 1854" (July); av. yr., 8.86".
TEMPERATURE: Av. min. and max., 50.8° to 76.1°; extremes, -5° to 106°.
FOG: Aug. to Mar.
FACILITIES: First-order weather station.
TRANSPORTATION:
RAILROADS: Mexico North-Western; Southern Pacific; Texas & Pacific; at El Paso. Sidings: On field.
ROADS: U.S. No. 54, 3.0 mi. NW; U.S. No. 62, 3.5 mi. S; paved.
FACILITIES: Bus, taxi, and trolley service.
OPERATED BY: Army Air Forces.
OWNED BY: U.S. Govt.

Fort Worth Army Airfield

U.S. Army Air Force Information Sheets
July 1944 (Formerly Restricted)

LOCATION:
FROM CITY: 6.25 mi. WNW (airline); 8.0 mi. (road)
POSITION: lat. 32°46'22". Long. 97°26'13".
ALTITUDE: 613'.
CITY POPULATION: 177,662.
DESCRIPTION:
TYPE: Army (Specialized Four-Engine Pilot School).
SIZE: 1,428 acres.
SHAPE: Irregular.
RUNWAYS: N/S 7,300' x 150', NE/SW 5,643' x 150', EW 4,100' x 150' (permanently closed), NW/SE 7,000' x 150', concrete.
DRAINAGE: Natural and artificial.
SURFACE THROUGHOUT YEAR: Good.
OBSTRUCTIONS: None within 30/1 glide angle.
MARKINGS: Tetrahedron.
CAMOUFLAGE: None.
LIGHTING: Beacon (rotating); obst.; boundary; contact; range; flood.
FACILITIES:
HANGARS: (1) 202' x 163', door 120' x 25'; (4) 122' x 80', door 120' x 25'; steel; (1) 122' x 80', door 120' x 25', wood.
SHOPS: Major repairs.
GASOLINE:
At Airport: 87, 91 and 100 octane, 71,000 gal.; tank capacity, 71,000 gal.; 18 servicing trucks, total capacity, 72,000 gal.
In Vicinity: At Fort Worth; 100 octane, 408,000 gal., at refineries (10.0 mi.).
OIL:
At Airport: SAE 1120, 20,000 qt., in underground storage.
In Vicinity: At Fort Worth.
COMMUNICATIONS:
Telephone; telegraph.
PERSONNEL ACCOMODATIONS:
At Airport: 22 officers; 120 enlisted men.
In Vicinity: At Fort Worth.
RADIO FACILITIES:
RANGE: 365 kcs.; ident. sig., FV;call KKJ; mag. bearing, station to field, 211°, 6.8 mi.
INSTRUMENT APPROACH AND LETDOWN PROCEDURE:
Min. safe initial approach alt., 2,000'. Final approach, N leg. Procedure turn alt., 2,000'. Alt. over range, final approach, 2,000'. Min. safe letdown alt. over field, 1,120'. Missed approach, climb to 2,000' on SW leg.
CONTROL TOWER: 201 kcs and 126.18 mcs; continuous.
WEATHER:
PREVAILING WIND: S, except Dec., Jan., Feb., NW.
PRECIPITATION: Av. mo, 1.83" (Jan.) to 4.53" (May); av. yr., 32.67".
TEMPERATURE: Av. min. and max., 57.7° to 76.2°; extremes, -8° to 112°.
FOG: Fall and winter.
FACILITIES: Class B weather station.
TRANSPORTATION:
RAILROADS: At Fort Worth. Sidings: Capacity, 55 cars, adjacent.
ROADS: U.S. No. 80, 3.6 mi. SSE; State No. 199, 2.4 mi. NE; paved.
FACILITIES: Bus and taxi service.
OPERATED BY: Army Air Forces.
OWNED BY: U.S. Govt.
AUXILIARY FIELDS: Olney Municipal Airport, 92.7 mi. WNW.

Lubbock Army Airfield

U.S. Army Air Force Information Sheets
July 1944 (Formerly Restricted)

LOCATION:
FROM CITY: 11.5 mi. W (airline); 13.0 mi. (road)
POSITION: lat. 33°36'30". Long. 102°02'00".
ALTITUDE: 3,330'.
CITY POPULATION: 31,853.

DESCRIPTION:
TYPE: Army (Advanced Twin-Engine Pilot School).
SIZE: 1,631 acres.
SHAPE: Rectangular.

RUNWAYS: N/S 6,500' x 150', NE/SW 6,500' x 150', E/W 6,540' x 150', asphalt.
DRAINAGE: Natural and artificial.
SURFACE THROUGHOUT YEAR: Good.
OBSTRUCTIONS: None within 40/1 glide angle.
MARKINGS: Tetrahedron.
CAMOUFLAGE: None.
LIGHTING: Beacon (rotating); obst.; contact; approach; runway (mobile); flood.

FACILITIES:
HANGARS: (3) 184' x 100', 2 doors 92' x 20'; (5) 122' x 80', metal.
SHOPS: Major repairs.

GASOLINE:
At Airport: 73 to 87 octane, 170,000 gal.; tank capacity, 539,000 gal.; 8 servicing trucks, total capacity, 14,000 gal.
In Vicinity: None reported.

OIL:
At Airport: SAE 1120, 20,000 qt., in underground storage.
In Vicinity: None reported.

COMMUNICATIONS:
Telephone; telegraph; teletype.

PERSONNEL ACCOMODATIONS:
At Airport: 50 officers; 50 enlisted men.
In Vicinity: At Lubbock.

RADIO FACILITIES:
RANGE: 224 kcs.; ident. sig., HH; mag. bearing, station to field, 173°, 3.5 mi.

INSTRUMENT APPROACH AND LETDOWN PROCEDURE:
Min. safe initial approach alt., 5,000'. Final approach, N leg. Procedure turn alt., 4,400'. Alt. over range, final approach, 4,100'. Min. safe letdown alt. over field, 3,800'. Missed approach, climb to 4,400' on S leg.

CONTROL TOWER: 396 kcs continuous.

WEATHER:
PREVAILING WIND: SW except May, June, July, Aug., Sept., SE; Oct., S.
PRECIPITATION: Av. mo, 0.38" (Jan.) to 2.70" (Oct.); av. yr., 19.04".
TEMPERATURE: Av. min. and max., 44.9° to 73.5°; extremes, -10° to 108°.
FOG: Not prevalent.
FACILITIES: Class A weather station.

TRANSPORTATION:
RAILROADS: Fort Worth & Denver City; Panhandle & Santa Fe; at Lubbock. Sidings: Capacity, 42 cars, on field.
ROADS: State No. 290, adjacent S, county road, adjacent E.; paved.
FACILITIES: Bus service.

OPERATED BY: Army Air Forces.
OWNED BY: City of Lubbock.

Bergstrom Field

U.S. Army Air Force Information Sheets
July 1944 (Formerly Restricted)

LOCATION:
FROM CITY: 6.4 mi. SE (airline); 7.5 mi. (road)
POSITION: lat. 30°12'00". Long. 97°40'00".
ALTITUDE: 515'.
CITY POPULATION: 87,930.
DESCRIPTION:
TYPE: Army.
SIZE: 2,300 acres.
SHAPE: Irregular.
RUNWAYS: N/S 6,000' x 300', N/S 5,300' x 150', NE/SW 6,000' x 300', E/W 6,500' x 300', NW/SE 7,000' x 300', NW/SE 5,500' x 150', bituminous.
DRAINAGE: Natural and artificial.
SURFACE THROUGHOUT YEAR: Good.
OBSTRUCTIONS: None within 40/1 glide angle.
MARKINGS: wind cone; tetrahedron.
CAMOUFLAGE: None.
LIGHTING: Beacon (rotating); contact; runway (mobile); flood.
FACILITIES:
HANGARS: (1) 200' x 121', door 121' x 29', wood.
SHOPS: Major repairs.
GASOLINE:
At Airport: 73 and 91 octane, 165,000 gal.; tank capacity, 200,000 gal.; 7 servicing trucks, total capacity, 20,000 gal.
In Vicinity: At Austin.
OIL:
At Airport: SAE 1100 and 1120, 40,000 qt., in drums.
In Vicinity: At Austin.
COMMUNICATIONS:
Telephone; telegraph; teletype.
PERSONNEL ACCOMODATIONS:
At Airport: 50 officers; 50 enlisted men.
In Vicinity: At Austin.
RADIO FACILITIES:
RANGE: None.
INSTRUMENT APPROACH AND LETDOWN PROCEDURE: None.
CONTROL TOWER: 396 kcs and 126.18 mcs.; continuous.
WEATHER:
PREVAILING WIND: SE, except Nov., Dec., Jan., Feb., N.
PRECIPITATION: Av. mo, 1.97" (Jan.) to 4.42" (May); av. yr., 33.78".
TEMPERATURE: Av. min. and max., 53.7° to 78.4°; extremes, -1° to 109°.
FOG: Nov. to Apr.
FACILITIES: First-order weather station.
TRANSPORTATION:
RAILROADS: Missouri-Kansas-Texas; Missouri Pacific; Southern Pacific; at Austin.
Sidings: On field.
ROADS: U.S. No. 290, 0.6 mi. NE; State No. 29, adjacent W, paved.
FACILITIES: Bus service.
OPERATED BY: Army Air Forces.
OWNED BY: City of Austin

Big Spring Army Airfield

U.S. Army Air Force Information Sheets
July 1944 (Formerly Restricted)

LOCATION:
FROM CITY: 3.0 mi. WSW (airline and road)
POSITION: lat. 32°13'25". Long. 101°31'00".
ALTITUDE: 2,541'.
CITY POPULATION: 12,604.

DESCRIPTION:
TYPE: Army (Bombardier School).
SIZE: 1,284 acres.
SHAPE: Rectangular.

RUNWAYS: N/S 6,200' x 150', NE/SW 6,200' x 150', E/W 6,200' x 150', NW/SE 6,200' x 150', asphalt.
DRAINAGE: Artificial.
SURFACE THROUGHOUT YEAR: Good.
OBSTRUCTIONS: 20' pole line, N; 308' hill, E.
MARKINGS: Wind cone; wind tee.
CAMOUFLAGE: None.
LIGHTING: Beacon (rotating); obst.; contact; flood.

FACILITIES:
HANGARS: (1) 200' x 150', door 120' x 29'; (2) 120' x 80', door 120' x 27'; tile and wood.
SHOPS: Major repairs.

GASOLINE:
At Airport: 87, 91, and 100 octane, 220,000 gal.; tank capacity, 220,000 gal.; 16 servicing trailers, total capacity, 32,000 gal.
In Vicinity: 72 octane, ample, 6.0 mi.

OIL:
At Airport: SAE 50 to 60, 72,000 qt., in underground storage.
In Vicinity: At Big Spring.

COMMUNICATIONS:
Telephone; telegraph; teletype.

PERSONNEL ACCOMODATIONS:
At Airport: 30 officers; 200 enlisted men.
In Vicinity: At Big Spring.

RADIO FACILITIES:
RANGE: 326 kcs.; ident. sig., BZ; call KCAP; mag. bearing, station to field, 70°, 3.8 mi.

INSTRUMENT APPROACH AND LETDOWN PROCEDURE:
Min. safe initial approach alt., 4,000'. Final approach, SW leg. Procedure turn alt., 4,000'. Alt. over range, final approach, 3,100'. Min. safe letdown alt. over field, 3,100'. Missed approach, climb to 4,000' on E leg.
CONTROL TOWER: 278 kcs; continuous.

WEATHER:
PREVAILING WIND: S.
PRECIPITATION: Av. mo, 0.44" (Jan.) to 2.61" (May); av. yr., 18.60".
TEMPERATURE: Av. min. and max., 49.9° to 78.2°; extremes, -4° to 117°.
FOG: Not prevalent.
FACILITIES: First-order weather station.

TRANSPORTATION:
RAILROADS: Texas & Pacific at Big Spring.
Sidings: Capacity, 25 cars, adjacent.
ROADS: U.S. No. 80, 0.6 mi. N, paved; county road, adjacent W, dirt.
FACILITIES: Bus and taxi service.

OPERATED BY: Army Air Forces.
OWNED BY: U.S. Govt.

Ellington Airfield

U.S. Army Air Force Information Sheets
July 1944 (Formerly Restricted)

LOCATION:
FROM CITY: 15.7 mi. SE (airline); 19.0 mi. (road)
POSITION: lat. 29°36'20". Long. 95°10'06".
ALTITUDE: 34'.
CITY POPULATION: 384,514.
DESCRIPTION:
TYPE: Army (Advanced Twin-Engine Pilot School).
SIZE: 1,825 acres.
SHAPE: Rectangular.
RUNWAYS: (2) N/S 5,000' x 150', (2) NE/SW 5,000' x 150', (2) NW/SE 5,000' x 150', concrete.
DRAINAGE: Natural and artificial.
SURFACE THROUGHOUT YEAR: Use runways only.
OBSTRUCTIONS: None within 40/1 glide angle.
MARKINGS: Tetrahedron.
CAMOUFLAGE: None.
LIGHTING: Beacon (twin beam); obst.; contact; range; runway (mobile); flood.
FACILITIES:
HANGARS: (1) 201' x 162', door 122' x 28', wood and metal.
SHOPS: Major repairs.
GASOLINE:
At Airport: 87 to 130 octane, 368,000 gal.; tank capacity, 350,000 gal.; 18 servicing trucks, total capacity, 36,000 gal.
In Vicinity: At Houston and Pasadena (12.0 mi.).
OIL:
At Airport: SAE 120, 48,000 qt., in underground storage.
In Vicinity: At Houston and Pasadena.
COMMUNICATIONS:
Telephone; telegraph; teletype; AACS station, call WYYR.
PERSONNEL ACCOMODATIONS:
At Airport: None.
In Vicinity: At Houston.
RADIO FACILITIES:
RANGE: None.
INSTRUMENT APPROACH AND LETDOWN PROCEDURE:
None reported.
CONTROL TOWER: 219 kcs; continuous.
WEATHER:
PREVAILING WIND: SE, except Dec., Jan., N; July, Aug., S.
PRECIPITATION: Av. mo, 2.97" (Feb.) to 4.68" (May); av. yr., 46.00".
TEMPERATURE: Av. min. and max., 59.8° to 78.3°; extremes, 5° to 108°.
FOG: Oct. to May.
FACILITIES: Class B weather station.
TRANSPORTATION:
RAILROADS: Missouri-Kansas-Texas; Missouri Pacific; Southern Pacific; at Houston. Sidings: 4,174' in lgth., on field.
ROADS: U.S. No. 75, adjacent SW, paved.
FACILITIES: Bus and taxi service.
OPERATED BY: Army Air Forces.
OWNED BY: U.S. Govt.
AUXILIARY FIELDS: No. 1 (Red Bluff Field, 7.5 mi. NE; No. 3 (League-Davis Field) 8.2 mi. SE.

Photographs and specifications of the principal training and operational aircraft flown from the eight army airfields featured in this book.

— All photo information courtesy U.S. Air Force Museum —

North American T-6G "Texan"

The AT-6 advanced trainer was one of the most widely used aircraft in history. Evolving from the BC-1 basic combat trainer ordered in 1937, 15,495 Texans were built between 1938 and 1945. The USAAF procured 10,057 AT-6s; others went to the navy as SNJs and to more than thirty Allied nations. Most AAF fighter pilots trained in AT-6s prior to graduation from flying school. Many of the "Spitfire" and "Hurricane" pilots in the Battle of Britain trained in Canada in "Harvards," the British version of the AT-6. To comply with neutrality laws, U.S.-built Harvards were flown north to the border and were pushed across.

In 1948 Texans still in USAF service were redesignated as T-6s when the AT, BT, and PT aircraft designations were abandoned. To meet an urgent need for close air support of ground forces in the Korean Conflict, T-6s flew "mosquito missions," spotting enemy troops and guns and marking them with smoke rockets for attack by fighter-bombers.

The aircraft on display is one of 1,802 T-6s remanufactured under a 1949 USAF modernization program, redesignated as T-6Gs, and given new serial numbers. It was acquired from the Pennsylvania Air National

Guard in 1957 and is painted as an AT-6 based at Randolph Field, Texas, in 1942.

SPECIFICATIONS:
Span: 42 ft.
Length: 29 ft., 6 in.
Height: 10 ft., 10 in.
Weight: 5,617 lbs. loaded.
Armament: None (some AT-6s used for gunnery/bombing training).
Engine: Pratt & Whitney R-1340 of 600 hp.
Cost: $27,000

PERFORMANCE:
Maximum speed: 210 mph.
Cruising speed: 145 mph.
Range: 770 miles.
Service Ceiling: 23,200 ft.

Beech C-45H "Expeditor"

The C-45 was the WWII military version of the popular Beechcraft Model 18 commercial light transport. Beech built a total of 4,526 of these aircraft for the Army Air Forces between 1939 and 1945 in four versions, the AT-7 "Navigator" navigation trainer, the AT-11 "Kansan" bombing-gunnery trainer, the C-45 "Expeditor" utility transport anf the F-2 for aerial photography and mapping. The AT-7 and AT-11 versions were well-known to WWII navigators and bombardiers, for most of these men received their training in these aircraft. Thousands of AAF pilot cadets also were given advanced training in twin-engine Beech airplanes.

During the early 1950s, Beech completely rebuilt 900 C-45s for the air force. They received new serial numbers and were designated C-45Gs and C-45Hs, remaining in service until 1963 for administrative and light-cargo duties.

The aircraft on display is one of 432 rebuilt as C-45Hs. It was transferred to the U.S. Air Force Museum from the Federal Reformatory at Chillicothe, Ohio, in 1966.

SPECIFICATIONS:
- Span: 47 ft. 8 in.
- Length: 34 ft. 2 in.
- Height: 9 ft. 2 in.
- Weight: 9,300 lbs. maximum
- Armament: None
- Engines: Two Pratt & Whitney R-985s of 450 hp. ea.
- Cost: $57,838
- Serial Number: 210893

PERFORMANCE:
- Maximum speed: 219 mph.
- Cruising speed: 150 mph.
- Range: 1,140 miles
- Service Ceiling: 18,200 ft.

Douglas C-47D "Skytrain"

Few aircraft are as well-known or were so widely used for so long as the C-47, or "Gooney Bird" as it was affectionately nicknamed. The aircraft was adapted from the DC-3 commercial airliner, which appeared in

1936. The first C-47s were ordered in 1940 and by the end of WWII, 9,348 had been procured for AAF use. They carried personnel and cargo, and in a combat role they towed troop-carrying gliders and dropped paratroops into enemy territory.

After WWII, many C-47s remained in USAF service, participating in the Berlin Airlift and other peacetime activities. During the Korean War, C-47s hauled supplies, dropped paratroops, evacuated wounded, and dropped flares for night bombing attacks. In Vietnam, the C-47 served again as a transport, but it was also used in a variety of other ways, including flying ground attack (gunship), reconnaissance, and psychological warfare missions.

The C-47D on display, the last C-47 in routine USAF use, was flown to the museum in 1975. It is displayed as a C-47A of the 88th Troop Carrier Squadron, 438th Troop Carrier Group, which participated in the invasion of Europe on D-Day, June 6, 1944.

SPECIFICATIONS:
- Span: 95 ft. 0 in.
- Length: 64 ft. 5 in.
- Height: 16 ft. 11 in.
- Weight: 33,000 lbs. loaded
- Armament: None
- Engines: Two Pratt & Whitney R-1830s of 1,200 hp. ea.
- Crew: Six
- Cost: $138,000
- Serial Number: 43-49507
- C/N: 15313/26768
- Displayed As: 43-15174

PERFORMANCE:
- Maximum speed: 232 mph.
- Cruising speed: 175 mph.
- Range: 1,513 miles
- Service Ceiling: 24,450 ft.

Curtiss AT-9 "Fledgling"/"Jeep"

The AT-9 advanced trainer was used to bridge the gap between single-engine trainers and twin-engine combat aircraft. The prototype first flew in 1941, and the production version entered service in 1942. The prototype had a fabric-covered steel-tube fuselage and fabric-covered wings, but production AT-9s were of stressed metal skin construction. The AT-9 was not easy to fly or land, which made it particularly suitable for teaching new pilots to cope with the demanding flight characteristics of a new generation of high-performance, multi-engine aircraft such as the Martin B-26 and Lockheed P-38. Although the AT-9 originally bore the nickname "Fledgling," it was more widely known as the "Jeep." Four hundred ninety-one AT-9s and three hundred AT-9As were built before production ended in February 1943.

The aircraft on display was not complete when the USAF Museum acquired it. Some of the parts used to restore it were taken from another incomplete AT-9, while other parts had to be built from "scratch" by museum restoration specialists.

SPECIFICATIONS:

Span: 40 ft. 4 in.
Length: 31 ft. 8 in.
Height: 9 ft. 10 in.
Weight: 6,062 lbs. loaded
Armament: None
Engines: Two Lycoming R-680-9s of 295 hp. ea.
Crew: Two
Cost: $34,900

Serial Number: 41-12150
C/N: 362

PERFORMANCE:
Maximum speed: 197 mph.
Cruising speed: 173 mph.
Range: 750 miles
Service Ceiling: 19,000 ft.

Beech AT-11 "Kansan"

The AT-11 was the standard WWII bombing trainer; about 90 percent of the more than 45,000 AAF bombardiers trained in AT-11s. Like the C-45 transport and the AT-7 navigation trainer, the Kansan was a military version of the Beechcraft Model 18 commercial transport. Modifications included a transparent nose, a bomb bay, internal bomb racks, and provisions for flexible guns for gunnery training.

Student bombardiers normally dropped 100-pound sand-filled practice bombs. In 1943 the AAF established a minimum proficiency standard of 22 percent hits on target for trainees. Combat-training missions were flown taking continuous evasive action within a ten-mile radius of the target and final target approaches had to be straight and level and no longer than sixty seconds. After September 30, 1943, these missions were generally flown using the Norden Bombsight and the C-1 automatic pilot, the aircraft being guided by the bombardier student during the bombing run.

The AT-11 on display is one of 1,582 ordered by the AAF between 1941 and 1945, thirty-six of which were modified as AT-11A navigation trainers. It was donated to the museum by the Abrams Aerial Survey Corp., Lansing, Michigan, in 1969 and is painted to represent a trainer in service during the autumn of 1943.

SPECIFICATIONS:
- Span: 47 ft. 7 3/4 in.
- Length: 34 ft. 1 7/8 in.
- Height: 9 ft. 7 3/4 in.
- Weight: 9,300 lbs. maximum
- Armament: Two .30-cal. machine guns when used as a gunnery trainer
- Engine: Two Pratt & Whitney R-985 of 450 hp. each
- Cost: $67,000

PERFORMANCE:
- Maximum speed: 215 mph.
- Cruising speed: 150 mph.
- Range: 745 miles
- Service Ceiling: 20,000 ft.

Cessna UC-78B "Bobcat"

The UC-78 is a military version of the commercial Cessna T-50 light transport. Cessna first produced the wood and tubular steel, fabric covered T-50 in 1939 for the civilian market. In 1940 the air corps ordered them under the designation AT-8 as multi-engine advanced trainers.

Thirty-three AT-8s were built for the air corps, and production continued under the designation AT-17 reflecting a change in equipment and engine types. In 1942 the AAF adopted the Bobcat as a light personnel transport, and those delivered after January 1, 1943, were designated UC-78s. By the end of WWII, Cessna had produced more than 4,600 Bobcats for the AAF, 67 of which were transferred to the U.S. Navy as JRC-1s. In addition, 822 Bobcats had been produced for the Royal Canadian Air Force as Crane 1s.

Dubbed the "Bamboo Bomber" by the pilots who flew them, it was one of the aircraft featured in the popular television series "Sky King" of the 1940s and 1950s.

The UC-78 on display is one of the 1,806 Bs built for the AAF. It was acquired by the museum in 1982.

SPECIFICATIONS:
- Span: 41 ft. 11 in.
- Length: 32 ft. 9 in.
- Height: 9 ft. 11 in.
- Weight: 5,700 lbs. max.
- Armament: None
- Engines: Two Jacobs R-755-9s of 245 hp. each
- Cost: $31,000
- Serial Number: 42-71626
- C/N: 4322
- Other Registrations: N43BB, N4403N

PERFORMANCE:
- Maximum speed: 175 mph.
- Cruising speed: 150 mph.
- Range: 750 miles
- Service Ceiling: 15,000 ft.

This aircraft is awaiting restoration.

Boeing B-17G "Flying Fortress"

The Flying Fortress is one of the most famous airplanes ever built. The B-17 prototype first flew on July 28, 1935. Few B-17s were in service on December 7, 1941, but production quickly accelerated. The aircraft served in every WWII combat zone but is best known for daylight strategic bombing of German industrial targets. Production ended in May 1945 and totaled 12,726.

In March 1944 this B-17G was assigned to the 91st Bomb Group—"The Ragged Irregulars"—and based at Bassingbourn, England. There it was named *Shoo Shoo Baby* by its crew, after a popular song. It flew twenty-four combat missions in WWII, receiving flak damage seven times. Its first mission (Frankfurt, Germany) was on March 24, 1944, and last mission (Posen, Poland) on May 29, 1944, when engine problems forced a landing in neutral Sweden, where the airplane and crew were interned. In 1968 *Shoo Shoo Baby* was found abandoned in France; the French government presented the airplane to the USAF. In July 1978 the 512th Military Airlift Wing moved it to Dover AFB, Delaware, for restoration by the volunteers of the 512th Antique Restoration Group. The massive ten-year job of restoration to flying condition was completed in 1988 and the aircraft was flown to the museum in October 1988.

SPECIFICATIONS
Span: 103 ft. 10 in.
Length: 74 ft. 4 in.
Height: 19 ft. 1 in.
Weight: 55,000 lbs. loaded
Armament: Thirteen .50-cal. machine guns with normal bomb load of 6,000 lbs.
Engines: Four Wright "Cyclone" R-1820s of 1,200 hp. ea.
Cost: $276,000
Serial Number: 42-32076

PERFORMANCE
Maximum speed: 300 mph.
Cruising speed: 170 mph.
Range: 1,850 miles
Service Ceiling: 35,000 ft.

Douglas B-18A "Bolo"

The Douglas Aircraft Company developed the B-18 to replace the Martin B-10 as the Army Air Corps' standard bomber. The Bolo's design was based on the Douglas DC-2 commercial transport. During air-corps bomber trials at Wright Field in 1935, the B-18 prototype competed with the Martin 146 (an improved B-10) and the four-engine Boeing 299, forerunner of the B-17. Although many air-corps officers believed the Boeing design was superior, only 13 YB-17s were initially ordered. Instead, the Army General Staff selected the less costly Bolo and, in January 1936, ordered 133 as B-18s. Later, 217 more were built as B-18As with a "shark" nose in which the bombardier's position was extended forward over the nose gunner's station.

By 1939, underpowered and with inadequate defensive armament, the Bolo was the air corps' primary bomber. Some B-18s were destroyed by the Japanese on December 7, 1941. By early 1942, improved aircraft replaced the Bolo as first-line bombardment aircraft. Many B-18s were then used as transports, or modified as B-18Bs for anti-submarine duty. The B-18A on display was stationed at Wright Field from 1939 to 1942. The museum acquired it in 1971 and restored it as a B-18A serving in 1939 with the 38th Reconnaissance Squadron.

SPECIFICATIONS:

Span: 89 ft. 6 in.
Length: 57 ft. 10 in.
Height: 15 ft. 2 in.
Weight: 27,000 lbs. loaded

Armament: Three .30-cal. guns (in nose, ventral and dorsal positions), plus 4,500 lbs. of bombs carried internally
Engines: Two Wright R-1820-53s of 1,000 hp. ea.
Crew: Six
Cost: $80,000
Serial Number: 37-469
C/N: 2469
Other Registrations: N58674

PERFORMANCE:
Maximum speed: 215 mph. at 15,000 ft.
Cruising speed: 167 mph.
Range: 2,100 miles
Service Ceiling: 23,900 ft.

Consolidated B-24H "Liberator"

The B-24H was the result of a design effort to improve the defensive firepower of the basic B-24D design. Combat experience showed that even the late-model B-24Ds with three nose-mounted .50-caliber machine guns were vulnerable to head-on attacks. Some B-24Ds had power nose turrets (modified Emerson A-6 tail turrets) added at depot facilities and had greater success fending off frontal assaults.

The Army Air Force wanted this improvement incorporated into the B-24s coming off the production lines, so Emerson and Consolidated engineers redesigned the aircraft to accept the turret. The results were sent to the Ford Willow Run plant for manufacture. The nose-turret addition required more than fifty airframe changes, including a new bombardier compartment. Other improvements incorporated to improve the defensive strength of the aircraft included a new tail turret design with larger plexiglass windows, a higher top turret bubble for increased visibility, and offset waist gunner positions (starting with block 20 aircraft) to prevent the waist gunners from interfering with each other in battle.

The H-model design was sent to North American, where it was built as the B-24G-1. Ford also sent B-24H subassemblies to Consolidated and Douglas for final assembly.

Type	Number Built/Converted	Remarks
B-24H	3100	Imp. for greater def. firepower

Notes:

Serial numbers: 41-28574 to 41-29006; 41-29116 to 41-29608; 42-50277 to 42-50451; 42-51077 to 42-51225; 42-52077 to 42-52776; 42-64432 to 42-64501; 42-7465 to 42-7769; 42-94729 to 42-95503

1780 built by Ford at their Willow Run plant in 7 production blocks
738 assembled by Consolidated at their Fort Worth plant.
582 assembled by Douglas at their Tulsa plant.

SPECIFICATIONS:

Span: 110 ft. 0 in.
Length: 67 ft. 2 in.
Height: 18 ft. 0 in.
Weight: 56,000 lbs. design gross weight
Armament: Ten .50-cal. and 12,800 lbs. of bombs
Engines: Four Pratt & Whitney R-1830-65 supercharged radials of 1,200 hp. each (take-off power)
Crew: Ten

PERFORMANCE:

Maximum speed: 290 mph.
Cruising speed: 215 mph.
Range: 3,700 miles (max. ferry range); 2,100 miles w/ 5,000 lbs. bomb load
Service Ceiling: 28,000 ft.

North American B-25C "Mitchell"

The B-25C was an improved version of the -B model, featuring improved Wright R-2600-13 radial engines, de-icing and anti-icing equipment, a sighting blister for the navigator, and increased nose armament of one fixed and one flexible .50-caliber machine gun. The -C model was the first mass produced B-25 version and 1,625 were built with 1941 and 1942 serial numbers. The B-25C was also used by Great Britain as "Mitchell II," the Netherlands, China, Russia, and Canada (later models would be used by Brazil and Australia).

A few B-25Cs were modified for special purposes or to become prototype testbed aircraft. One was modified for use as a staff transport by General H. H. "Hap" Arnold and was redesignated RB-25C. Three more aircraft were modified and redesignated XB-25E, -F, and -G, while another was to become the prototype B-25H. Five more aircraft were rebuilt to become the first production B-25Gs.

Type	Number Built/Converted	Remarks
B-25C	1625	Imp. B-25B

Notes:

Serial numbers: 41-12434 to 41-13296; 42-32233 to 42-53493; 42-64502 to 42-64801

B-25C-1-NA S/N 42-13251 modified for use by Gen. Arnold and staff as RB-25C

B-25C-10-NA S/N 42-32281 modified to become XB-25E

One B-25C modified to become XB-25F

B-25C-1-NA S/N 41-13296 modified to become XB-25G

Five B-25C-10-NA S/N 42-32384 to 42-32388 modified to become B-25G-1-NA
B-25C-10-NA S/N 42-32372 modified to become the prototype B-25H
Some B-25Cs converted to Advanced Trainer AT-24C became TB-25C in 1945.

SPECIFICATIONS:
Span: 67 ft. 7 in.
Length: 52 ft. 11 in.
Height: 15 ft. 10 in.
Weight: 34,000 lbs. (max.)
Armament: Six .50-cal. machine guns plus 5,200 lbs. of bombs (max. for short range mission)
Engines: Two Wright R-2600-13 turbo-supercharged radials of 1,700 hp. each (take-off power)
Crew: 5
PERFORMANCE:
Maximum speed: 284 mph. at 15,000 ft.
Cruising speed: 233 mph.
Range: 1,500 miles w/ 3,000 lbs. bomb load
Service Ceiling: 21,200 ft.

Martin B-26B-10 to B-26B-55 "Marauder"

Major changes were incorporated into the B-26 design beginning with the block 10 -B model (and block 5 -C model). The wing span was increased from 65 to 71 feet to decrease the high wing loading and improve the handling of the aircraft, particularly at landing speeds. The wing was also modified by adding flaps outboard of the engine nacelles to further improve takeoff and landing performance. The vertical stabilizer was heightened by 20 inches to 21 ft. 6 in. and made the late-model B-26s easily distinguished from the 'short tail' early models.

Like the B-25, the forward armament of the B-26 was increased for ground-strafing missions. The nose featured one fixed and one flexible .50-caliber machine gun while four fixed fuselage-mounted .50-caliber package guns were added just behind and below the cockpit.

Differences between late-production -B models included a switch from manually operated tail guns to powered types, relocation of the waist-gunner positions, and various engine cowling changes. Many aircraft were modified in the field, incorporating improvements from later model production. Armor plating was added to the aircraft's exterior just below and slightly forward of the wind screen to protect the pilot and copilot. Block 45 and later B-26Bs had a larger windscreen designed for better forward visibility.

1,883 B-26Bs were built, and 1,242 of these were block 10 or later.

TYPE	Number Built/Converted	Serial Numbers
B-26B-10-MA	150	41-18185 to 41-18334
B-26B-15-MA	100	41-31573 to 41-31672
B-26B-20-MA	100	41-31673 to 41-31772
B-26B-25-MA	100	41-31773 to 41-31872
B-26B-30-MA	100	41-31873 to 41-31972
B-26B-35-MA	100	41-31973 to 41-32072
B-26B-40-MA	101	42-43260/43357; 43360/43361
B-26B-45-MA	91	43459
B-26B-50-MA	200	42-95738 to 42-95828
B-26B-55-MA	200	42-95829 to 42-96028
		42-96029 to 42-96228

SPECIFICATIONS (B-26B-10-MA):
- Span: 71 ft. 0 in.
- Length: 58 ft. 3 in.
- Height: 21 ft. 6 in.
- Weight: 38,200 lbs. (max.)
- Armament: Twelve .50-cal. machine guns plus 5,200 lbs. of bombs (max. overload) or one externally mounted torpedo
- Engines: Two Pratt & Whitney R-2800-43 "Double Wasp" radials of 2,000 hp. each (take-off power)
- Crew: 7

PERFORMANCE:
- Maximum speed: 282 mph at 15,000'

Cruising speed: 214 mph.
Range: 1,150 miles w/ 3,000 lbs. bomb load; 2,850 miles (max.)
Service Ceiling: 21,700 ft.

Boeing B-29B "Superfortress"

The Boeing B-29B was a modification of the basic B-29 design for use in the Pacific during World War II for low-level bombing raids against Japan. The army leadership, particularly Gen. Curtis LeMay, felt that a lighter and faster bomber would be more effective, since fighter opposition over Japan was minimal by late 1944 and flak was the most serious threat to U.S. bombers. The B-29B had all defensive armament removed except for the tail turret. The 20mm cannon was removed, and the two .50-caliber machine guns were aided by the installation of an AN/APG-15B radar fire-control system. Bell aircraft built 311 -B models at their Marietta, Georgia, plant between January and September 1945.

One B-29B, "PACUSAN Dreamboat," was flown by Colonel Irvine and his crew on October 4–6, 1946, on an unrefueled, nonstop, 9,500-mile flight from Honolulu to Cairo, Egypt, over the Arctic regions in 39 hours, 36 minutes. The route was chosen for its hazards of winter weather and complicated navigation and communications problems.

Type	Number Built/Converted	Remarks
B-29B	311	Improved B-29

Notes:

All B-29B-BA built by Bell at their Atlanta, Georgia, plant.

SPECIFICATIONS:

Span: 141 ft. 2 in.
Length: 99 ft. 0 in.

Height: 27 ft. 9 in. (at rest) 27 ft. 6.7 in. (taxi position)
Weight: 137,500 lbs. (max. overload)
Armament: Two .50-cal. machine guns plus 20,000 lbs. of bombs.
Engines: Four Wright R-3350-23 "Cyclone" radials each equipped with two type B-11 turbo superchargers and each producing 2,200 hp. at takeoff power.
Crew: Normal crew of seven consists of Pilot, Co-Pilot, Flight Engineer, Bombardier, Navigator, Radio Operator and Tail Gunner.

PERFORMANCE:
Maximum speed: 364 mph at 25,000 ft.
Cruising speed: 228 mph
Range: 4,200 miles with 18,000 lbs. of bombs
Service Ceiling: 32,000 ft.

Convair B-36A "Peacemaker"

Twenty-two B-36As were built in four production blocks. The -A model featured the domed canopy first seen on the YB-36 and a redesigned four-wheel main landing-gear system, which replaced the single-wheel main landing gear of the two earlier aircraft (XB-36 and YB-36).

The first flight of the B-36A was on August 28, 1947. The -A model actually flew six months earlier than the YB-36, but this was because the first production B-36A (S/N 44-92004) was completed with just enough equipment to make a ferry flight to Wright Field, Ohio. Once at Wright Field, the aircraft was used as a testbed for structural tests. These tests were often conducted to test maximum loads until structural failure occurred. Thus, the first B-36A was destroyed.

Although the B-36A was technically a production aircraft, no defensive armament was installed. The -A model was used by the 7th Bomb Group at Carswell AFB, Texas, for crew training and testing only.

TYPE	Number Built/Converted	Remarks
B-36A	22	Initial production block

Notes:

Serial numbers: 44-92004 to 44-92025
First flight was 28 August 1947
B-36A S/N 44-92004 used for destructive structural ground testing.
All B-36As (except for 004) were later modified to RB-36E

SPECIFICATIONS:

Span: 230 ft. 0 in.
Length: 162 ft. 1 in.
Height: 46 ft. 8 in.
Weight: 310,380 lbs. (max. gross weight)
Armament: Designed for ten .50-cal. machine guns and five 37mm cannon plus 72,000 lbs of bombs. (No defensive armament was actually installed)
Engines: Six Pratt & Whitney R-4360-25 radials of 3,000 hp. each (takeoff power)
Crew: 15

PERFORMANCE:

Maximum speed: 345 mph. at 32,000 ft.
Cruising speed: 202 mph.
Range: 3,380 miles with 10,000 lbs. bomb load. (estimated combat radius); 9,136 mile ferry range
Service Ceiling: 39,100 ft.

Texas and World War II

For those readers interested in expanding their knowledge of the role the Lone Star State played during World War II, below are some museums, historic sites, memorials, monuments, libraries, archives, and organizations that contain some great information. The list is by no means exhaustive, but it will get you started on your path to learning more about Texas and World War II.

MUSEUMS AND HISTORICAL SITES:

1st Cavalry Division Museum
56th Street, 761st Tank Battalion Avenue
Fort Hood, TX 76544
254.287.3626
http://www.first-team.us/tableaux/apndx_13/

12th Armored Division Memorial Museum
1289 N. 2nd Street
Abilene, TX 79601
325.677.6515
http://www.12tharmoredmuseum.com/

American Freedom Museum
The Brook Hill School
1051 N. Houston Street
Bullard, TX 75757
903.894.5252
http://www.americanfreedommuseum.org/

Audie Murphy, American Cotton Museum
600 Interstate 30 East
Greenville, TX 75043
903.450.4502
http://www.cottonmuseum.com/

Aviation Museum at Garner Field
201 Sul Ross Drive
Uvalde, TX 78801
830.278.2552

Battleship *Texas* State Historic Site
3523 Independence Parkway South
LaPorte, TX 77571
281.479.2431
https://tpwd.texas.gov/state-parks/battleship-texas

Building 98, International Women's Foundation
705 West Bonnie Street
Marfa, TX 79843
432.386.3212
http://www.internationalwomansfoundation.org/

Camp Hearne – World War II P.O.W. Camp in Texas
12424 Camp Hearne Road
Hearne, TX 77859
979.314.7012
http://camphearne.com/

Cavanaugh Flight Museum
4572 Claire Chennault
Addison, TX 75001
972.380.8800
https://www.cavflight.org/

Central Texas Wing (Commemorative Air Force)
1841 Airport Drive, Bldg. 2249
San Marcos, TX 78666
512.396.1943
http://www.centraltexaswing.org/

Chinati Foundation, Fort D. A. Russell
1 Cavalry Row
Marfa, TX 79843
432.729.4362
https://chinati.org/

Club Victoria
806 Frisco Avenue
Menard, TX 76859
325.396.2365

Commemorative Air Force Airpower Museum
5661 Mariner Drive
Dallas, TX 75237
877.767.7175
https://commemorativeairforce.org/

Dallas Holocaust Museum Center for Education and Tolerance
211 N. Record Street, Suite 100
Dallas, TX 75202-3361
214.741.7500
http://www.dallasholocaustmuseum.org/

DFW Wing (Commemorative Air Force)
Lancaster Airport
720 Ferris Road
Lancaster, TX 75146
817.269.4081
http://www.dfwwing.com/

Don Freeman Memorial Museum
Paint Rock Street on the Square
Eden, TX 76837
325.869.2211
http://www.edentexas.com/articles/view/edens-museum

Dyess Heritage Museum, Memorial Park, and Linear Air Park
800 Arnold Blvd.
Dyess Air Force Base
Abilene, TX 79607
325.793.2199
http://www.dyess.af.mil/

Eisenhower Birthplace State Historic Site
609 S. Lamar Ave.
Denison, TX 75021
903.465.8908
http://www.thc.texas.gov/historic-sites/eisenhower-birth-place-state-historic-site

El Paso Holocaust Museum and Study Center
715 N. Oregon Street
El Paso, TX 79902
915.351.0048
http://www.elpasoholocaustmuseum.org/

Flight of the Phoenix Aviation Museum
Fox Stephens Field
43 Aviation Drive
Gilmer, TX 75644
http://www.flightofthephoenix.org/

Fort Bliss Museums
Building 1735, Marshall Road
ATS-GC-M
Fort Bliss, TX 79916-3802
915.568.5412

Fort Travis Park
900 State Highway 87
Port Bolivar, TX 77650
409.934.8100

Fort Worth Aviation Museum
3300 Ross Avenue
Fort Worth, TX 76106
855.733.8627
http://fortworthaviationmuseum.com/

Freedom Museum USA
600 North Hobart Street
Pampa, TX 79065
806.669.6066
http://www.freedommuseumusa.com/

Frontiers of Flight Museum
Dallas Love Field
6911 Lemmon Avenue
Dallas, TX 75209
214.350.3600
https://www.flightmuseum.com/

Hangar 25 Air Museum
1911 Apron Drive
Big Spring, TX
432.264.1999

Heart of Texas Historical Museum
117 North High
Brady, TX 76825
325.597.0526
http://www.heartoftexasmuseum.com/

H.E.A.R.T.S. Veterans Museum of Texas
463 State Highway 75 N.
Huntsville, TX 77320
936.295.5959
http://www.heartsmuseum.com/index.html

High Sky Wing Complex (Commemorative Air Force) and the Midland Army Air Field (MAAF) Museum
9612 Wright Drive
Midland, TX 79706
432.235.7007
http://highskywing.org/

Holocaust Museum Houston
Morgan Family Center
9220 Kirby Drive, Suite 100
Houston, TX 77054
713.942.8000
http://www.hmh.org/

Holocaust Memorial Museum of San Antonio
12500 N.W. Military Hwy.
San Antonio, TX 78231
210.302.6807
http://texasindependencetrail.com/plan-your-adventure/historic-sites-and-cities/sites/holocaust-memorial-museum-san-antonio

Iwo Jima Monument and Memorial Museum
320 Iwo Jima Blvd.
Harlingen, TX 78550
956.421.9234
http://texastropicaltrail.com/plan-your-adventure/historic-sites-and-cities/sites/iwo-jima-mounument-and-memorial-museum

Laughlin Heritage Foundation Museum
309 South Main Street
Del Rio, TX 78841
830.719.9380
http://www.laughlinheritagefoundationinc.org/

Lone Star Flight Museum at Ellington Joint Reserve Base
11511 Aerospace Ave.
Houston, TX 77034
888.359.5736
http://www.lonestarflight.org/

Medina County Museum
2202 18th St.
Hondo, TX
800.426.3037

Midland County Historical Museum
301 W. Missouri Ave.
Midland, TX 79701
432.688.8947

Military Heritage Collection of North Texas
20798 County Road 590
Nevada, TX 75173
469.434.0396
http://www.fubarmotorpool.com/home.html

Museum of the American G.I.
19124 Highway 6 South
College Station, TX 77845
979.690.0501
http://americangimuseum.org/

National Border Patrol Museum
4315 Transmountain Road
El Paso, TX 79924
915.759.6060
http://www.borderpatrolmuseum.com/

National Museum of the Pacific War
340 East Main Street
Fredericksburg, TX 78624
830.997.8600
http://www.pacificwarmuseum.org/

National Women Airforce Service Pilots (WASP) World War II Museum, Avenger Field
210 Avenger Field Rd.
Sweetwater, TX 79556
325.235.0099
http://waspmuseum.org/

No. 1 British Flying Training School Museum, Inc.
119 Silent Wings Blvd.
Terrell, TX 75160
972.551.1122
http://www.bftsmuseum.org/bfts16/

Old Post Office Museum and Art Center
510 Third Street
Graham, TX 76450
940.549.1470
http://www.opomac.net/index.html

Rattlesnake Bomber Base Museum
1500 E. Sealy Avenue
Monahans, TX 79756
432.943.8401

Rio Grande Wing (Commemorative Air Force)
955 South Minnesota Avenue
Brownsville, TX 78521
956.541.8585
http://www.rgvcaf.org/

Sabine Pass Battleground State Historic Site
6100 Dowling Road
Port Arthur, TX 77640
512.463.7948
http://www.thc.texas.gov/historic-sites/sabine-pass-battleground-state-historic-site

Silent Wings Museum
6202 N. I-27
Lubbock, TX 79403-9710
806.775.3046
https://www.mylubbock.us/departmental-websites/departments/silent-wings-museum/home

Texas Air & Space Museum
10001 American Drive
Amarillo, TX 79111-1213
806.335.9159
http://www.texasairandspacemuseum.org/

Texas Air Museum
Slaton Municipal Airport
806.224.3601
http://www.thetexasairmuseum.org/

Texas Air Museum at Stinson Field
1234 99th Street
San Antonio, TX 78214
210.977.9885
http://www.texasairmuseum.org/

Texas Heritage Museum
112 Lamar Drive
Hillsboro, TX 76645
254.659.7750
http://www.hillcollege.edu/museum/

Texas Military Forces Museum at Camp Mabry
3038 West 35th Street
Austin, TX 78763
512.782.5659
http://texasmilitaryforcesmuseum.org/

The Harlingen Arts and Heritage Museum
2425 Boxwood Street
Harlingen, TX 78550
956.216.4901
http://www.myharlingen.us/page/hahm.home

Third Coast Squadron (Commemorative Air Force)
1309 South Airport Road
Alice, TX 78332
361.356.4918
https://thirdcoastcaf.org/wordpress/

U.S. Army Medical Department Museum, Fort Sam Houston Museum, Randolph Army Airfield
3898 Stanley Road, Bldg. 1046
Fort Sam Houston
San Antonio, TX 78234
210.221.6358
http://ameddmuseum.amedd.army.mil/

USS *Cavalla*, American Undersea Warfare Center
100 Seawolf Parkway
Galveston, TX 77554
409.770.3196
http://www.americanunderseawarfarecenter.com/

USS *Lexington*
2914 N. Shoreline Blvd.
Corpus Christi, TX 78403
800.LADY LEX or 361.888.4873
http://www.usslexington.com/

Victory Grill
1104 E. 11th Street
Austin, TX 78702
512.291.6211
http://atxhistoricvictorygrill.org/

Vintage Flying Museum
505 N.W. 38th Street
Hangar 33 South
Meacham International Airport
Fort Worth, TX 76106
817.624.1935
http://vintageflyingmuseum.org/

Zilker Botanical Garden
2220 Barton Springs
Austin, TX 78746
512.477.8672
http://www.zilkergarden.org/

MEMORIALS AND MONUMENTS:

103rd Infantry Division Memorial
N 33° 41.572 W 097° 09.761
14S E 670291 N 3729617
4901 N. I-35
Gainesville, TX 76240

Burleson County in World War II
Historical Marker #14272
E 721321 N 3379985
Burleson County Courthouse Grounds
100 W. Buck Street
Caldwell, TX
Calhoun County Participation During World War II
Historical Marker #17137
E 732108 N 3167428
Calhoun County Courthouse Grounds
Port Lavaca, TX
Camp Alto, World War II Prisoner of War Camp
Historical Marker #13703
E 302391 N 3503352
0.9 mi west of intersection of State Highway 21 and Highway 294
Alto, TX
Camp Center, World War II Prisoner of War Camp
Historical Marker #14723
Center, TX
Camp Chireno, World War II Prisoner of War Camp
Historical Marker #15445
E 371605 N 3485734
near intersection of Main Street and Depot Street
Chireno, TX
Camp Fannin Internment Camp World War II P.O.W. Camp
Historical Maker #14566
Tyler, TX
Camp Fannin Veterans Memorial
University of Texas Health Center at Tyler
11937 U.S. 271
Tyler, TX 75708
Camp Hearne, World War II Prisoner of War Camp
Historical Marker #14755
Hearne, TX
Camp Huntsville, World War II Prisoner of War Camp
Historical Marker #13707
E 267331 N 3412021
Approximately 8 miles northeast of Huntsville on State Highway 19
Huntsville, TX
Camp San Augustine World War II P.O.W. Camp
Historical Marker #14190
San Augustine, TX

Crystal City Family Internment Camp, World War II
Historical Marker #13720
E 420011 N 3173987
Crystal City, TX

Heritage Plaza
E. Methvin Street and N. Green Street
Longview, TX 75601

Italian P.O.W. Chapel at Camp Hereford
3.5 miles south of Hereford on the Deaf Smith and Castro County line
Hereford, TX

John H. Reagan World War II Memorial Plaza
Heights Boulevard and East 11th Street
Houston, TX 77008

Moulton's World War II Observation Tower
Historical Marker #18168
E 680755 N 3272239
FM 532 E
1 mile east of the intersection of Texas Highway 95 and FM 532 E
Moulton, TX

Randall County World War II Memorial
Historical Markers #4191, 14782, 15164
E 233075 N 3873887
19th Street and 11th Avenue
At the entrance to Conner Park
Canyon, TX

Riverside Addition: World War II Housing in Orange
Historical Marker #13970
E 429976 N 3329104
Green Avenue and Simmons Drive
Orange, TX

Site of Palestine Service Men's Club, World War II
Historical Marker #13656
E 250494 N 3517045
400 W. Spring Street
Palestine, TX

Site of World War II Camp Bowie
Historical Marker #4918
E 500709 N 3504621
At entrance to 36th Division Memorial Park, Burnett Street near Morris Sheppard Road
Brownwood, TX

Site of World War II P.O.W. Camp
Historical Marker #11557
E 422860 N 3331391
4 miles west of Orange on US 90 ROW at Womack Road
Orange, TX

Site of World War II Prisoner of War Camp
Historical Marker #4917
E 782497 N 3247457
marker is located in front of Ladien Technology Center at the corner of Junior College Blvd. and FM 1301
2015 Junior College Blvd.
Wharton, TX

Site of World War II Prisoner of War Camp
Historical Marker #6222
E 732208 N 3674439
community park
W. College Street
Princeton, TX

Stephen F. Austin State Teachers College During World War II
Historical Marker #12107
Stephen F. Austin State University campus between Business & Education buildings
Raguet Street
Nacogdoches, TX

Texas Petroleum in World War II
Historical Marker #15180
Midland, TX

Texas World War II Memorial in Austin
N 30° 16.553 W 097° 44.441
14R E 621125 N 3350027
On the northwest corner of the Texas Capitol grounds
201 E. 14th Street
Austin, TX 78701

The Texas World War II Home Front
Historical Marker #15646
Next to Civic Center
Cleburne, TX

Veterans' Memorial Monument in Noonday
16662 CR 196
Noonday, TX 75703

Veteran's War Memorial of Texas
3129 Galveston Ave.
McAllen, TX 78501
956.631.2511
http://www.mcallen.net/veterans/default.aspx
War Memorial in Atlanta
100 N. East Street
Atlanta, TX 75551
William Haddad World War II Memorial
9500 Gateway Blvd. N
El Paso, TX 79924
World War II Air Training School Brayton Flying Field
Historical Marker #5907
E 666477 N 3219150
200 block East Main Street in City Park
Cuero, TX
World War II Coastal Defenses at Sabine Pass
Historical Marker #13116
E 416240 N 3287990
1.5 miles south via FM 3322 in Sabine Pass Battleground State Historic Park
Sabine Pass, TX
World War II Coastal Defenses at the Aransas Pass
Historical Marker #15267
E 690691 N 3081116
Roberts Point Park
311 J. C. Barr Blvd.
Port Aransas, TX
World War II Prisoner of War Camp at McLean
Historical Marker #5908
E 360033 N 3900811
2 miles east of McLean on IH-40 to exit #146; 1 mile north on CR 5280 (county line road)
McLean, TX

LIBRARIES AND ARCHIVES:

Archives of the Big Bend, Bryan Wildenthal Memorial Library, Sul Ross State University
P.O. Box C-109
Alpine, TX 79832
432.837.8123
https://library.sulross.edu/archives/

Border Heritage Center, El Paso Public Library
501 N. Oregon
El Paso, TX 79901
915.212.0355
http://www.elpasolibrary.org/research/border-heritage-section

C. L. Sonnichsen Special Collections Department, The University of Texas at El Paso Library
500 W. University Ave.
El Paso, TX 79968-0582
915.747.5697
http://libraryweb.utep.edu/special/

Fort Worth Branch, National Archives and Records Administration
1400 John Burgess Drive
Fort Worth, TX 76140
817.551.2051
https://www.archives.gov/fort-worth

George H. W. Bush Presidential Library Center
1000 George Bush Drive West
College Station, TX 77845
979.691.4000
https://bush41.org/

J. Conrad Dunagan Library Archives, The University of Texas of the Permian Basin
4901 E. University Blvd.
Odessa, TX 79762
432.552.2397
https://www.utpb.edu/library/services/archives/index

Nimitz Education and Research Center, National Museum of the Pacific War
340 East Main Street
Fredericksburg, TX 78624
830.997.8600
http://www.pacificwarmuseum.org/your-visit/nimitz-education-and-research-center/

Southwest Collection, Texas Tech University Special Collections Library
15th and Detroit
Box 41041
Lubbock, TX 79409-1041
http://swco.ttu.edu/

Special Collection Division, The University of Texas at Arlington
702 Planetarium Place
Arlington, TX 76019
817.272.3393
http://library.uta.edu/special-collections/collections

Texas Room, Houston Metropolitan Research Center, Houston Public Library
500 McKinney
Houston, TX 77002
832.393.1662
http://www2.houstonlibrary.org/hmrc/index.html

Texas State Library and Archives Commission
1201 Brazos Street
Austin, TX 78701
512.463.5455
https://www.tsl.texas.gov/

WASP Collection, Blagg-Huey Library, Texas Women's University
304 Administration Drive
Denton, TX 76204
940.898.3701

ORGANIZATIONS:

Commemorative Air Force (CAF)
Dallas, TX 75376
877.767.7175
https://commemorativeairforce.org/

Texas Historical Commission
1511 Colorado Street
Austin, TX 78701
512.463.6100
http://www.thc.texas.gov/

VETERANS CEMETERIES:

Houston National Cemetery
10410 Veterans Memorial Drive
Houston, TX 77038
281.447.8686
https://www.cem.va.gov/cems/nchp/houston.asp

Texas State Cemetery
909 Navasota Street
Austin, TX 78702
512.463.0605
http://www.cemetery.state.tx.us/

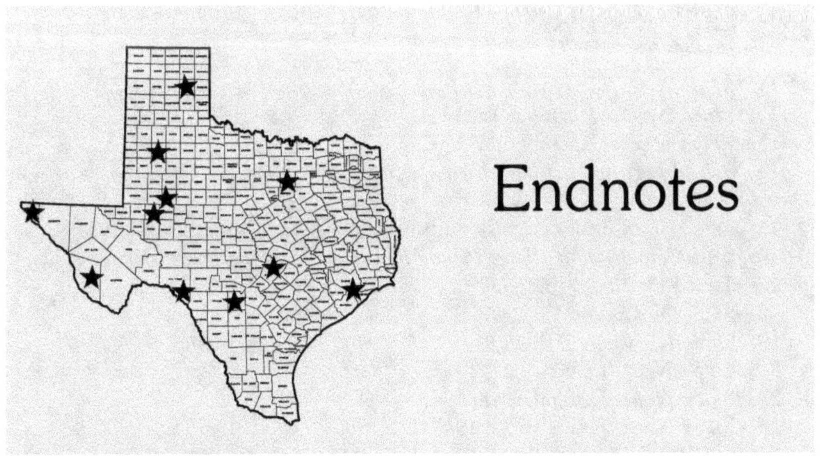

Endnotes

NOTES TO CHAPTER I

1. Jacqueline L. Mayo, interview with author, Austin, Texas, March 9, 2000.
2. Jerold E. Brown, *Where Eagles Land: Planning and Development of U.S. Army Airfields*, 1910–1941, 92.
3. Ibid., 115.
4. J. Frank Davis, *Randolph Field: A History and Guide*, 2.
5. *Fort Worth Star-Telegram*, July 3, 1948.
6. *Texas Almanac and State Industrial Guide, 1943–1944*, 93.
7. Ibid., 316.
8. Ibid., 334.
9. *Texas Almanac and State Industrial Guide, 1939–1940*, 264–65.
10. Ron Tyler, ed., *The New Handbook of Texas*, vol. 6, 1079.
11. *Texas Almanac*, 1943–1944, 87.
12. Robert D. Thompson, *We'll Find the Way*, 20.
13. *The Hondo Anvil Herald*, March 9, 1944.
14. Thomas Leonard, *Day By Day: The Forties*, 217.
15. Arnold Frank Simpson, interview with author, Abilene, Texas, June 9, 1998.
16. *San Antonio Light*, December 8, 1946.

NOTES TO CHAPTER II

1. Ron Tyler, ed., *The New Handbook of Texas*, vol. 5, 33.
2. Ibid., 33.
3. *Pampa News*, March 14, 1942.
4. *Pampa News*, May 15, 1942.
5. *Pampa News*, May 17, 1942.
6. *Pampa News*, May 23, 1942.
7. *Pampa News*, July 9, 1942.
8. *Pampa News*, July 23, 1942.
9. *Pampa News*, September 11, 1942.
10. *Pampa News*, November 3, 1942.

11. *Pampa News*, November 29, 1942.
12. *Pampa News*, December 15, 1942.
13. *Pampa News*, December 24, 1942.
14. W. C. Ferguson Jr., *Who's Who: Pampa Army Airfield Association Reunion Directory*, 30.
15. Mike Porter, interview with author, Pampa, Texas, October 15, 1999.
16. Jamie Gough, *Who's Who: Pampa Reunion Directory*, 35.
17. Harold H. Noah, Ibid., 66.
18. Roger G. Ritchey, Ibid., 80.
19. William T. Wagner, Ibid., 93.
20. *Pampa News*, February 23, 1943.
21. *Pampa News*, December 15, 1942.
22. *Pampa News*, February 28, 1943.
23. Daniel S. Campbell, *Who's Who, Pampa Reunion*, 19.
24. *Texas Almanac and State Industrial Guide, 1939–1940*, 93.
25. *Pampa News*, March 7, 1943.
26. Ibid.
27. *Pampa News*, February 21, 1943.
28. *The Pampa Flyer*, November 1, 1944.
29. *The Pampa Flyer*, December 29, 1944.
30. *The Pampa Flyer*, December 27, 1944.
31. *The Pampa Flyer*, December 22, 1944.
32. *Pampa News*, January 28, 1943.
33. *Pampa News*, May 13, 1943
34. *Pampa News*, June 20, 1943.
35. *Pampa News*, December 15, 1943.
36. *Pampa News*, January 6, 1944.
37. *Pampa News*, July 25, 1943.
38. *Pampa News*, September 3, 1943.
39. Ibid.
40. *Pampa News*, November 28, 1944.
41. *Pampa News*, May 7, 1945.
42. *Pampa News*, July 31, 1945.
43. *Pampa News*, September 6, 1945.
44. *Pampa News*, September 13, 1945.
45. *Pampa News*, September 23, 1945.
46. Ibid.
47. Tyler, ed., 33.
48. Mike Porter interview.
49. Ibid.
50. Rod "Doc" Savage, *Who's Who*, 82.

NOTES TO CHAPTER III

1. Robert D. Thompson, *We'll Find the Way*, 9.
2. *Texas Almanac and State Industrial Guide, 1943–1944*, 77.
3. *Hondo Anvil Herald*, April 10, 1997.
4. Ibid.

5. Amos O. Beasley, interview with author, San Antonio, Texas, September 12, 1999.
6. Thompson, 8.
7. *Hondo Anvil Herald*, January 23, 1942.
8. Ron Tyler, ed., The New Handbook of Texas, vol. 3, 681.
9. *Hondo Anvil Herald*, March 2, 1942.
10. *Hondo Anvil Herald*, April 3, 1942.
11. Tyler, ed., 681.
12. *Hondo Anvil Herald*, April 10, 1942.
13. Thompson, 14.
14. Ibid., 17.
15. *Hondo Anvil Herald*, April 19, 1942
16. Ibid.
17. Tyler, ed., 682.
18. John Wentz, interview with author, Hondo, Texas, September 12, 1999.
19. Tyler, ed., 682.
20. *Hondo Anvil Herald*, August 14, 1942.
21. Ibid.
22. Chief Justice William H. Rehnquist, letter to author, June 11, 1999.
23. Ibid.
24. Wentz interview.
25. *Hondo Anvil Herald*, November 30, 1945.
26. *Hondo Anvil Herald*, May 21, 1943.
27. *Hondo Anvil Herald*, June 25, 1943.
28. *Hondo Anvil Herald*, October 2, 1942.
29. *Hondo Anvil Herald*, October 9, 1942.
30. *Hondo Anvil Herald*, June 25, 1943.
31. Ibid.
32. Thompson, 63–67.
33. *Hondo Anvil Herald*, August 2, 1945.
34. *Hondo Anvil Herald*, September 30, 1999.

NOTES TO CHAPTER IV

1. *A Guide to Historic Del Rio, Texas*, 1.
2. Ron Tyler, ed., *The New Handbook of Texas*, vol. 2, 578.
3. E. Roebuck Daughtery, *U.S. Air Force Activities In and Near Del Rio, Val Verde County, Texas*, 3.
4. Ibid., 4.
5. *Del Rio News-Herald*, August 8, 1945.
6. James H. Doolittle, *I Could Never Be So Lucky Again*, 63.
7. *Del Rio News-Herald*, April 2, 1942.
8. *Del Rio News-Herald*, May 15, 1942.
9. Ibid., May 22, 1942.
10. Daughtery, 9.
11. Ibid., 10.
12. *Tarfu*, March 12, 1943.
13. Gerald C. Brant, Dedicatory Address, March 28, 1942.

14. Laughlin Heritage Foundation (LHF) Files.
15. Gerald L. Stephens, interview in LHF Files.
16. James K. Stepp, interview in LHF Files.
17. John P. McNeese, interview in LHF Files.
18. George M. Carnahan to Paul O. Russell, April 13, 1997, in LHF Files.
19. Ibid.
20. Allard E. Stevens to Paul O. Russell, December 1, 1997, in LHF Files.
21. Ibid.
22. *Del Rio News-Herald,* June 24, 1945.
23. *Summary of Aircraft Accidents At Laughlin Army Air Field*, in LHF Files.
24. Ray Wagner, *American Combat Planes*, 226–27.
25. Stevens letter.
26. Paul O. Russell, *Reminiscences of Laughlin*, in LHF Files.
27. Ibid.
28. Gene Fowler and Bill Crawford, *Border Radio*, 34.
29. Stevens letter.
30. *Tarfu*, June 18, 1943.
31. Russell, *Reminiscences*.
32. Ibid.
33. *Tarfu*, September 12, 1944.
34. Whitehead Memorial Museum, Vertical File.
35. *Tarfu*, August 20, 1943.
36. *Tarfu*, October 5, 1943.
37. *Tarfu*, December 31, 1943.
38. *Tarfu*, August 27, 1943.
39. *Tarfu*, May 19, 1944.
40. *Del Rio News-Herald,* August 27, 1945.
41. *Del Rio News-Herald*, September 7, 1945.
42. *Report of the 47th Comptroller Flight*, 1998.

NOTES TO CHAPTER V

1. Ron Tyler, ed., *The New Handbook of Texas*, vol. 4, 706–707.
2. *Midland Reporter-Telegram*, June 9, 1921.
3. *Odessa American*, February 6, 1942.
4. *Reporter-Telegram*, June 13, 1940.
5. Ibid., July 15, 1940.
6. Ibid., November 19, 1940.
7. *Odessa American*, October 18, 1940.
8. Ibid., April 3, 1941.
9. *Midland Reporter-Telegram*, June 13, 1941.
10. Ibid., October 24, 1941.
11. Ibid., August 11, 1942.
12. James L. Colwell, “Hell From Heaven Midland Army Airfield in World War II,” *The Permian Historical Annual XXV*, 32.
13. *Life* Magazine, May 18, 1942, 64.
14. Bruce Callander, “The Short Heyday of the Bombardier,” *Air Force Times*, April 9, 1984, 4.

15. *Midland Reporter-Telegram*, January 13, 1991.

16. Ibid.

17. Walter Prescott Webb, ed., *The Handbook of Texas*, 187.

18. Ibid.

19. *Midland Reporter-Telegram*, December 1, 1991.

20. *Odessa American*, August 8, 1943.

21. James L. Colwell, "Hell From Heaven, Midland Army Airfield in World War II," *The Permian Historical Annual XXVI*, 68.

22. Irene Paulette, "Odessa During the War Years," *The Permian Historical Annual XXI*, 22.

23. *Odessa American*, March 20, 1988.

24. Colwell, "Hell From Heaven, Part II," 71.

25. "History of Childress Army Airfield," 2.

26. Colwell, "Hell From Heaven, Midland Army Airfield in World War II," Part III, 76.

27. Ibid., 77.

28. Midland International Airport Press Release.

29. Colwell, "Hell From Heaven," Part III, 115.

NOTES TO CHAPTER VI

1. Ron Tyler, ed., *The New Handbook of Texas*, vol. 4, 503–504.

2. Ibid., 503.

3. Susanne Grube, "A Brief History of Camp Marfa and Fort D. A. Russell," 1.

4. Ibid., 2.

5. Tyler, ed., *The New Handbook of Texas*, vol. 2, 1096.

6. Cecilia Thompson, *History of Marfa and Presidio County*, vol. 2, 493.

7. *The Big Bend Sentinel*, May 22, 1942.

8. Ibid., May 29, 1942.

9. Ibid.

10. *Texas Almanac and State Industrial Guide, 1949–1950*, 107.

11. *The Big Bend Sentinel*, May 1, 1942.

12. Ibid.

13. Tyler, ed., vol. 4, 504.

14. C. M. (Frtiz) Kahl, interview with author, October 11, 1999.

15. *The Big Bend Sentinel*, August 8, 1942.

16. Kirby F. Warnock, "Wings West of the Pecos," *Big Bend Quarterly*, Summer 1999, 14.

17. Kahl interview.

18. *The Big Bend Sentinel*, October 10, 1942.

19. Ibid., November 23, 1942.

20. Tyler, ed., vol. 4, 504.

21. *The Big Bend Sentinel*, December 28, 1942.

22. Ibid., December 14, 1942

23. *United States Army Air Forces Directory of Airports*, vol. 3, 1945, 202.

24. *The Big Bend Sentinel*, February 8, 1943.

25. Tyler, ed., vol. 4, 504.

26. Thompson, 505.

27. *The Big Bend Sentinel*, August 20, 1943.
28. Ibid., September 17, 1943.
29. Ibid., June 8, 1943.
30. Thompson, 506.
31. Ibid., 507.
32. Warnock, 14.
33. *The Big Bend Sentinel*, September 15, 1944.
34. Kahl interview.
35. Ephraim Katz, *The Film Encyclopedia*, 793.
36. *The Big Bend Sentinel*, August 10, 1945.
37. Thompson, 515.
38. Ibid., 517.
39. *The Big Bend Sentinel*, May 6, 1945.
40. Ibid., May 13, 1945.
41. Thompson, 530.
42. *Marfacts*, June 30, 1944.
43. *The Big Bend Sentinel*, August 3, 1945.
44. Thompson, 531.
45. Kahl interview.
46. "Life After Giant," *LIFE Magazine*, January 3, 1957, 86.

NOTES TO CHAPTER VII

1. Ron Tyler, ed., *The New Handbook of Texas*, vol. 2, 846.
2. Ibid.
3. Paul Horgan, *Great River: The Rio Grande in North American History*, 18.
4. *A Brief History of El Paso County*, Texas, 3.
5. *The Story of Old Fort Bliss*, 9.
6. E. L. Robertson, *Villa Rides!*, 88.
7. *El Paso Times*, June 12, 1916.
8. Maurer Maurer, *Aviation in the U.S. Army*, 99.
9. *Old Fort Bliss*, 13.
10. *El Paso Times*, October 28, 1956.
11. C. Forrest Wilson, *A History of Biggs Field and Early Border Aviation*, 26.
12. *El Paso Times*, August 13, 1945.
13. "Biggs Field Fact Sheet," Fort Bliss History Office, 10.
14. *History of Biggs Field*, 36.
15. "Biggs Field Fact Sheet," 12.
16. *U.S. Army Air Forces Directory of Airports*, July 1944, 203.
17. *History of Biggs Field*, 48.
18. *El Paso Times*, February 27, 1943.
19. *The Air Officer's Guide* 1953, 115.
20. Alicia Gonzalez, Oral History Transcript.
21. Ibid.
22. Elisa Martinez, Oral History Transcript.
23. Ysidro Cervantes, Oral History Transcript.
24. George Saucier, Oral History Transcript.
25. *El Paso Times*, September 13, 1945.

26. "Fact Sheet," 3.
27. Ibid., 4.
28. *El Paso Times*, November 24, 1964.
29. "Fact Sheet," 3.
30. Ibid., 4.
31. "Economic Survey Bulletin," *El Paso Convention and Visitors Bureau Bulletin, 1999.*

NOTES TO CHAPTER VIII

1. Ron Tyler, ed., *The New Handbook of Texas*, vol. 2, 1122.
2. Ibid., 1123.
3. "Tarrant County Web Site," 3.
4. *Texas Almanac and State Historical Guide, 1939–1940*, 33.
5. *Fort Worth Star-Telegram*, June 25, 1955.
6. Jerry Flemmons, *Amon: The Life of Amon Carter, Sr. of Texas*, 433.
7. "History of Fort Worth Army Air Field," *Lone Star Scanner*, February 16, 1946, 4.
8. Flemmons, 434–35.
9. Ibid., 436.
10. *Star-Telegram*, January 4, 1941.
11. "History of Fort Worth Army Air Field," *Lone Star Scanner*, 6.
12. Flemmons, 436.
13. J'nell Pate, "Impact of the Military Base Called Carswell," 2.
14. Ibid., 3.
15. "A Look Back," *Consolidated-Vultee Annual Report, 1952*.
16. *Star-Telegram*, June 8, 1991.
17. Star-Telegram, October 12, 1942.
18. Star-Telegram, December 10, 1942.
19. Ibid.
20. The Tarranteer, January 9, 1943.
21. *Star-Telegram*, February 6, 1943.
22. *Star-Telegram*, October 25, 1942.
23. Ibid.
24. *Star-Telegram*, November 2, 1942.
25. Star Telegram, October 3, 1943.
26. The Tarranteer, November 8, 1943.
27. The Tarranteer, September 13, 1943.
28. *Star-Telegram*, February 8, 1943.
29. *Star-Telegram*, February 20, 1944.
30. Flemmons, 429.
31. Ibid., 429.
32. Oliver Knight, *Fort Worth: Outpost On The Trinity*, 216–26.
33. *Star-Telegram*, September 3, 1943.
34. *Star-Telegram*, September 22, 1944.
35. *Star-Telegram*, November 27, 1942.
36. Ray Wagner, *American Combat Planes*, 213.
37. Ibid., 404.

38. The Tarranteer, August 1, 1945.
39. Ibid.
40. *Star-Telegram*, August 2, 1945.
41. Ibid.
42. *Fort Worth Press*, September 21, 1945.
43. *Star-Telegram*, October 14, 1945.
44. Pate, 9.
45. *Socioeconomic Impact Analysis Study of Disposal and Reuse of Carswell AFB*, 8.
46. *Star-Telegram*, July 11, 1978.
47. Ibid.
48. *Star-Telegram*, June 9, 1994.
49. Pate, 11.

NOTES TO CHAPTER IX

1. Ron Tyler, ed., *The New Handbook of Texas*, vol. 4, 321.
2. Tyler, ed., vol. 6, 436.
3. *The Hub*, vol. 3, No 5, 5.
4. *Texas Almanac and State Industrial Guide, 1939–1940*, 110.
5. A. B. Davis to Brig. Gen. G. C. Brant, letter dated September 8, 1936.
6. A. B. Davis, notation dated June 29, 1941.
7. *Fort Worth Star-Telegram*, March 6, 1939.
8. Davis to T. L. Patterson, letter dated May 31, 1940.
9. Davis to R. D. Shinkle, telegram dated May 26, 1940.
10. Gerald C. Brant to Davis, letter dated September 6, 1945.
11. W. T. Spurgin to Davis, letter dated April 9, 1941.
12. *Lubbock Avalanche-Journal*, April 16, 1941.
13. Department of Defense (DOD), "Legacy Resource Management Film," 1997.
14. Davis to Charles H. Dowman, letter dated May 6, 1941.
15. *Avalanche-Journal*, June 21, 1941.
16. *Avalanche-Journal*, June 22, 1941.
17. DOD Legacy Film.
18. *Avalanche-Journal*, June 13, 1941.
19. Ibid.
20. *United States Army Air Forces Directory of Airports, 1944.*
21. *Avalanche-Journal*, January 4, 1942.
22. Ibid.
23. DOD, "Legacy Film."
24. Ibid.
25. Ibid.
26. Ibid.
27. *The History of Lubbock Army Air Field Through September 1945*, 9.
28. Ibid., 15.
29. *Avalanche-Journal*, October 5, 1945.
30. Tyler, ed., vol. 4, 321.
31. *The Hub*, vol. 4, No 1, 6.

32. Ibid., 7.
33. *Avalanche-Journal*, March 15, 1992.
34. Ibid.
35. DOD, "Legacy Film."
36. "Reese AFB Historic Building Inventory and Expansion," 3–24.
37. Ibid.
38. *History of Reese Air Force Base and 64th Flying Training Wing*, 9.
39. George Mahon to Davis, letter dated November 6, 1945.
40. Davis to Mahon, letter dated November 10, 1945.
41. Ibid.
42. *History of Reese AFB*, 9.
43. Ibid.
44. *Avalanche-Journal*, November 12, 1949.
45. *Avalanche-Journal*, June 4, 1991.
46. Ibid.
47. Bill G. Gregory, interview with author, March 26, 2000.
48. *Avalanche-Journal*, November 6, 1967.
49. *History of Reese AFB*, 26.

NOTES TO CHAPTER X

1. Ron Tyler, ed., *The New Handbook of Texas*, vol. 1, 299.
2. Ibid.
3. E. J. Hargraves, *Austin: From Republic Days to Statehood*, 18.
4. Ibid., 19.
5. Mark M. Boatner III, *The Civil War Dictionary*, 832.
6. L. Patrick Hughes, "To Meet Fire With Fire: Lyndon Johnson, Tom Miller, and Home-Front Politics," *Southwestern Historical Quarterly*, vol. C, no. 4, 456.
7. "Bergstrom Field History," 1.
8. Tyler, ed., vol. 2, 584.
9. Robert A. Beggs, "Del Valle Army Air Field," 2.
10. Tom Miller to Lyndon Johnson, letter dated April 9, 1941.
11. "Bergstrom Field History," 2.
12. Robert Sligh, *Bergstrom AFB: A History*, 2.
13. Beggs, 3.
14. Ibid.
15. *The Austin Statesman*, February 17, 1942.
16. Ibid.
17. *The Austin Statesman*, March 4, 1942.
18. *The Austin Statesman*, March 8, 1942.
19. *The Austin Statesman*, March 14, 1942.
20. Mrs. Lyndon B. Johnson, Oral History Interview, February 1, 1980.
21. *The Austin Statesman*, March 4, 1942.
22. *The Austin Statesman*, May 27, 1942.
23. *United States Army Air Forces Directory of Airports*, Vol. 3, 1945, 19.
24. Beggs, 6.
25. Sligh, 4.
26. Beggs, 7.

27. Sligh, 5.
28. Beggs, 9.
29. Ibid., 10.
30. Sligh, 5.
31. Beggs, 13.
32. Ibid., 11.
33. Ibid., 15.
34. Ibid., 16.
35. Robert Mueller, *Air Force Bases*, vol. 1, *Active Air Force Bases Within the United States of America*, 29.
36. Beggs, 17.
37. Robert McHenry, ed., *Webster's American Military Biographies*, 100.
38. Beggs, 17.
39. Ibid., 22.
40. Sligh, 18.
41. Ibid., 19.
42. Ibid., 36.
43. Ibid., 37.
44. Ibid., 40.
45. "City of Austin: Bergstrom Air Force Base History," 3.
46. *Austin American-Statesman*, January 9, 1992.
47. "City of Austin: Austin-Bergstrom International Airport: Aviation Milestones 2000," 2.

NOTES TO CHAPTER XI

1. Ron Tyler, ed. *The New Handbook of Texas*, vol. 1, 538.
2. *Texas Almanac and State Industrial Guide, 1939–1940*, 96.
3. *Big Spring-Howard County Centennial Souvenir-Album*, 5.
4. Ibid., 6.
5. Ibid., 14.
6. *Midland Reporter-Telegraph*, July 18, 1991.
7. *Big Spring Herald*, April 22, 1942.
8. *United States Army Air Forces Directory of Airports, 1944*, 33.
9. Bill Steagald, "The Big Spring Army Air Force Base or Big Spring Bombardier School: Some Recollections," 3.
10. *History of the 812th Bombardier Training Squadron*, n.d.
11. Ibid.
12. Ibid.
13. Steagald, 3.
14. Ibid., 3.
15. *Midland Reporter-Telegram*, July 7, 1991.
16. Steagald, 4.
17. *Big Spring Herald*, January 9, 1945.
18. Steagald, 6.
19. Ibid., 1.
20. *Gyro: The Yearbook of Class 43-G*, Big Spring Bombardier School, 22.
21. *El Rodeo, Yearbook of Big Spring High School, Class of 1945*, 64.

22. Steagald, 9.
23. Ibid., 10.
24. *History of Big Spring Air Force Base*, 6.
25. *Gyro, The Yearbook of Cadet Class 44–10*, 38.
26. *Big Spring Herald*, September 16, 1946.
27. Ibid.
28. Souvenir-Program, 49.
29. Tyler, ed., vol. 6, 864.
30. Ibid., 864.
31. *Big Spring Herald*, March 10, 1976.
32. Ibid.
33. *Lubbock Avalanche-Journal*, August 1, 1999.

NOTES TO CHAPTER XII

1. Ron Tyler, ed., *The New Handbook of Texas*, vol. 3, 721.
2. Ibid.
3. Ibid.
4. Ibid.
5. *Texas Almanac and State Industrial Guide*, 1943–1944, 77.
6. George Sessions Perry, Texas: *A World In Itself*, 247–48.
7. *Houston Chronicle*, May 17, 1917.
8. Ibid., September 30, 1917.
9. *The Houston Post*, December 31, 1942.
10. *Houston Chronicle*, December 3, 1917.
11. Ibid.
12. Erik Carlson, *Ellington Field: A Short History, 1917–1963*, 16.
13. "Historical Background-Ellington Air Force Base," Ellington File, Houston Public Library.
14. Drury M. Phillips, *Texaco Star* 6, 15.
15. "Historical Background"
16. *Ellington Field Yearbook, 1943*, 28.
17. *Houston Chronicle*, June 6, 1940.
18. *The Houston Post*, December 31, 1942.
19. *Houston Chronicle*, October 26, 1941.
20. *Houston Press*, August 22, 1941.
21. *Ellington Field Yearbook*, 27.
22. *Houston Press*, May 28, 1941.
23. Carlson, 45.
24. *Houston Chronicle*, March 18, 1945.
25. Ibid.
26. Thomas B. Allen, interview with author, May 15, 2000.
27. Theodore Sherman, interview with author, June 12, 2000.
28. C. William Blanchard, interview with author, April 20, 2000.
29. *Houston Press*, May 25, 1944.
30. *Houston Chronicle*, July 28, 1948.
31. Ibid., July 27, 1948.
32. Author's reminiscences.

NOTES TO CHAPTER XIII

1. *Fort Worth Star-Telegram*, October 12, 1945.
2. Barton K. Jennings, "Texans at War," *Texaco Star 38*, 16.
3. *Kilgore News-Herald*, April 9, 1944.
4. Thomas Leonard, *Day By Day: The Forties*, 253.
5. *Star-Telegram*, January 1, 1946.
6. *Texas Almanac and State Industrial Guide 1950–1951*, 97.

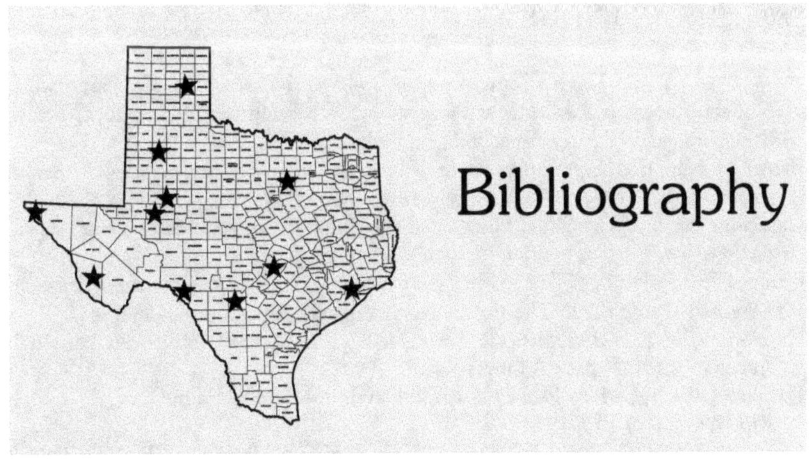

Bibliography

The Air Officers Guide. Harrisburg, PA: The Telegraph Press, 1951.

Allen, Thomas B. Interview with author. San Antonio, Texas. May 15, 2000.

Annual Report of the 47th Comptroller Flight. Laughlin Air Force Base, Texas, 1998.

Arnschuler, Ernest E. Interview with author. San Antonio, Texas. June 9, 1999.

The Austin American-Statesman, January 9, 1992.

The Austin Statesman: February 17, 1942; March 4, 1942; March 8, 1942; March 14, 1942; May 27, 1942.

Baumgart, Vernon. *Who's Who: Pampa Army Airfield Association Reunion Directory.* Pampa, TX: The Pampa Army Airfield Association, 1988.

Beasley, Amos O. Interview with author. San Antonio, Texas. September 12, 1999.

Beggs, Robert A. "Del Valle Army Air Field." Austin, 1944.

Bellingham, Thomas F. Interview with author. Dallas, Texas. November 12, 1999.

"Bergstrom Field History." Pamphlet. n.d.

The Big Bend Sentinel: May 1, 1942; May 22, 1942; May 29, 1942; June 5, 1942; October 10, 1942; December 14, 1942; December 28, 1942; June 8, 1943; August 20, 1943; September 17, 1943; May 6, 1945; May 13, 1945; August 3, 1945; August 10, 1945.

"Biggs Field Fact Sheet." El Paso: Fort Bliss History Office. n.d.

Big Spring Herald: April 22, 1942; January 9, 1945; September 16, 1946; March 10, 1976.

Big Spring–Howard County Souvenir Album. Big Spring, TX: Howard County Heritage Museum, 1981.

Blanchard, C. William. Interview with author. Dallas, Texas. April 20, 2000.

Blumenthal, Ernie L. Interview with author. January 9, 2000.

Boatner, Mark M., III. *The Civil War Dictionary, Revised Edition*. New York: Vintage Books, 1991.

Bonifield, J. R. *Reminiscences of a Buffalo Hunter.* Fort Worth: Greenwood Book Publishing Company, 1903.

Brant, Gerald C. *Dedicatory Address at Laughlin Army Airfield,* March 28, 1942.

———. to A. B. Davis. September 6, 1945. Davis File 15-8C. Southwest Collection/Special Collections Library. Texas Tech University, Lubbock, Texas.

A Brief History of El Paso, Texas. n.d.

Brown, Jerold E. *Where Eagles Land: Planning and Development of U.S. Army Airfields, 1910-1941.* New York: Greenwood Press, 1990.

Callander, Bruce. "The Short Heyday of the Bombardier." *Air Force Times,* April 9, 1984.

Campbell, Daniel S. *Who's Who: Pampa Army Airfield Association Reunion Directory.* Pampa, TX: The Pampa Army Airfield Association, 1988.

Carlson, Erik. *Ellington Field: A Short History, 1917–1963.* Houston: National Aeronautics and Space Administration, 1999.

Carnahan, George M. to Paul O. Russell. Laughlin Heritage Foundation Files. Del Rio, Texas, April 13, 1997.

Cervantes, Ysidro. *Transcript From An Oral History Project of El Paso Public Libraries.* n.d.

Chapman, Arthur. *The Denver Times.* n.d.

"City of Austin: Bergstrom Air Force Base History." 2000.

"City of Austin: Austin-Bergstrom International Airport Aviation Milestones, 2000."

Colwell, James L. "'Hell From Heaven': Midland Army Airfield in World War II, Part I." *The Permian Basin Historical Annual, Vol. XXV.* Odessa, Texas: The Permian Basin Historical Association, 1985.

———. "'Hell From Heaven': Midland Army Airfield in World War II, Part II." *The Permian Basin Historical Annual, Vol. XXVI.* Odessa, Texas: The Permian Basin Historical Association, 1986.

———. "'Hell From Heaven': Midland Army Airfield in World War II, Part III." *The Permian Basin Historical Annual, Vol. XXVII.* Odessa, Texas: The Permian Basin Historical Association, 1987.

Daughtery, E. Roebuck. *U.S. Air Force Activities In and Near Del Rio, Val Verde County, Texas.* Del Rio, Texas: Val Verde County Historical Commission. n.d.

Davis, A. B. to Gerald C. Brant. September 8, 1938. Davis File 15-8C. Southwest Collection/Special Collections Library. Texas Tech University, Lubbock, Texas.

———. to R. D. Shinkle. May 26, 1940. Davis File 15-8C.

———. to T. L. Patterson. May 31. 1940. Davis File 15-8C.

———. to Charles H. Dowman, May 6, 1941. Davis File 15-8C.

———. to George Mahon, November 10, 1945. Davis File 15-8C.

———. Personal notation. June 28, 1941. Davis File 15-8C.

Davis, J. Frank. *Randolph Field: A History and Guide.* New York: The Devin-Adair Company, 1942.

Del Rio News-Herald: May 15, 1942; May 22, 1942; June 24, 1945; August 17, 1945; September 7, 1945.

Department of Defense Legacy Management Resource Film. 1997.

Doolittle, James H. *I Could Never Be So Lucky Again.* New York: Bantam Books, 1991.

"Economic Survey Bulletin." El Paso Convention and Visitors Bureau, 1999.

Eisenhower, John S. D. *So Far From God: The U.S. War With Mexico 1846-1848.* New York: Doubleday, 1989.

Ellington Field Yearbook, 1943. Baton Rouge (LA): Army and Navy Publishing Company of Louisiana, 1944.

El Paso Times: June 12, 1916; February 27, 1943; August 13, 1945; September 13, 1945; November 24, 1964.

El Rodeo: Yearbook of Big Spring High School, Class of 1944. Big Spring, Texas, 1944.

Ferber, Edna. *Giant.* Garden City, NY: Doubleday & Company, 1952.

Ferguson, W. C., Jr. *Who's Who: Pampa Army Airfield Association Reunion Directory.* Pampa: The Pampa Army Airfield Association, 1988.

Flemmons, Jerry. *Amon: The Life of Amon Carter, Sr. of Texas.* Austin: Jenkins Publishing Company, 1978.

Forstmann, Ardella. Interview with author. October 12, 1999.

Fort Worth Press, September 21, 1945.

Fort Worth Star-Telegram: March 6, 1939; January 4, 1941; October 12, 1942; October 25, 1942; November 2, 1942; November 27, 1942; December 10, 1942; February 6, 1943; February 8, 1943; September 3, 1943; September 13, 1943; October 3, 1943; November 8, 1943; February 20, 1944; September 22, 1944; August 2, 1945; October 12, 1945; October 14, 1945; January 1, 1946; July 3, 1948; June 25, 1955; July 11, 1978; June 8, 1991; June 9, 1994.

For Your Information. Del Rio Chamber of Commerce Pamphlet, 1999.

Fowler, Gene and Bill Crawford. *Border Radio.* Austin, Texas: Texas Monthly Press, Inc., 1987.

Franklin, James G. *The Story of Old Fort Bliss.* El Paso, Texas: Privately published, 1963.

Gilmore, Eugene R. Interview with author. Lubbock, Texas. March 28, 2000.

Gonzalez, Alicia. *Transcript From An Oral History Project of El Paso Public Libraries,* n.d.

Gough, Jamie. *Who's Who: Pampa Army Airfield Association Reunion Directory.* Pampa: The Pampa Army Airfield Association, 1988.

Gregory, Bill G. Interview with author. Lubbock, Texas. March 26, 2000.

Grube, Susanne. "A Brief History of Camp Marfa and Fort D. A. Russell." Chinati Foundation Fact Sheet. n.d.

A Guide To Historic Del Rio, Texas. Del Rio: The Val Verde County Historical Commission. n.d.

Gyro: The Yearbook of Cadet Class 43-G, Big Spring Bombardier School. Big Spring, Texas, 1943.

Gyro: The Yearbook of Cadet Class 44-10. Big Spring Bombardier School. Big Spring, Texas, 1944.

Hargraves, E. J. *Austin: From Republic Days to Statehood.* Austin: Lone Star Press, 1936.

Henderson, L. K. Interview with author. Houston, Texas. June 11, 2000.

Hewlett, Ernest. Letter reprinted in *The Pampa Flyer,* July 14, 1943.

"Historical Background, Ellington Air Force Base." Ellington File, Texas Room. Houston Public Library. Houston, Texas. n.d.

History of the 812th Bombardier Training Squadron. On file. Hangar 25 Museum. Big Spring, Texas. n.d.

History of Big Spring Air Force Base. Maxwell, Alabama: United States Air Force Research Center, 1979.

"The History of Childress Army Airfield." n.d.
"History of Fort Worth Army Airfield." in *Lone Star Scanner*, February 16, 1946.
The History of Lubbock Army Airfield Through September 1945. n.d.
History of Reese Air Force Base and 64th Flying Training Wing. Lubbock: Office of the Wing Historian, 1993.
Hondo Anvil Herald: March 9, 1944; April 10, 1999; January 23, 1942; March 6, 1942; April 3, 1942; April 10, 1942; August 14, 1942; November 30, 1945; June 25, 1943; October 2, 1942; October 9, 1942; August 2, 1945; September 30, 1999.
Horgan, Paul. *Great River: The Rio Grande in North American History.* New York and Toronto: Rinehart & Company, Inc., 1954.
Houston Chronicle: June 6, 1940; October 26, 1941; March 18, 1945; July 27, 1948; July 28, 1948.
The Houston Post, December 31, 1942.
Houston Press: May 28, 1941; August 22, 1941; May 25, 1944.
The Hub. Vol. 3. No. 5. Lubbock: The Lubbock Chamber of Commerce.
———. Vol. 4. No. 1.
Hughes, L. Patrick. "To Meet Fire With Fire: Lyndon Johnson, Tom Miller, and Home-Front Politics." *Southwestern Historical Quarterly.* Vol. C. No. 4. Austin: The Texas State Historical Association, 1997.
Jennings, Barton K. "Texans At War." *Texaco Star,* 38. Houston, Texas, 1945.
Johnson, Mrs. Lyndon B. Interview XVI. Interviewed by Michael Gillette. Casa Leonore, Acapulco, Mexico. February 1, 1980.
Kahl, C. M. (Fritz) Interview with author. Marfa, Texas. October 11, 1999.
Katz, Ephraim. *The Film Encyclopedia. Third Edition.* New York: HarperCollins, 1998.
Kilgore News Herald. April 9, 1944.
Kleinschmidt, Alton. Interview with author. San Antonio, Texas. November 19, 1999.
Knight, Oliver. *Fort Worth: Outpost On The Trinity.* Fort Worth: TCU Press, 1989.
Leonard, Thomas. *Day By Day: The Forties.* New York: Facts on File. 1977.
"Life After Giant." *LIFE Magazine,* January 3, 1957.
LIFE Magazine, May 18, 1942.
"A Look Back." Consolidated-Vultee Corporation Annual Report, 1952.
Lubbock Avalanche-Journal: April 16, 1941; June 13, 1941, June 21, 1941; June 22, 1941; January 4, 1942; October 5, 1945; November 12, 1949; November 6, 1967; March 15, 1992.
Lubbock Avalanche-News, August 1, 1999.
McHenry, Robert, ed. *Webster's American Military Biographies.* Springfield, Mass: G & C Merriam Company, 1978.
McNeese, John P. Interview in Laughlin Heritage Foundation Files, Del Rio, Texas. n.d.
Mahon, George, to A. B. Davis. November 6, 1945. Davis File 15-8C. Southwest Collection/Special Collections Library. Texas Tech University, Lubbock, Texas.
Marfacts. Marfa Army Airfield, June 30, 1945.
Martinez, Elisa. *Transcript From An Oral History Project of El Paso Public Libraries,* n.d.

Maurer, Maurer. *Aviation in the U.S. Army, 1919–1939.* Washington, D.C.: U.S. Government Printing Office, 1986.
Mayo, Jacqueline L. Interview with author. Austin, Texas. March 9, 2000.
Midland International Airport Press Release. n.d.
Midland Reporter-Telegram: June 9, 1921; June 13, 1940; July 15, 1940; June 13, 1941; October 24, 1941; August 11, 1942; January 13, 1991; July 7, 1991; July 18, 1991; December 1, 1991.
Miller, Tom, to Lyndon Johnson. April 8, 1941. Letter Box 27. Lyndon B. Johnson Library. Austin, Texas.
Mueller, Robert. *Air Force Bases Vol. 1, Active Air Force Bases Within the United States of America on 17 September, 1982.* Washington: Department of the Air Force, 1989.
Neale, Felix B., Jr. Interview with author. Houston, Texas. June 12, 2000.
Noah, Harold H. *Who's Who: Pampa Army Airfield Association Reunion Directory.* Pampa: The Pampa Army Airfield Association, 1988.
The Odessa American: February 6, 1940; April 3, 1941; August 8, 1943; March 20, 1988.
Oliphant, Mary Kate. Interview with author. San Antonio, Texas. May 11, 1999.
The Pampa Flyer: November 1, 1944; December 22, 1944; December 27, 1944; December 29, 1944.
Pampa News: May 15, 1942; May 17, 1942; May 23, 1942; July 9, 1942; July 23, 1942; September 11, 1942; November 3, 1942; November 29, 1942; December 15, 1942; December 23, 1942; January 28, 1943; February 21, 1943; February 28, 1943; March 7, 1943; May 13, 1943; June 20, 1943; July 25, 1943; September 3, 1943; January 6, 1944; November 28, 1944; May 7, 1945; July 31, 1945; September 6, 1945; September 13, 1945; September 23, 1945.
Pate, J'nell. "Impact Of The Military Base Called Carswell." Paper given at the annual meeting of the Texas State Historical Association, Dallas, Texas, March 3, 1999.
Paulette, Irene. "Odessa During the War Years 1941-1945: A Microcosm of the Nation." *The Permian Historical Annual, Vol. XXI.* Odessa: The Permian Historical Association, 1981.
Perry, George Sessions. *Texas: A World In Itself.* Gretna (LA): Pelican Publishing Company, Inc., 1975.
Phillips, Drury M. *Texaco Star 6.* Houston: The Texaco Petroleum Company, July 1919.
Porter, Mike. Interview with author. Pampa, Texas. October 15, 1999.
Pringle, Elliott. Interview with author. El Paso, Texas. October 11, 1999.
"Reese AFB Historic Building Inventory and Expansion." Washington: Department of the United States Air Force, 1997.
Rehnquist, William H. Letter to author. June 11, 1999.
Ritchey, Roger G. *Who's Who: Pampa Army Airfield Association Reunion Directory.* Pampa: The Pampa Army Airfield Association, 1988.
Robertson, E. L. *Villa Rides!* New York: Paisley Press, 1943.
Russell, Paul O. "Reminiscences of Laughlin." Laughlin Heritage Foundation Files. Del Rio, Texas. n.d.
San Antonio Light, Dec. 8, 1946.

Saucier, George. *Transcript From An Oral History Project of El Paso Public Libraries.* n.d.

Savage, Rod "Doc." *Who's Who: Pampa Army Airfield Association Reunion Directory.* Pampa, Texas: The Pampa Army Airfield Association, 1988.

Schaeffer, W. Harris. Paper presented at East Texas Historical Association meeting. Navasota, Texas. March 4, 1953.

Schnelling, Lorene. Interview with author. December 6, 1999.

Sherman, Theodore. Interview with author. Houston, Texas. June 12, 2000.

Simmons, Mrs. Everett P. (Elva). Interview with author. Pasadena, Texas. June 11, 2000.

Simpson, Arnold Frank. Interview with author. June 9, 1998.

Sligh, Robert. *Bergstrom AFB: A History.* Austin: Bergstrom/Austin Community Council, 1993.

Spurgin, W. T. to A. B. Davis. April 9, 1941. Davis File 15-8C. Southwest Collection/Special Collections Library. Texas Tech University, Lubbock, Texas.

Steagald, Bill. "The Big Spring Army Air Force Base or Big Spring Bombardier School: Some Recollections." Big Spring: Unpublished Memoir. n.d.

Stephens, Gerald L. Interview in Laughlin Heritage Foundation Files. Del Rio, Texas. n.d.

Stevens, Allard E. to Paul O. Russell. Laughlin Heritage Foundation Files. Del Rio, Texas. December 1, 1997.

Summary of Aircraft Accidents at Laughlin Airfield. Laughlin Heritage Foundation Files. Del Rio, Texas. n.d.

Tarfu: March 1, 1943; June 8, 1943; September 12, 1944; August 20, 1943; December 31, 1943; August 27, 1943; May 19, 1944.

"Tarrant County Information Website," April 2000.

Tarranteer. Fort Worth: Fort Worth Army Airfield. August 1, 1945.

Texas Almanac and State Industrial Guide, 1939–1940. Dallas: A. H. Belo Corporation, 1939.

Texas Almanac and State Industrial Guide, 1943–1944. Dallas: A. H. Belo Corporation, 1943.

Texas Almanac and State Industrial Guide, 1950–1951. Dallas: A. H. Belo Corporation, 1950.

Thompson, Cecilia. *History of Marfa and Presidio County, Texas 1535-1946, Vol. 2.* Austin: Nortex Press, 1986.

Thompson, Robert D. *We'll Find the Way: The History of Hondo Army Air Field During World War II.* Austin: Eakin Press, 1992.

Timmons, Mrs. J. A. Interview with author. Midland, Texas. October 8, 1999.

Tyler, Ron, ed. *The New Handbook of Texas.* 6 vols. Austin: The Texas State Historical Association, 1996.

United States Army Air Forces Directory of Airports, Vol. 3. Washington, D.C.: War Department, 1945.

U.S. Army Air Forces Directory of Airports. Washington D.C.: War Department, 1944.

Wagner, Ray. *American Combat Planes.* Garden City, NY: Doubleday Company, 1960, 1968, 1982.

Wagner, William T. *Who's Who: Pampa Army Airfield Association Reunion Directory.* Pampa, Texas: The Pampa Army Airfield Association, 1988.

Warnock, Kirby F. "Wings West of the Pecos." *Big Bend Quarterly,* Summer, 1999.

Webb, Walter Prescott, ed. *The Handbook of Texas,* Vol. II. Austin: The Texas State Historical Association, 1952.

Wentz, John. Interview with author. September 12, 1999.

Whitehead Memorial Museum Vertical Files. "The Military in Del Rio." Del Rio, Texas.

Wilson, C. Forrest. *A History of Biggs Field and Early Border Aviation.* El Paso: Texas Western University, 1952.

Index

D

E

F

www.ingramcontent.com/pod-product-compliance
Lightning Source LLC
Chambersburg PA
CBHW071724080526
44588CB00013B/1887

* 9 7 8 1 9 3 3 3 3 7 7 3 9 *